OHIO WINE COUNTRY EXCURSIONS

OHIO WINE COUNTRY EXCURSIONS

UPDATED EDITION

Patricia Latimer

RINGTAW BOOKS
AKRON, OHIO

All rights reserved • Manufactured in the United States of America. •
All inquiries and permission requests should be addressed to the
Publisher, The University of Akron Press, Akron, Ohio 44325-1703.

15 14 13 12 11   5 4 3 2 1

LIBRARY OF CONGRESS CATALOGING-IN-PUBLICATION DATA
Latimer, Patricia.
Ohio wine country excursions / Patricia Latimer. — Updated ed.
   p. cm.
First published: Cincinatti, OH : Emmis books, c2005.
Includes bibliographical references.
ISBN 978-1-935603-99-3 (pbk. : alk. paper)
1. Wine and wine making—Ohio—Guidebooks. 2. Wineries—Ohio--
Guidebooks. 3. Ohio—Wine—Guidebooks. I. Title.
TP557.L366 2010
641.2′209771—dc22
                       2010045010

The paper used in this publication meets the minimum requirements of
American National Standard for
Information Sciences—Permanence of Paper for Printed Library Materials,
ANSI Z39.48–1984. ∞

Cover: Photo by Tyler Stableford.
Ohio Wine Country Excursions was designed and typeset by Amy Freels. The text was
set in Arno Pro with Avenir LT Standard display. *Ohio Wine Country Excursions* was
printed on 60# white and bound by BookMasters of Ashland, Ohio.

Photo facing title page: White grapes on the vine at The Winery at Wolf Creek. ©
2010 by Amy Freels. Used with permission.

Contents

Preface

This book is dedicated to the men and women in my family who over three generations sought adventure and opportunity as they journeyed across the United States. It is a story of chance and choice from Connecticut to Ohio and on across the plains and mountains to their destination, California. They passionately pursued their dreams, and were challenged by the lure of California to live them, but ultimately were called home to Ohio to replenish them.

The record of this historic adventure began in Harrisburg, Iowa, March 2, 1850, as seven men and my great-grandfather, Leonard Straight, started west by horse and wagon, traveling for more than one hundred days through hardship and struggle to give reality to their dream of finding gold in the Sierra Nevada. Returning to Ohio with pockets of plenty, my great-grandfather purchased a farm, to serve both his avocation and vocation, in northern Ohio for his wife and eight children.

But the dream did not die. In the early twentieth century, my grandmother, Lenore Straight Latimer, the youngest daughter of Leonard Straight, headed west, and she and her physician husband settled in Pomona, California, in 1918. During the height of the Spanish flu pandemic, while trying to save his patients, the young doctor became ill and suddenly died. This time California offered no gold. The young wife was left a widow with a son of ten. Her anguished letters are witness to her decision to return to Ohio, where a large family would help her.

Her son, Vernon Straight Latimer, grew up in Cleveland and attended Case Western Reserve and then Harvard Business School, yet he remembered his California childhood amongst the orange groves and olive orchards. Stories of the 1920s inspired me, Vernon's youngest daughter, to make a mid-twentieth-century trip to California after college. For several decades I remained in San Francisco, where I became a writer and author on California wine, then later an entrepreneur, representing the wineries of Napa, Sonoma, and Mendocino, each with its own thrilling story.

By the late 1990s, my life took a dramatic turn when my father became ill. I found myself traveling back and forth between California and Ohio. In Ohio I reacquainted myself with my family's heritage and my own interest in

A vineyard at dawn. *Courtesy OSU/OARDC*

viticulture. I brought with me the gift of inquiry, interviewing people and penning Ohio's untold wine story.

Thus, three generations later, influenced by my extraordinary California wine experience, there is new hope in the Buckeye State to share the vision of Ohio families, past and present, who believe in an Ohio wine empire. This book is dedicated to those in my family who came before and encouraged me to pursue my dreams in my two favorite places.

Foreword

Arnie Esterer

Welcome to Ohio, with all its wines and the people who make them.

Historically, Ohio ranks as a great wine state, and this book covers both the wonderful early story and the amazing rebirth by the current generation.

You will enjoy details that cover the Buckeye State's two major winegrowing regions, Lake Erie and the Ohio River Valley, and interesting people and wineries in between. Like the world wine business, the Ohio industry grows from family interests and their long-term views. As winery owners happily pour their vintages, they share their personal winemaking philosophies and cultural heritage. By touring Ohio with this book, you will discover the wine heartland and the colorful families and members who built it.

Today, I believe wine to be a food, both healthy and nutritious, the beverage of moderation, to be consumed with meals but not to be misused. This tradition goes back ages to when bread and wine were staples used as offerings, and later became sacraments.

"Americans should drink the best wines!" Dr. Konstantin Frank said, and he demonstrated how to grow wine grapes to make the most of each vintage in the Finger Lakes region in upstate New York. Winegrowing at Markko Vineyard, in Conneaut, adapted his practice to Ohio's Lake Erie. Now his influence shows that wines from Lake Erie grapes can complement the daily meals we share at home and when dining out as well as any.

Remember, every wine differs by vintage, winery, and bottling. No two wines are the same. Each wine has its own personality, just like people, and changes occur with age—some better than others.

Let this book be your guide as you find, meet, and follow these Ohio wines each year. As you buy, drink, and then grow to understand and appreciate each wine, you can share your feelings. Your feedback gives growers and winemakers important guidance on which direction to take. And by doing this, you shape Ohio wines; it becomes your own region.

What an exciting experience! Just enjoy the fun of discovering the beauty of these heartland wines and the human hands that make them.

Gladden your heart. Cheers to the wines, the dreams, and the memories!

Elegant bunches of blue grapes on trellised vines. *Photo by John Waraksa, Sapphire Falls Web design Courtesy Harpersfield Vineyard*

Introduction

The diversity of Ohio's landscape invites guests, visitors, residents, and tourists to explore its beautiful grape vineyards, appellation by appellation and viticultural district by viticultural district.

As you drive along the south shore of Lake Erie, the lake serves as a spectacular backdrop for acres of gently rolling green vineyards. Its cerulean-blue waters share 262 miles of northern Ohio's border, all the way from the port at Conneaut past Cleveland and Sandusky Bay to Toledo and the Maumee estuary.

The Lake Erie Plains, a fertile swath of land, are part of the Great Lakes Plains, which sweep southward from Lake Erie into Ohio. Farther inland, the fertile farmlands of the dramatic, rolling Central Plains and the sweeping corn belt are intermittently dotted with lush vineyards. The Allegheny Plateau to the east, which merges with the hills and valleys of the Appalachian Mountains, is planted to vines and descends to the Bluegrass along the winding waters of the Ohio River Valley, home to more breathtaking vineyards.

Whenever you visit the Ohio wine country, there is a chance to observe the cycle of life in the vineyards. In the spring, the sleeping vines burst with buds; in the summer, the vines form branches of leafy green; in the fall, the celadon and purple clusters glisten amid the burgundy and gold vineyards; and in the winter, the dormant, darkened, earthy vines rest. Then the cycle repeats itself.

Early on, the Ohio River Valley attracted the paleo-Indians: the Archaic, the Woodland, and the Hopewell. Although they were followed later by the Shawnee, the Miami, the Wyandot, and others, it was the arrival in 1788 of early settlers who had fought in the Revolutionary War and were given land for their service that stimulated the rush to settle Ohio and promote its agriculture.

Traveling by flatboat down the Ohio River, or by horse and wagon over the Appalachian Mountains, these eager young pioneers were determined to build settlements. This led to their planting small crops—fruits, vegetables, orchards, and vineyards. The determination and experimentation by one Nicholas Longworth, a prominent lawyer and horticulturist, in 1813 in and around Cincinnati laid the foundation

Young grapes. *Courtesy OSU/OARDC*

for experimental grape trials, resulting in the making of champagne and still wine from the Catawba grape.

During the heyday of wine in Ohio during the 1850s, Cincinnati and its environs were the center of American wine production. By the late 1860s, powdery mildew and black rot devastated the vineyards. The wine industry moved from the Ohio River Valley in the south to the shores of Lake Erie around Sandusky and the Erie Islands.

This region gained prominence in 1869, and it became Ohio's new grape-growing and wine-producing capital. By the early 1900s, the largest wineries in the Lake Erie Island region were situated there. The eastern grape belt, of which this was a part, started by migrations of Germans, French, Italians, Czechs, Hungarians, Slovenians, and Shakers, extended from Sandusky to Conneaut and into Pennsylvania and western New York. From 1920 to 1933, Prohibition closed many wineries and vineyards. Wineries that produced sacramental wines and vineyards making nonalcoholic grape-based products were the exception. The sixties wine revolution in California inspired viticulturists to experiment with vinifera, labrusca, and hybrids and vintners to practice better winemaking in Ohio.

Today, the ribbon of towns, villages, and cities that crisscrosses the Buckeye State has defined its wine country. Just off of I-90 along Lake Erie, there are wineries and vineyards that appeal to wine aficionados, families, friends, and neighbors from around the globe. They range across the Lake Erie Plains around Bryan, Toledo, Sandusky, Port Clinton, Kelleys Island, Put-in-Bay, Oregon, Avon Lake, Cleveland, Madison, Geneva, Ashtabula, and to Conneaut. These communities generate a lifestyle-workstyle for their citizenry and provide their patrons with lodging, fine dining, wine tasting, recreation, and relaxation.

As wine lovers travel any of the three north-south corridors, I-75, I-71, or I-77, they pass through some of the most gorgeous farm country in America, the heart of Amish Country, where horse and buggies are de rigueur and huge barns, tall silos, well-manicured crops, and herds of cattle catch the imagination. Here the wineries and vineyards are tucked among hills and valleys or grace the flat plains in towns like Versailles, Dover, Newcomerstown, Coshocton, Aurora, Valley City, West Lafayette, Wooster, Kent, Navarre, and Norton. Farther to the southwest, wine towns include Manchester, Ripley, Bethel, Cincinnati, Morrow, and Silverton.

Proprietors of these wineries encourage the public to stop by and experience the Ohio wine country. Some seventy to eighty-plus wineries—sometimes occupying elegant chateaus, old castles, threshing barns, bank barns, modern wonders, or humble cottages—are located on hilltops or in valleys alongside lakes, rivers, and streams. The

Flint Ridge Vineyards. *Courtesy Carl Jahnes, owner of Flint Ridge Vineyards*

public can taste and compare some of the most eclectic wines in the world, whether from estate-grown vineyards or farm wineries. Ohio is on the rise as a major player in the American wine industry!

Everywhere, there are restaurants, bistros, and delis for romantic picnics or family outings. Clubs, resorts, hotels, lodges, and bed and breakfasts make for inviting accommodations. Throughout this book, a quick guide included with each winery profile details contact information, owners, directions, hours, tours, events, winemaking procedures, best wines, and nearby places to visit. To all who explore the pages of this wine book, here is an invitation to join us in an Ohio wine country adventure!

Courtesy Cincinnati Museum Center, Cincinnati Historical Society Library

First of the Ohio River Valley Visionaries

What we know as Ohio was once a vast unexplored region. Prior to the 1780s, except for traveling Indian tribes, Ohio was a wilderness of forests, rivers, fertile deltas, grasslands, rolling hills, and beautiful valleys.

In 1787, the United States Congress passed the Northwest Ordinance, which encouraged the settlement of the lands between the Allegheny Mountains and the Mississippi River. By 1788, John Cleves Symmes had been granted a charter to develop the Miami Purchase, a tract between the Great Miami and Little Miami rivers. In November of that year, Benjamin Stites and a party of twenty-six settled Columbia, just west of the Little Miami River's mouth. By December, Colonel Robert Patterson, along with eleven families and twenty-four men, colonized the 747-acre site called Losantiville opposite the Licking River. But it was Arthur St. Clair, the first governor of the Northwest Territory, who renamed it Cincinnati.

Ohio's penetration by larger numbers of settlers increased when participants of the Revolutionary War were given land as payment for their services. Rivers provided cheap and relatively easy means of transportation. Cincinnati grew rapidly, settled by people who arrived by flatboat or overland by horse and cart.

The southern hillsides along the Ohio River were used for experimental vineyards and grape trials. Swiss-born Jean Jacques Defour, a viticulturist, had read about the possibilities of grape growing in the United States given its geography, climate, soil, and native varieties. Upon his arrival in America, he embarked on a campaign to educate Americans about the benefits of viticulture. In 1799, Defour established the Kentucky Wine Company, which at first failed due to vineyard disease and reduced yields.

When Defour visited Washington, D.C., he made a proclamation to the United States Congress that one day the Ohio River would rival the Rhine River for growing outstanding vines. Many representatives were dubious. In 1802, Defour's luck changed, and he successfully planted grapes on a land grant along the Ohio River.

In 1804, the dashing Nicholas Longworth departed Newark, New Jersey, and arrived in Cincinnati, the shining hillside city, where the realization of one's dreams often led to great fortune. Though a gifted lawyer, he preferred horticulture, especially grape

Nicholas Longworth. *Courtesy Cincinnati Museum Center, Cincinnati Historical Society Library*

growing, which led to his wealth and ability to support his passion.

From 1813 onward, Longworth tested the best varietals suitable for the Ohio River Valley. The cumulative effect of the fertile limestone soils, the modified continental climate, and the gently rolling topography were ideal for quality grapes and intensely flavored wines. He just had to find the right match. A four-acre vineyard planted to Cape and Alexander resulted in the production of a good white wine. Longworth's cellar yielded a Madeira copycat, which he fortified with brandy and sugar to make it more palatable. He planted European varieties by type, variety, and species for the next three decades. He persevered until the late 1840s, ever hopeful that his vitis vinifera would one day thrive in the Ohio River Valley.

Vintage after vintage, Longworth cultivated new native American

varieties, shipped by friendly viticulturists from across the states. But it wasn't until 1825 that John Adlum, a wine patriarch, gave Longworth a gift of Catawba grape cuttings. Mistakenly identified as Hungarian Tokay, the Catawba, which grew wild near Asheville, was named for the Catawba River, which flows from the mountains of the Carolinas. Adlum gained national fame for his discovery that the native Catawba made good wine, which he simultaneously publicized in his *Memoir on the Cultivation of the Vine in America and the Best Mode of Making Wine.*

Longworth wrote in the *Horticulturist,* "Major Adlum had a proper appreciation of the value of the Catawba grape. In a letter to me he remarked: 'In bringing this grape into public notice, I have rendered my country a greater service than I would have done, had I paid off the national debt.' I concur in this opinion."

Classified as vitis labrusca, the Catawba reflected nuances of classic vitis vinifera. A coveted 150-year-old eastern variety, the grape had bold-textured, dark-green foliage with flowers that self-fertilized. Its purplish-red medium-sized berries produced a clean, austere wine with an aroma of spice and a distinctive flavor. This fast-growing climber survived both heat and cold and loved the sun. Grown throughout the United States, the Catawba flourished best along the Ohio River, southern

Lake Erie, and in the Finger Lakes. It was originally used for making sparkling wine, still wine, and grape juice.

Longworth mapped out a business plan for the establishment of Longworth's Wine House and Vineyards. He planted the best native American varieties, from which he produced a substantial dry table wine. His investments placed Cincinnati and the Ohio River Valley as the center of the American wine industry. Skilled German immigrants who produced his Rhine-style wines added taste and cachet to the mix.

Beginning in the 1830s Cincinnati and the agricultural lands along the Ohio River became famous as the home of America's first commercial vineyards. The viticultural district was later dubbed "Rhineland of America." During this time, Longworth was a reputable 3,000-gallon premium producer, winning prizes for his Catawba. The Ohio wine boom took place after 1842, when Longworth accidentally produced a terrific sparkling Catawba. Convinced of the potential of this style of wine, he hired a French champagne-maker in the late 1840s to produce pure, natural sparkling Catawba in quantity to market outside of Cincinnati.

By 1848, Longworth had designed a 60,000-bottle cellar for the production of classic methode champenoise sparkling Catawba. After completion of the first fermentation, a dose of sugar was added to the wine. A second fermentation was completed in the bottle; the sediment was cleared by riddling, the process of turning the bottles stored in racks by hand. In 1851, Longworth built a second 75,000-bottle cellar and hired a second French champagne-maker from Rheims. Sparkling Catawba became a rising star on the national wine scene, and Longworth's Wine House and Vineyards prospered.

A promoter, Longworth curried favor with the press by sending a letter and a wine sample. He also entered his Catawba in state, national, and international competitions. Longworth presented wine to Henry Wadsworth Longfellow, America's most noted nineteenth-century poet, and in return he received a poem, "Ode to Catawba Wine."

While Longworth was revered as an American wine industry leader and Cincinnati wine entrepreneur, other commercial growers quickly followed in his footsteps. Prominent names included Robert Buchanan, C. W. Elliott, A. H. Ernest, John Motier, Stephen Mosher, Louis Rehfuss, William Resor, and John A. Warder. Other Catawba vineyards flourished in Hamilton, Brown, and Clermont counties, as did vineyards along the Ohio River in Kentucky and Indiana. Soon, there were some three hundred established vineyards in southwest Ohio.

As had Longworth, the proprietors of Cincinnati's wine houses employed

Ode to Catawba Wine 🍇

by Henry Wadsworth Longfellow

This song of mine
  Is a song of the vine
  To be sung by the glowing embers
  Of wayside inns,
  When rain begins
  To darken the drear Novembers.

It is not a song
  Of the Scuppernong,
  From warm Carolinian valleys,
  Nor the Isabel
  And the Muscadel
  That bask in our garden alleys.

Nor the red Mustang,
  Whose clusters hang
  O'er the waves of the Colorado,
  And the fiery flood
  Of whose purple blood
  Has a dash of Spanish bravado.

For richest and best
  Is the wine of the West,
  That grows by the Beautiful River,
  Whose sweet perfume
  Fills all the room
  With a benison on the giver.

And as hollow as trees
  Are the haunts of the bees,
  Forever going and coming,
  So the crystal hive
  Is all alive
  With a swarming and buzzing and
  humming.

Very good in its way
  Is the Verzenay
  Or the Sillery soft and creamy;
  But Catawba wine
  Has a taste more divine,
  More dulcet, delicious and dreamy.

There grows no vine
  By the haunted Rhine,
  By Danube or Guadalquivir,
  Nor on island or cape,
  That bears such a grape
  As grows by the Beautiful River.

Drugged is their juice
  For foreign use,
  When shipped o'er the reeling Atlantic,
  To rack our brains
  With fever pains,
  That have driven the Old World Frantic.

To the sewers and sinks
  With all such drinks,
  And after them tumble the mixer,
  For poison malign
  Is such Borgia wine,
  Or at best but a Devil's elixir.

While pure as spring
  Is the wine I sing,
  And to praise it, one needs but name it;
  For Catawba wine
  Has need of no sign,
  No tavern bush to proclaim it.

And this Song of the Vine,
  This greeting of mine,
  The winds and the birds shall deliver
  To the Queen of the West,
  In her garlands dressed,
  On the banks of the Beautiful River.

German workers. Though for each vintage they cultivated the grapes and made the wine, there was no consistent standard for quality. The national demand for Catawba coerced large owners to upgrade production, distribution, and storage. Smaller wine operations fell by the wayside. Advocates of natural wine typically harvested and sorted the grapes by hand. The clusters were destemmed, crushed, and fermented naturally without sugar. If the sugar level was acceptable, the fermentation was completed. Early on, if the sugar level was unacceptable, vintners were permitted to add sugar to complete the fermentation.

The 1850s were the heyday of Ohio wine. One of the first organizations of its kind, the American Wine Growers Association of Cincinnati published viticultural information and promoted natural wine. As America's leading wine center, Cincinnati produced 245,000 bottles of sparkling wine (at $1.50 a piece) and 205,000 bottles of still wine (at 40 cents a piece), valued at around $400,000.

The Ohio River Valley growers and vintners were buoyed by the prospect of healthy vineyards and huge profits. John Michael Meier came from the vineyards of Bavaria in 1856 and established a 164-acre homestead and vineyard in Kenwood, which he planted to German rootstock that failed. His son John Conrad Meier sought advice from

John Michael Meier. *Courtesy Meier's Wine Cellars*

Nicholas Longworth and replaced their German varietals with Catawba. This decision influenced winegrowing and wine-making at Meier's Wine Cellars for more than 140 years.

The greater Cincinnati wine community became alarmed, however, by the rise and fall of black rot (reddish-brown circular to angular spots) and powdery mildew (small grayish-white patches) which attacked the vine and the fruit. Black rot was often mistakenly attributed to soil, climate, cultivation, or other factors. The native American powdery mildew, on the other hand, had ravaged vineyards in Europe before it wiped out ones in Ohio, so growers recognized the problem. These intruders reduced vine growth, yield, fruit, quality, and winter hardiness. At the end of the 1860s, grape growing had diminished in the Ohio River Valley, and the Catawba no longer reigned as king.

Viticulture of Sandusky and the Erie Islands

After the Civil War, Ohio grape growing moved from the Ohio River Valley in southern Ohio to the shores and islands of Lake Erie and to other areas of the state. The southern rim of Lake Erie became home to German immigrants. In 1830, Clevelander H. C. Coit made a prediction that one day Lake Erie would become a world-famous viticultural district. Growers and vintners organized the Lake Shore Grape and Wine Growers' Association (later renamed the Ohio Grape Growers Association to quiet the prohibitionists) and showcased their best wines at the fashionable Paris Exhibition and other international festivals. The growers promoted the Catawba vineyards, which were later dominated by the Concord vineyards east of Cleveland. Popular wineries included Dover Bay Grape Wine Company, Lake View Wine Farm, and Louis Harris Winery.

The most distinctive winegrowing area was the region centered in the Lake Erie Islands, which dot the lake's western basin. The region consists of North Bass, Middle Bass, and South Bass islands, Catawba Island, Kelleys Island, Danbury Township on the Marblehead Peninsula, and the city of Sandusky.

Harlan Hatcher writes in *Lake Erie,* "The Lake Erie Islands, though often visited, were settled relatively late. The discovery that they were uniquely adaptable to grape culture attracted settlers in numbers around the middle nineteenth century."

From 1865 up to the advent of Prohibition in 1920, Ottawa and Erie Counties dominated wine production in Ohio, accounting for two-thirds or more of the state's production. Wines from the Lake Erie Islands were distributed in overseas markets and domestic markets in the South, Midwest, and along the East Coast. Lake Erie Island wines won medals and commendations in competitions in the United States and abroad.

The Erie Islands, also called the Wine Islands, distinguished themselves for having the longest growing season in the north-eastern United States. The islands' growing season averaged 190 days, while inland Ohio's growing season averaged 178 days or less. Island wine grapes are typically harvested up to six weeks later than mainland grapes. Lake Erie absorbs heat four times more slowly than the land and, conversely, retains heat four times longer than the land. Subsequently, the air over the lake reflects the water's more moderate

Wine casks from Kelleys Island wineries were brought across Lake Erie to Sandusky by horse and sleigh in the nineteenth and twentieth centuries. *Courtesy Sandusky Library*

temperature. In the Lake Erie American Viticultural Area, the regional autumn temperatures are warmer than Ohio's interior districts. The first harsh frost of fall is delayed by the warmer temperatures. Catawba and other late-ripening grapes thrived in these conditions.

In spring, the air around Lake Erie causes the shoots and buds to develop slowly, after the spring frosts. The fog and dew-free air over the islands eliminates any conditions for fungus, rot, and mildew during the growing season. The air over the islands is in constant motion because of the differences in temperatures between the land and water. The low rainfall compares favorably with Germany's winegrowing region along the Rhine River.

Datus Kelley planted Isabella cuttings on Kelleys Island in 1842 and founded the wine-growing industry in the Lake Erie Islands. His son-in-

law, Charles Carpenter, developed the first commercial vineyard in 1845 and pressed the district's first wine in 1850. Kelleys Island wine was taken to Cincinnati, where it was judged to be of comparable quality to wine that was produced in the Ohio River Valley. Carpenter built the first wine cellar on Kelleys Island in 1854.

The Erie Islands proved to be one of the better viticultural districts to cultivate some eighty varieties of grapes. The loamy topsoil with its porous underpan of cracked limestone was ideal because it absorbed Lake Erie water in the hot summer to moisten the roots. John Adlum's remarkable discovery of the Catawba's potential for good wine awakened a new spirit, and jump-started the economy.

From the 1840s until after World War II, Ohio winegrowers planted native American labrusca grapes, such as Catawba, Delaware, and Concord.

French-American hybrids were introduced, such as Baco Noir, Chlois, and Seyval Blanc. More recently, European vitis vinifera varietals have thrived, including Chardonnay and Johannisberg Riesling. Traditionally, the best wines produced on the islands were Catawba, Delaware, Niagara, Baco Noir, and Johannisberg Riesling.

The region held the greatest appeal to hordes of German newcomers, who believed the climate and soil matched that of their native Germany. They gambled everything to purchase land and plant grapes. The prosperity of the grape culture spread from Kelleys Island to the nearby Bass Islands to the Marblehead Peninsula between Lake Erie and Sandusky Bay and the outskirts of Sandusky. During the 1860s and 1870s, speculative grape growing started at $50 an acre and rose to a high of $1,500 an acre.

Gradually, as the black rot and powdery mildew destroyed the vineyards in Cincinnati and its environs, the Lake Erie Island region became the new center of Ohio grape growing. Cincinnati wine merchants established new business patterns: purchasing grapes or finished wine from the island region, or building wineries there themselves. John G. Dorn founded a winery in Sandusky in 1869, outfitting it with ancient oak casks from Longworth's wine cellar. Queen City wine wholesalers, the Rheinstrom Brothers started a Sandusky winery. Alsatian Vintner

Michael Werk invested in a Middle Bass winery. Joseph R. Peebles, a grocer and wine merchant, developed vineyards on North Bass Island. Nicholas Longworth, who is often remembered as the father of winegrowing on South Bass Island, is said to have given Philip Vroman, also a friendly grower, grape stock from his Cincinnati vineyards. Vroman planted them on South Bass Island, getting $400 for the first vintage and $3,000 for the second vintage.

In the excitement, small American wineries took root, and winemaking traditions originated in the Lake Erie Islands. Growers harvested and aged their wine in press houses on their farms or in the cellars of their homes. Across the United States and Europe, different generations have emulated this practice, from the home industries in Cleveland to the boutique wineries in Napa Valley to the garagistes in Bordeaux.

In 1866, the Kelleys Island growers founded the Kelley's Island Wine Company, a cooperative that allowed them to control their grape prices. Located in a stone castle with twin turrets, the 350,000-gallon winery was the largest on the island. Growers on North Bass, Middle Bass, and South Bass also started cooperatives, bridging the relationship between the small producer and the large producer. Several wineries rose to great heights—William Mills, Diamond Wine Company, M. Hommel Wine Company, Sweet Valley Wine Company, Thaddeus Lorch,

Conrad Ernest, Duroy & Haines Wine Company, and John Andrews. Others included Steuk Wine Company, Engles & Krudwig, Lenk Wine Company, Golden Eagle Winery, Lonz Wine Company, and Gustav Heineman.

In the early twentieth century, Kurt Boker wrote that professor W. B. Alwood, head of the United States Bureau of Chemistry, had studied the content of Lake Erie grapes and discovered that the most superb Delaware grapes in the world were grown in the Lake Erie Islands. He rated the Catawbas as second. Alwood continued that the overall growing conditions, soil, and climate favored the Erie Islands to produce some of the best basics for wine, surpassing the most famous winegrowing regions of Europe.

Arnold F. Elfers, a poet, author, and longtime Kelleys Islander until his death, always felt that "Earth hath no fairer spot than this!" In tribute, he wrote several poems, such as this one:

The rose may bloom in England,
The lily for France unfold;
Ireland may honor the Shamrock,
And Scotland her thistle bold;
But the shield of Kelleys Island
Shall be with Grapes inscrolled.

The popular Lonz Winery on Middle Bass Island has been a landmark since the 1800s. Launched during the Civil War as the Golden Eagle Winery, it became a 500,000-gallon wine and juice producer, one of the largest in America, by 1875. In 1884, Peter Lonz produced wines on Middle Bass Island, and then his son George Lonz designed the magnificent Gothic castle and vineyard estate that became Lonz Winery. It was visited by no fewer than five United States presidents and countless dignitaries. They were captivated by the winery's huge fireplace made from island stone and its hand-painted ceiling murals with poetry about the fruit of the vine. President Theodore Roosevelt once enjoyed a game of billiards in the tower room, which was also an observatory. In the mid-1970s, the late wine statesman Robert S. Gottesman, president of Cleveland's Paramount Distillers, Inc., purchased the Lonz Winery and several Erie Island vineyards. The facility remained open until July 2000, when tragically one afternoon a side terrace of the castle caved to the ground. One person was killed, and seventy people were injured.

In 2003, John Kronberg, a real estate developer, and Claudio Salvador, a respected winemaker, formed a holding company that they called Lonz Winery, Inc. It bought the Lonz name and other wine and vineyard properties from Paramount Distilleries, Inc. Though wine is no longer produced on the island, the current owners maintain Concord and Catawba vineyard contracts and send the wine grapes to the mainland for processing.

In 2004, Ohio Governor Bob Taft acquired 87 percent of 677-acre North

Antique Engles and Krudwig Winery poster featuring the commuter airline between Sandusky and the Lake Erie Islands. *Courtesy Phil Masturzo and Sandusky Library*

Bass for $17.4 million in state and federal funds from the island's longtime owner, Meier's Wine Cellars, Inc. (a division of Paramount Distilleries, Inc.) The purchase price was well below market value and reflected Gottesman's desire to preserve the island's grape heritage, undeveloped shoreline, natural coastal wetlands, geologic features, and habitats for endangered species and spawning grounds for the benefit of all Ohioans. In addition, the purchase protected North Bass Island as the last undeveloped island of its size in Lake Erie. Wine grape production has been a major part of the island's heritage and will continue on eighty-seven acres remaining under lease to Firelands Winery in Sandusky.

In northwest Ohio, the Lenk Wine Company was one of Toledo's most distinguished institutions. Brothers Peter and Carl Lenk started a nursery with F. C. Hansen. It was modeled after nurseries in Bavaria, where Peter had learned to grow grapes and make fine German wines. In 1862, the brothers harvested fruit from their vines and purchased Catawba from Put-in-Bay.

In 1868, Lenk & Company built the first wine cellar in Toledo and produced 15,000 gallons of wine. By 1887 the winery with the arched cellars covered two acres, processed 3,000 tons of grapes, and made 700,000 gallons of wine annually. Fruit was sourced from the Lake Erie Islands and the south shore of Lake Erie. The cellar consisted of four hundred casks, holding from 1,000 to 36,000 gallons. Its largest cask was also the largest one in existence, built by Mueller Brothers, Toledo coopers.

By the early 1900s, the largest wineries in the Lake Erie Island region were situated around Sandusky. While the winery proprietors were dependent on the island vineyards for grapes, they were lured by the city's extensive railroads and lake shipping, which provided easy, affordable access to out-of-state markets. On the eve of Prohibition, Sandusky was billed as the third-largest winegrowing center in America.

Winegrowing East of Cleveland

The expansion of commercial winegrowing east of Cleveland, home to vineyards as early as the 1830s, played a significant but lesser known role in developing Ohio's wine and grape industry. The Lake Erie viticultural district stretched west to Sandusky and east to Conneaut and into Pennsylvania and eastern New York. Identified as the eastern grape belt, the growing area has a history of being the largest in the United States outside of California. While western Sandusky and the Erie Islands became known for Catawba, eastern Geneva and Ashtabula became known for Concord.

The 1840s and 1850s were experimental growth years. Although the early 1860s were stifled by the Civil War, by the late 1860s wine entrepreneurs were passionate about winegrowing. Cleveland developed as a burgeoning city center with vineyards displaced by neighborhoods and industry. A significant number of varietal plantings and wineries were built to the east.

"In the mid-nineteenth century, like the rest of East Cleveland's Township, the area that became Cleveland Heights was farmland, quarries, and vineyards, owned by men and women of northern and western European descent who had come from New England, Ohio, and neighboring states and had acquired substantial property," Mary J. Morton wrote in *Cleveland Heights, The Making of an Urban Suburb*. "In 1864, John Peter Preyer bought 75 acres of farmland, moved his family into a spacious home built in the 1820s of local sandstone, and planted vineyards for his Lake View Wine Farm."

Other successful grape growers were the Shakers, members of a religious community influenced by the Quakers. Two Shaker communities existed in Ohio: Union Village in Lebanon, 1805, and North Union in Shaker, 1822. They designed their lives to bring heaven to earth, expressed through their creativity and industry. The Shaker Vineyards Land Company was one such example.

In 1892, Joseph Shingleland, head elder of the Western Shakers, settled in Wickliffe when raising grapes along Lake Erie had become profitable business. In one Shaker Historical Society letter, a Wickliffe resident wrote, "Elder Shingleland was not imbued with the Shaker simplicity, but had been bitten by a 'get rich quick' desire...He was building a handsome dwelling

Joseph Golomb atop his tractor. *Courtesy Judith Orkin Rosenthal*

For more than forty years, the Geneva Jewish farmers flourished in agriculture. During the 1900s, the Geneva farmers, also recognized as the Lake Erie Jewish Community, comprised ninety families who had departed Cleveland for a better life. Wealthy European financier Baron Maurice de Hirsch, a humanitarian, was concerned about the welfare of Russian Jews after the assassination of Czar Alexander the II. In 1881, de Hirsch gave $2.4 million to fund farm colonies; the Geneva farmers were one such group. They constructed homes surrounded by grape vineyards and fruit orchards. During the week, the men were employed in the Cleveland garment and needle trades, and on the weekends they commuted to their farms, where they grew Concord in Lake and Ashtabula counties. At one time, this enterprising community produced 60 percent of the area's grape crop.

Cleveland families such as that of Judith Orkin Rosenthal were among the first Jewish farmers to settle in Unionville in 1902. Rosenthal's maternal grandparents, Joseph and Rachael Golomb, came to Cleveland from the Ukraine in 1910. They established a two-hundred-acre farm in Cork, just outside of Geneva, where they cleared the woods for a Concord vineyard and pastured horses and cows. It was an example of a model vineyard, used by the Ohio State University Department of Agriculture. Golomb and his friend Morris Brody

and administrative building at Union Village and needed ready money." Shingleland bought some 1,000 acres of vineyards and two packing houses. "It takes three years for a vine to mature, and the first crop was harvested in 1897, when four carloads of grapes went out daily," the letter continues. "Here the work went on night and day in season."

Shingleland later converted the packing houses into wineries, where he installed presses and wooden vats. He hired an expert winemaker and for a time made money, but this was contrary to Shaker beliefs. A frost destroyed many of the vineyards, and the death of the chief overseer caused Shingleland to sell the property.

headed the wine cooperative so they could monitor grape prices. During depressed years, a bushel of grapes sold for two cents. After a late frost when grapes were scarce, they went for $100 a ton.

Also notable in Geneva was the Cohodas Brothers Produce Company, founded by Morris and Bessie Cohodas. They raised grapes, corn, strawberries, tomatoes, peas, potatoes, and other crops. Later, their son Norman Cohodas purchased Highland Farms from Rosenthal's paternal grandparents, and his brother Alvin became an agricultural consultant with a keen interest in grapes and wine.

At the turn of the twentieth century, Morris and Anne Brody established the 118-acre Brody's Fruit Farm on South River Road in Geneva. Brody was a leader in the affairs of the Jewish farm community and one of the most prominent fruit growers in eastern Ohio. The Ohio State Experimental Station used his orchards for tests to manage insects and diseases.

The community prospered until the Depression, when small farms failed and people moved into the city for work. After World War II, the community's farming activities ceased because the younger generation went on to college under the G.I. Bill. After observing how hard their parents had worked to live on a farm, the younger generation was never committed to perpetuating their dreams.

As northeast Ohio shifted from "truck farming" to "grape growing," people of all nationalities and cultures settled there. Far from home, these immigrants shared their treasured traditions, customs, rituals, and lore—specifically as they related to wine and food—with each other. They included the English, the Italians, the French, the Germans, the Austrians, the Hungarians, the Slovenians, the Czechoslovakians, and the Scandinavians. Families such as the Ferrantes, the Virants, the Debevcs, and the Grubers loved the land; they planted orchards and vineyards and built farmhouses and barns for horses, cattle, sheep, chickens. As wine pioneers, these families blazed the trail for grape growing and winemaking to produce bulk wines and, later, private-label wines.

In the early 1960s, Joseph Gruber Sr., a pioneering Geneva grape grower, read about the tradition of grape festivals in other wine states. Joseph and his brother Ray presented the idea for a similar event in 1963 to the Tri-County Grape Growers Association and the Geneva Area Chamber of Commerce. What resulted was the now-historic Jamboree Grape Festival, a two-day celebration of the grape harvest first started in 1964, held the last weekend of September. People and grapes are featured in parades, contests, exhibits, arts and craft fairs, and a farmer's market.

Vintner's Challenge

In 1806, Edward Phelps and his family moved from Windsor, Connecticut, to five hundred fertile acres of farmland along Alum Creek in the frontier town of Westerville, Ohio. Ten years later, they were joined by the Westervelt brothers from New York, and by the late 1840s there was a sizeable settlement. In 1858, the town was officially incorporated and a year later legally banned "the sale, barter, or gift of wine, fermented cider, beer, and spirituous liquors." That controversial decision was to affect the history of Westerville and the United States for more than a century.

Henry and Phyloxena Corbin, proprietors of a new saloon on Westerville's Main Street, vehemently challenged the law. In the Westerville Whiskey War of 1875, the citizenry demonstrated and blew out the saloon's windows and roof with gunpowder. For four years, this act stopped the war until 1879, when it was revived. Afterward, Westerville became a dry town, and no fermented spirits have been sold there since.

Over time, grape growing and wine-making gradually declined in the Buckeye State. By the mid-1870s, inexpensive California wine was shipped to the Midwest and East. In the 1880s, Henry Howe, a historian, wrote how the adulteration of wine and the California competition had dramatically affected Ohio's standing in the world. The Erie Island producers, Ohio's premiere viticulturists, could no longer be compared favorably to France. In addition, older grape growers in the most productive regions were faced with aging vineyards, where quality and yields were threatened. Crop failures due to unexpected plagues hit the island growers at random over many decades.

From the late 1880s to the late 1890s, Ohio growers and vintners witnessed the increase of viticulture and vinification in Michigan, Pennsylvania, and New York. Ohio entrepreneurs were troubled by the competition's low pricing. As a strategy to win back their clientele, Ohio vintners lowered the price of their wine, which was made from the same amount of juice, but added alcohol, water, sugar, and berries.

In 1893, a national temperance movement was founded in Oberlin, Ohio. Later headquartered in Washington, D.C., the Anti-Saloon League of America vowed to close the country's saloons and promote abstinence by agitation, legislation, and enforcement. The league and the town joined forces when Westerville offered a permanent location for establishing the league's publishing center for anti-alcohol publications, booklets, and posters. Westerville was chosen because it was a viewed as a socially clean and morally upright community.

This partnership, dubbed the noble experiment, and Prohibition, in effect from 1920 to 1933, contributed to the Ohio wine industry's decline. During the early 1920s, the Erie Island winegrowers benefited from Prohibition because grape prices for Catawba peaked at around $100 a ton as demand for nonalcoholic grape juice replaced wine sales. People converted grape juice into homemade wine. But by the late 1920s, commercial winegrowers were confronted with a surplus of grapes. Soon, vineyards around the Erie Islands region and the state were abandoned.

Interestingly, several Ohio and California bulk wineries were permitted by law to produce wine for the sacrament or medicine. Cleveland's Hammer Company, an importer and distributor of wine from around the world, was founded in 1914 by Alfred Joseph Hammer. "With Prohibition in 1920, my grandfather realized he would be out of a job; his older brother, a priest in the Cleveland Diocese, suggested that he sell sacramental wines to churches. So, he bought Muscatel, Port, Tokay, Chablis, and Burgundy from Beaulieu Vineyard in the Napa Valley and other wineries," says A. J. Hammer, former president of the company, now owned by Glazer Distributors, Inc.

The repeal of Prohibition in 1933 brought hope to a handful of Ohio wineries, who applied for licenses and planted new vineyards. But the demand for grapes never materialized, and the commercial winegrowers left the industry in droves. World War II brought a renewed interest in grapes and an upturn in wine sales, but it was the tumultuous sixties that brought dramatic change to the Ohio wine industry. The U.S. government spearheaded a campaign to reach new and existing winegrowers. Wine legend Dr. Garth A. Cahoon, professor emeritus at Ohio State University, led the charge and spent ten years, from 1953 to 1963, at University of California, Riverside, conducting research on citrus physiology before coming to Ohio. Plant nutrition was his research emphasis throughout his career.

He writes, "I began my work in Ohio with grapes in 1963 and retired in 1992. I did extensive work with several hundred hybrids at many locations around the state during this period of time. I consider my venture back into the southern part of this state, where the industry originally began, to be the start of the revival of the grape and wine industry in Ohio. The number of wineries grew rapidly during this period…To further test the value of the hybrids I established a series of plots with growers, in 15 counties adjoining the Ohio River, which I called 'Research Demonstration Vineyards'…

I don't anticipate that the acreage of new vineyards will increase in any major way under the present industry environment but hope that I am wrong. Vinifera wines now seem to receive the major emphasis and have the best sales appeal. Looking back at where we started in the sixties current Ohio wines are now light years ahead."

An enologist of high merit, Dr. James F. Gallander, professor emeritus at Ohio State University for thirty-five years, is the winner of awards from the American Wine Society and the Eastern Section of Enologists and Viticulturists. He writes, "Much of our early research, mid-1960s, dealt with the evaluation of French hybrids, selections from eastern institutions, and a few vinifera varieties for their table wine quality. Attention was given to those grapes which yielded high-quality wines without the characteristic flavors and aromas of American species. Some of the most successful grapes included: Seyval, Vidal, Riesling, Chardonnay, Foch, and De Chaunac."

Dr. Gallander stated his vision for Ohio for the twenty-first century. "Continue the growth of small boutique wineries and strive to produce superior table wines, particularly white wines that are distinguishable from other regions. An emerging challenge to the Ohio wine industry will be the discovery of a premium red variety."

The Ohio State University Viticulture and Enology research program provides the commercial grape and wine industry and its citizens practical research in viticulture and enology to enhance quality Ohio wine. Viticulture trials research crop levels, training systems, clones, rootstock, and cold hardiness. Enology trials show how these viticultural practices enhance quality by evaluating yeast strains, malolactic fermentation, and pressing treatments. The annual Ohio Grape-Wine Short Course founded by Cahoon and Gallander serves as a major avenue of distribution of these findings.

Commercial experiments are conducted in viticulture and enology at Ohio's research centers in Kingsville, Ripley, and Wooster, all different climates and growing conditions. The research plots consist of two American hybrid, six French-American hybrid, and eight vitis vinifera vineyards. To ensure quality Ohio premium wine, the Ohio Grape Industries Committee and Ohio Agriculture Research and Development Center (OARDC) have partnered in offering wine analysis and trouble-shooting free to the Ohio wine industry. The Ohio Wine Competition, part of the OARDC Enology program, provides Gold, Silver, or Bronze Medal winners a complete wine analysis in the interest of education and excellence. Ohio is once again reclaiming its rightful reputation for improved standards.

Arnie Esterer and Tim Hubbard, founders of Markko Vineyard in Conneaut, planted the first all-vitis vinifera vineyard in 1968. During the

Glasses set up for comparative wine tasting in Wooster. *Courtesy OSU/OARDC*

seventies, new commercial grape growing commenced in southern Ohio, where viticulture had begun in the early 1800s. In 1970, Wistar and Ursula Marting, pioneers of several new and experimental vineyards, founded the Tarula Farm Winery near Clarksville. The Martings had an interest in French hybrids, then later vitis vinifera. They shared an association with Ken Schuchter Sr., owner of Valley Vineyards, twelve miles west in Morrow, and the two families actively planted grapes and made wine. Nearby, Meier's Wine Cellars in Silverton developed a 125-acre vineyard of an experimental French hybrid.

Encouraged by the results, others followed their lead until large tracts of considerable size were under cultivation in the Ohio River Valley. The grapes produced wines on a caliber of classic European vitis vinifera varietals. The rebirth of the Ohio wine industry in the south caused a shift in the north on the Erie Islands and around Sandusky, where new French-American hybrid and vitis vinifera vineyards were developed.

The Ohio Wine Producers Association (OWPA), an eclectic group of growers and vintners, was organized in 1975 supported by leadership from researchers at the Ohio State University Research and Development Center. Its early founders included Ray Gruber, Arnie Esterer, Tony Debevc, Ken Schuchter, Sr., Ken and Mary Rush, Estel Cloud, Louis Heineman, Dr. James Gallander, and Dr. Garth A. Cahoon. The association aims to produce quality grapes and wines, build a positive public awareness of Ohio wines, encourage unity within the industry, ensure a climate that sustains its long-term viability, and coordinate other member services.

Donniella Winchell, executive director of the Ohio Wine Producers Association, assesses the future of Ohio wines: "Our industry faces several major tasks in the coming decades: We must continue to identify appropriate clonal selections of world-class varietals and to locate more amenable growing sites for that fruit. We must find a way to protect those unique vineyard plots against urban encroachment. In the cellar, we must improve winemaking techniques to attract the most sophisticated palates and find more ways to attract visitors to 'wine country.' We must establish additional off-site tasting opportunities at restaurants, seminars, and festivals."

In the 1980s the Ohio General Assembly passed legislation that created the Ohio Grape Industries Program, a vehicle for vintners and viticulturists to access marketing and research programs. In the 1990s Governor George Voinovich established programs to increase grape acreage such as tax credits, planting grants, and the addition of a state viticulturist. Ohio wines have regained name recognition and goodwill at local, state, national, and international festivals and competitions.

The establishment of Ohio American Viticultural Areas specifies the precise geographic location or origin of grapes used to produce a specific wine type. The appellations reflect the *terroir,* or the sum of the characteristics of the place that include the vineyard site and its history, geography, climate, soil, and grape variety. In Ohio, there are five distinct viticultural districts. The Lake Erie American Viticultural Area, the first, consists of grapes grown along or near the shores of Ohio, Pennsylvania, and New York. Its two sub-viticultural districts are the Isle St. George, the second, and the Grand River Valley, the third. Ohio River Valley American Viticultural Area, the fourth, parallels the Ohio River from Wheeling, West Virginia, to Evansville, Indiana. The Loramie Creek American Viticultural Area, the fifth, in Shelby County is bordered by Loramie and Tuttle creeks on State Route 47 but has no vineyard or winery within its parameters.

The Lake Erie Quality Wine Alliance (LEQWA) was formed in 1993 to represent farm wineries in Ohio, Pennsylvania, and western New York. The association espouses standards and practices in viticulture and the production of grape-based products. "Creating elegant wines through the reflections of our unique *terroir,* The Lake Erie Quality Wine Alliance expresses international excellence through regional character," LEQWA President Ken Tarsitano says.

Ohio Vineyard Lands

The Ohio Wine Country provides unique advantages for winegrowing. The Lake Erie Plains expand in a rolling band along the banks of the lake and then widen into fertile lowlands some fifty miles west in the Maumee Valley. The Ohio shoreline parallels Lake Erie from Conneaut in the east, where there are high clay bluffs, to Toledo farther west, where there are sandy clay beaches, a total of 262 miles. One of America's most fertile farming districts, the Till Plains in western Ohio are sporadically planted with grapes in what is called the corn belt. The Appalachian or Allegheny Plateau comprises the half of Ohio to the south of the Lake Erie Plains. The ruggedly beautiful, mineral-rich plateau has thin, depleted soils contrasted with its northern hills and valleys and its much steeper southern hills and deeper valleys. A small triangular section of the Bluegrass Region, which spills north from Kentucky, includes the thin soils that make up that part of southern Ohio.

Dedicated Ohio winegrowers, vintners, and scientists have collaborated to discover which types of grapes grow best in which districts. In 1983, American wines were formally identified with specificity by the distinct regions of the

Ohio at a Glance

Land Area 40,953 square miles
Waterway Area 3,875 square miles
Average Elevation 850 feet above sea level
Primary Rivers Ohio, Cuyahoga, Miami, Sandusky
Primary Lakes Lake Erie, Grand Lake
Seasons: Cold winters and warm, humid summers
Average Temperature 52 degrees Fahrenheit
Monthly Average Temperatures Range from low of 15.5 degrees to high of 85.8 degrees Fahrenheit

United States where the grapes were cultivated. These winegrowing regions were defined by the political subdivision by county and state, or by a viticultural district named for its particular climate, soil, topography, and history. These elements precisely mirror the personality and character of the locales where the grapes were cultivated.

Climate is the challenge with winegrowing in Ohio. Noble varieties such as Chardonnay, Riesling, Cabernet Sauvignon, and Pinot Noir are hard to grow in the cold climes of northern Ohio. Though the hardier, winter-resistant grapes like Catawba and Delaware produce quaffable Ohio table wine, a large percentage of consumers prefer the

An aerial view of lush vineyards in Harpersfield, with the winding Grand River in the background. *Courtesy Rebecca Wayman, photographer, and Robert Oxley, pilot, Oxley Photography*

gentler bouquet and taste of California and European wines. A native vitis labrusca varietal, an acidic Concord (used in jams, jellies, and juices), thrives in Ohio and is softened by the addition of sugar and water so it is drinkable.

Vintners have even gone so far as to blend native Ohio grapes with California wines. Wine expert and vitis vinifera advocate Dr. Konstantin Frank made history planting the noble varieties in the Finger Lakes in protected environments near large bodies of water. Through the decades his pioneering work has changed the thinking of serious Ohio winegrowers, and classical varietals are constantly changing the landscape of wines offered.

Following the phylloxera epidemic of the twentieth century, French wine growers grafted the delicate classic vines onto sturdy, disease-resistant American rootstocks. The grape species retained their original traits and did not acquire negative aspects. Further, the French crossed true grape species that resulted in vines that adapted to different growing conditions, the fruits of which would make good wine. The grapes are called French hybrids in the United States and Canada and American hybrids in France.

With its present 2,200 acres of grapes and five American viticultural areas, Ohio has produced some outstanding dry table wines from vitis vinifera grapes for more than thirty-five years. Specific to Ohio is its historic production of sweet table and dessert wines produced from vitis labrusca grapes and hardy French hybrids.

Lake Erie has the greatest annual temperature variation of any of the Great Lakes, resulting in a longer growing season. The history of major bodies of water located near top-quality vineyards is known throughout the world. The Guadalquivir in Spain's Sherry district, Jerez de la Frontera; Germany's Rhine and Mosel districts; France's Loire, Rhone and Gironde Estuary; California's Napa and Russian rivers; and New York's Finger Lakes have established unique appellations with regional climates. The larger the body of water, the greater its influence on the district's climate, weather, and vineyards. It is said that Lake Erie provides the foundation to produce wines of excellence. Weather variations continuously challenge the vintner, resulting in a marked difference in the style and variety of wine from vintage to vintage. Such variation is typical of the Lake Erie viticultural district, a cool climate region, but the nature of the wines there is awesome.

Today, Lake Erie is noted for its vitis viniferas and its French-American hybrids. The European varietals produce higher yields per acre than French-American hybrid varietals and a superior taste with more bottle aging. The white viniferas include Chardonnay, Riesling, Gewurztraminer, and Pinot Gris. The red viniferas are Cabernet Sauvignon, Pinot Noir, and Cabernet Franc. The French-American hybrid varietals were developed for winter hardiness and resistance to disease, enhanced by a complexity of flavors. The white hybrids highlighted are Vidal Vignoles, Seyval Blanc, and Cayuga. The red hybrid most featured is Chambourcin. The region's other noted hybrid varieties are Baco Noir, Chancellor, Chelois, Concord, De Chaunac, Ives Noir, and Marechal Foch.

Grand River Valley American Viticultural Area, situated in Lake, Geauga, and Ashtabula counties, is a sub-appellation. Again, Lake Erie's moderating effect on climate and the growing season is the dominant geographical feature. The Grand River

An aerial view of the world-famous North Bass Island, which has the distinction of being one of the few premium island winegrowing districts in the world with its own appellation, the Isle St. George America Viticultural Area, and the first official Ohio AVA. *Courtesy Ohio Wine Producers Association*

Valley viticultural district is confined to the portion of the Lake Erie viticultural district that is within two miles in any direction of the river. It consists of all the land west of Ohio State Route 45 in any direction of the river and within fourteen miles of the shore of Lake Erie. The climate is the river valley's most distinguishing feature. The Grand River Valley's excellent air drainage supercedes that of the Lake Erie area. And the isobars, the exact place where the pressure of air is the same, for the 170-day and 180-day growing seasons pass directly through the Grand River Valley American Viticultural Area.

A second sub-appellation, Isle St. George is a small viticultural area in the western part of Lake Erie in Ottawa County. This appellation is the northernmost of the Bass Islands. It is one-and-one-half miles wide and slightly less that in length, and is eighteen miles from Port Clinton on the mainland. The first grapes were planted on the island in 1853 by Peter and Simon Fox. Catawba and other grapes have flourished here for more than 117 years. At its conception as an appellation, half of the island was devoted to vineyards. At the turn of the twentieth century, there were only two wineries that processed these grapes: one North Bass Island winery and Cincinnati's Meier's Wine Cellars. All the grapes on the island are sent by boat to the Ohio mainland

Kinkead Ridge Vineyards in the spring. *Photo by Nancy Bentley, courtesy Kinkead Ridge*

for processing as no wineries currently exist on the island.

Isle St. George has distinctive topography, soils, and climate from other identified regions for the cultivation of grapes. It is basically flat; no point is more than fourteen feet above the surface of Lake Erie. The soil comprises shallow sandy loam and silt loam with limestone bedrock twenty to thirty inches deep in some places. The lake-influenced climate allows for a frost-free period of 206 days, longer than any other place in Ohio, and annual precipitation is less than the adjacent areas. Isle St. George has 26.7 inches, while Kelleys Island has 31.7 inches and Sandusky has 32.1 inches.

The Ohio River Valley American Viticultural Area was established as a 26,000-squaremile viticultural area

in Ohio, Indiana, West Virginia, and Kentucky. At the onset, there were 570 acres of vines, grown by 463 grape growers and eighteen wineries. The Ohio River Valley viticultural region is known for its rare pattern of rainfall, the "Ohio type," in which water accumulates in excess of 2.3 inches within twenty-four hours. Robert De Courcy Ward in *The Climates of the United States* explains that this phenomenon, which occurs monthly except in October, could result in severe flooding but for two features. Gray-Brown Podzolic, the dominant soil type only to this area, has slow to moderate permeability, and the Ohio River Valley landscape drains rapidly. Within a few miles of the river, there is a more moderate climate that has fewer extremes during the growing season and is tempered by winds.

Ohio Wineries at a Glance

1. Al-Bi Winery
2. Biscotti Family Winery
3. Breitenbach Wine Cellars
4. Buccia Vineyard
5. Buckeye Winery
6. Burnet Ridge Winery
7. Camelot Cellars Winery
8. Candlelight Winery
9. Chalet Debonné Vineyards
10. Coffee Cake Winery
11. Cortland Wine Cellar
12. Emerine Estates Winery
13. Farinacci Winery
14. Ferrante Winery & Ristorante
15. Firelands Winery
16. Flint Ridge Vineyard & Winery
17. Georgetown Vineyards
18. Grand River Cellars
19. Grande Wine Cellars
20. Grape & Granary
21. Harmony Hill Vineyards
22. Harpersfield Vineyard
23. Heineman Winery
24. Henke Winery
25. Heritage Vineyard & Guest House
26. Hermes Vineyards
27. Hillside Winery
28. Jilbert Winery
29. John Christ Winery
30. Kelley's Island Wine Company
31. Kinkead Ridge Estate Winery
32. Klingshirn Winery
33. The Lakehouse Inn Winery
34. Lakeside Vineyard & Winery
35. Laleure Vineyards
36. Laurello Vineyards
37. Maize Valley Winery
38. Maple Ridge Vineyard
39. Markko Vineyard
40. Mastropietro Winery
41. Matus Winery
42. Meier's Wine Cellars
43. Meranda-Nixon Winery
44. Merry Family Winery
45. Mon Ami Restaurant & Historic Winery
46. Moyer Vineyards, Winery & Restaurant
47. Myrddin Winery
48. Old Firehouse Winery
49. Paper Moon Vineyards
50. Perennial Vineyards
51. Quarry Hill Winery
52. Rainbow Hills Vineyards
53. Raven's Glenn Winery
54. Ravenhurst Champagne Cellars
55. Red Horse Vineyards
56. Sarah's Vineyard
57. Shamrock Vineyard
58. Shawnee Springs Winery
59. Silver Moon Winery
60. Slate Run Vineyard
61. Soine Vineyards
62. South River Vineyard
63. St. Joseph Vineyard
64. Stone Crest Vineyard
65. Stoney Ridge Winery
66. Swiss Heritage Winery
67. Tarsitano Winery
68. Terra Cotta Vineyards
69. ThornCreek Winery and Gardens
70. Troutman Vineyards
71. Valley Vineyards
72. Vermilion Valley Vineyards
73. Viking Vineyards and Winery
74. Vinoklet Winery
75. Virant Family Winery
76. The Winery at Spring Hill
77. The Winery at Versailles
78. The Winery at Wolf Creek
79. Woodstone Creek Winery
80. Wyandotte Winery

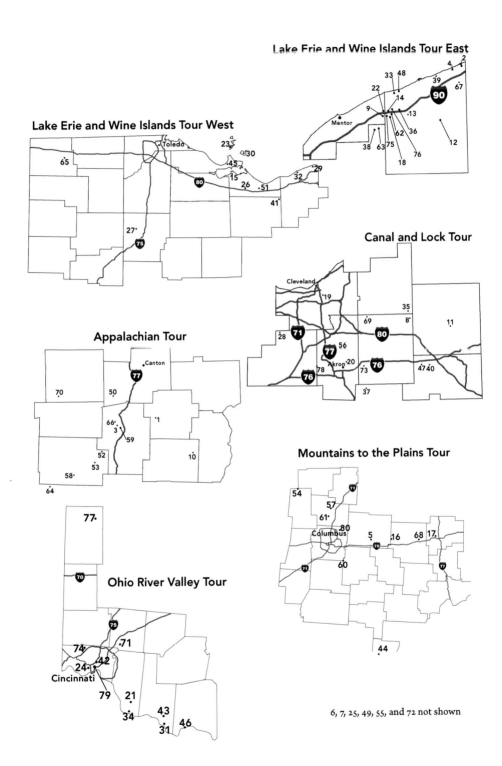

Lake Erie and Wine Islands Tour East

Lake Erie and Wine Islands Tour West

Canal and Lock Tour

Appalachian Tour

Mountains to the Plains Tour

Ohio River Valley Tour

6, 7, 25, 49, 55, and 72 not shown

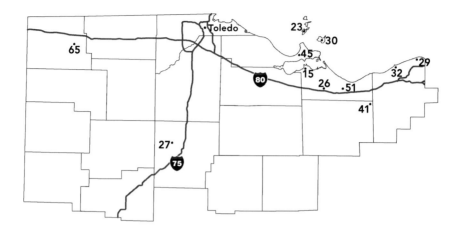

Lake Erie and Wine Islands Tour West

Firelands Winery

917 Bardshar Road
Sandusky, OH 44870
Tel (419) 625-5474 or (800) 548-wine
Fax (419) 625-4887
E-mail Info@firelandswinery.com
Web site www.firelandswinery.com
Owners Lonz Winery, includes John Kronberg and Claudio Salvador
Winemaker Claudio Salvador
Founded 1880

Between 1776 and 1783, Connecticut citizens whose domiciles were ravaged by the British during the Revolutionary War migrated to the Firelands region of north-central Ohio, where they were granted homesteads as compensation. These proud but practical New Englanders brought a tradition of growing grapes and making wine to the Midwest. One such gentleman, Edward Mantey, was enticed by the thriving wine industry along Lake Erie's south shore. He learned that this wine district, now the American Viticultural Area, had a promising reputation for its climate, soil, grapes, and wines.

In 1880, Mantey, a German settler, built a fruit farm that became Mantey Winery. Highly coveted, the Mantey wines, especially the Catawbas, were sold both locally and as far east as Pittsburgh and as far west as Chicago. Mantey and his two ambitious sons, Sylvester and Aloysius, expanded the winery's production to 50,000 gallons.

With the advent of Prohibition in 1920, Mantey Winery ceased to operate. The wine barrels and aging casks were destroyed, but the vineyards and orchards were maintained. Grapes were sold for fruit or juice. With the repeal of Prohibition in 1933, Sylvester rebuilt Mantey Winery. Demand soared for labeled wines packaged in glass bottles. Customers no longer filled their jugs with wine or purchased wine by the barrel.

By 1945, Paul and Norman Mantey, the grandsons of founder Edward, assumed leadership. They established a reputation for fine wines and loyal patrons. "Three generations of Manteys worked here for one hundred years," current vice president and winemaker Claudio Salvador says. In 1980, after the Manteys retired, they sold the jointly owned Mantey Winery and Mon Ami Restaurant & Historic Winery (of which Norman was the sole owner) to the late Robert Gottesman, founder of Cleveland's Paramount Distillers, Inc.

Claudio Salvador, winemaker, evaluating Firelands premium wines. *Courtesy Firelands Winery*

"Overnight, Gottesman transformed the place," Salvador says. "He named the venture Firelands, planted some of the region's early vitis vinifera wines, and retained the Mantey line of native American wines."

When Ohio vintners began to challenge themselves to grow new grape types, Gottesman, a wine pioneer in his own right, was quick to respond. He replaced fifty acres of Catawba and Concord at Firelands' vineyards on North Bass Island (once known as the Isle of St. George) with vitis vinifera. Gottesman planted and replanted a test vitis vinifera vineyard until he

achieved the right mix of grapes. It featured twenty-five acres of Riesling; five acres of Gewürztraminer; five acres of Chardonnay; five acres of Pinot Noir; five acres of Cabernet Sauvignon; and five acres of Petit Verdot, Alicante, Pommard, and other varieties.

"1984 was the first vintage of vinifera grapes that I processed in Ohio," says Salvador, who is originally from Italy. "It took me a couple of years to understand the growing season in this part of the world. We introduced a revolutionary and different style of Firelands wines. They were characterized as young, lighter, fruitier, drinkable, and

Firelands Winery. *Courtesy Firelands Winery*

affordable—whites such as Pinot Grigio and Riesling and good hearty reds such as Cabernet Sauvignon and Merlot."

Time and again, Salvador has changed his style of winemaking to meet the demands of the market. The late eighties were a period of experimentation and expansion. "I made a fruity Chardonnay, but consumers said they preferred a Chardonnay that was chewy with oak aging. So, that is the kind of Chardonnay I produced. Sales went up, and we began to win medals," he says.

In 2003, Salvador and John Kronberg, a real estate developer, formed Lonz Winery, Inc., a holding company that purchased Firelands Winery and Mon Ami Restaurant & Historic Winery from Paramount Distillers, Inc. "Our emphasis consists of creating quality wine products," Salvador says. "We make wine in the vineyard, but because of the Ohio weather, we must be prepared to help the wine in the cellar."

The Firelands wine-production center is equipped with the newest equipment and the latest technology. It is both a boutique winery and a juice processor for Firelands, Mon Ami, and Cincinnati's Meier's Wine Cellars, owned by Paramount Distillers, Inc.

Firelands Winery

Directions Take I-90 to Ohio 2 west. Exit at U.S. Route 6 toward Fremont/Sandusky. Turn left onto Fremont Avenue/U.S. 6, then right on Bardshar Road to the winery

Hours June–Sept., Mon.–Thurs., 9 AM–6 PM; Fri.–Sat., 9 AM–5 PM; Sun., 11 AM–5 PM; Oct.–May, Mon.–Sat., 9 AM–5 PM; Closed Sunday

Tours Self-guided tours; deluxe group tours for 20 or more cost $3 per person, which includes four wines, juices, cheese and crackers, and a souvenir glass

Tastings Daily

Gifts Wine and wine-related artifacts

Picnics Picnics are welcome in the gazebo overlooking the vineyard

Highlights at Winery Lovely outdoor picnic facilities; lively tasting room with lots of good wines; excellent winery video presentation

Events Christmas Open House, February Wine and Chocolate

Prices $5.99–$29.99; 10 percent case discount; UPS shipping in Ohio

Brand Names Firelands, Mantey, Lonz

Type of Production Traditional

Method of Harvesting Mechanical

Pressing and Winemaking Pressurized screw press for volume juice; bladder press for vinifera; traditional winemaking

Aging and Cooperage Stainless steel and oak cooperage

County Erie

AVAs Isle of St. George and Lake Erie

Acreage 50

Waterway Lake Erie

Climate Moderating lake effect; 200-day frost-free growing season

Soil Clay loam

Varieties Vitis vinifera, French-American hybrids, vitis labrusca

Wines Cabernet Sauvignon, Merlot, Cabernet Franc, Chardonnay, Chardonnay Select, Pinot Grigio, Pinot Noir, Country Estate Red, Country Estate White, Gewürztraminer, Riesling, Walleye White, Country Estate Blush, Ice White, Vin Rosé, Delaware, Niagara, Blue Face, Pink Catawba, Fifty-Fifty, Haut Sauterne, Crème Catawba, Mellow Concord, Blackberry, Cream Sherry, Firelands Champagne Brut, Firelands Champagne Brut Rosé, Firelands Riesling Champagne

Best Reds Merlot and Cabernet Sauvignon

Best White Pinot Grigio

Best Other Wine Gewürztraminer

Nearby Places to Visit Picturesque Sandusky; Historic Port Clinton

Heineman Winery

978 Catawba Avenue, Box 300
Put-in-Bay, OH 43456
Tel (419) 285-2811
Fax (419) 285-3412
Web site www.heinemanswinery.com
Owner Louis V. Heineman
Winemaker Edward Heineman
Founded 1888

The blue and white ferry boat from Catawba plied the choppy, white-capped waters and gusty winds at the western end of Lake Erie on its run to Put-in-Bay, the only town on South Bass Island. It was from the harbor called Put-in-Bay that Oliver Hazard Perry sailed to defeat the British fleet under Robert H. Barclay during the War of 1812. This gray morning, the skies accentuated the limestone cliffs as the ferry boat tooted its horn and pulled into the dock. A gentleman of distinction, Louis V. Heineman, third-generation owner of the family-owned and -operated Heineman Winery, awaited on shore, delighted to share tales of one of Ohio's most revered viticultural treasures.

Grape growing and winemaking commenced on this small, two-by-four-mile island in the early 1850s. Real estate mogul Joseph de Rivera, a Spanish merchant, purchased South Bass Island and its sister islands for $44,000, dividing the land into ten-acre parcels. As South

Bass Island's reputation grew as a fashionable resort, tourists from Canada and the Great Lakes came by steamship to stay at the popular Victory Hotel.

In 1880, Gustav Heineman, Louis's grandfather, left Freiburgim-Breisgau, a prized grape-growing district along the Rhine, and headed for America. With other German immigrants from that country's grape-growing district, he journeyed inland to Ohio. "Gustav worked at Golden Eagle Winery, later Lonz Winery, on Middle Bass Island, then visited Germany in 1882," Louis says. "Upon his return, the Erie Islands were prospering and valued by growers and producers as a highly recognized viticultural district. Simultaneously, Stephanie (Fanny) Zeller, a beauty from Baden-Baden, won Gustav's heart, and the newly married Heinemans relocated to the island."

The Heinemans found the legendary Lake Erie Islands, with their clay limestone soils and temperate climate, ideal for a vineyard. "The island temperatures are five degrees Fahrenheit warmer—more like Detroit and Toledo—than the east side of Cleveland," Louis says. His grandfather planted labrusca grapes, such as Concord, Niagara, Delaware, and Catawba, and then, in 1888, started the winery. By 1900, there were seventeen wineries on Put-in-Bay, close to eight varieties, and four hundred acres planted to vines. "Put-in-Bay had a street car line that transported tourists to the Heineman Winery," Louis says. "My father, Norman, who inherited the winery from Gustav, used to sell wine to visitors outside the winery."

With the advent of Prohibition in 1920, Norman focused his production on grape juice, offered in five- to fifty-gallon lots with a little bootlegged wine thrown in on the side. Stocks departed on the ferry boat from Put-in-Bay to arrive in Sandusky, then were shipped east by rail.

Tourists flocked to Crystal Cave on the Heineman property, which houses one of the world's largest known geodes (hollow rocks lined with crystals), some thirty feet in diameter. Samples of these crystals are on display at the Smithsonian Natural History Museum in Washington, D.C.

After Prohibition, Norman applied for a grower's permit to make wine. Louis outlines his entry into the business: "At nine in 1935, I cleared tables; after World War II, at twenty-two in

1948, I ran the bar." By 1953, his brother Harry Heineman bought the Port Clinton-headquartered Heineman Distributing Company from Otto Heineman, his cousin, and Heineman Trucking, a beverage wholesaler serving six counties. Today Louis runs the winery with his son Edward, the winemaker, and his daughter Angie, the retail shop manager. Grandson Dustin represents the fifth generation at the winery.

At 50,000 gallons, Heineman Winery considers itself a "small producer," selling 90 percent of its stocks—70 percent labrusca and 30 percent vinifera and French hybrid—at the winery at retail. "I grew up drinking labrusca wines, which are fruity and grapey. I aspire to make wines so they taste like the grape," says Edward, who graduated in enology and food technology from Ohio State University in 1980.

Heineman Winery produces a wide variety of wines from grapes grown on the island, with Sauterne being Louis's favorite blend of native grapes. Recently the Heineman Winery won the Director's Choice Award, the highest commendation in Ohio (given by the director of agriculture) for its White Riesling and its Put-in-Bay Ice Wine. "I love living on the island, where I was born and raised," Edward says. "I like making wine taste good and pleasing the people." That's exactly what his father, Louis, said, too: "It's all about the people!"

Heineman Winery 🍂

Directions Take I-80 to U.S. Route 250 north to U.S. Route 2 west to 53 north to ferry dock: 20-minute, $6 ferry ride by Miller Boat Line from Point Catawba or Port Jet Express from downtown Port Clinton; two cruise lines from Sandusky: Goodtime and City of Sandusky from Marblehead to Put-in-Bay

Hours May–October, 10 AM–7 PM daily

Tours Combined tours of winery and Crystal Cave, daily, May–September, 11 AM–5 PM

Tastings May–September, part of wine tour

Gifts Variety of mineral and fossil specimens and wine-oriented gifts

Picnics None

Highlights at Winery Beautiful "wine garden"; Crystal Cave featuring largest deposit of celestite crystals in world; wood carvings by artist Bruno Weber

Restaurant Light fare: cheese and wine

Prices $8–$22.50; 10 percent case discount

Brand Names Heineman's Winery

Type of Production Vitis vinifera, French-American hybrids, vitis labrusca, and grape juice

Method of Harvesting Hand and machine

Pressing and Winemaking German membrane press

Aging and Cooperage Stainless steel tanks and oak barrels

Vineyards Founded 1900

County Ottawa

AVA Lake Erie

Acreage 25

Waterway Lake Erie

Climate Moderated by Lake Erie

Soil Clay limestone, Put-in-Bay Dolomite

Varieties Vitis vinifera, vitis labrusca, French-American hybrids

Wines Sweet Belle, Sweet Concord, Sweet Catawba, Pink Catawba, Vidal Blanc, Merlot, Rosé, Traminette, Niagara, Gewürztraminer, Burgundy, Sauterne, Island Chablis, Pinot Grigio, Riesling, Cedar Woods Red, Chardonnay, Cabernet Sauvignon, Cabernet Franc, Iced Vidal Blanc, Crystal Cave Champagne, Crystal Cave Spumante, Concord Grape Juice, Catawba Grape Juice

Best Red Burgundy

Best White White Riesling

Other Best Wine Pink Catawba

Quote "We make wine the Old World way."—Louis V. Heineman

Nearby Places to Visit Perry's Victory and International Peace Memorial; Crystal Cave

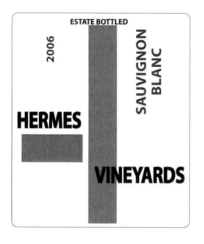

Hermes Vineyards

6413 South Hayes Avenue
Sandusky, OH, 44870
Tel (419) 626-8500
E-mail hermesvineyard@bex.net
Web site www.hermesvineyards.com
Owner David Kraus, MD
Winemaker David Kraus, MD
Founded 2002

Hermes Vineyards in Sandusky began as a boyhood vision of Ohio native, David Kraus, MD, now a New York resident and psychiatrist. "I had a lifelong dream to plant a vineyard and make wine," he says. After considering New York's Long Island and several other places, he returned to Ohio to plant 30 acres of vines on the Kraus family's 150-plus-year-old farm.

Hermes Vineyards was named for David's great-great-great-grandfather, Nicholas Hermes, who like David, descended from German winegrowers from the villages between Trittenheim and Cochem in the Moselle River Valley. Nicholas had heard of the Sandusky district's stellar reputation for winegrowing and winemaking in the mid-to-late 1800s.

Kraus was similarly inspired by Sandusky's lastingness as a choice viticultural wine district, and the benefits of starting a family wine venture. The winegrowing region surrounding Lake Erie was once dubbed the Ohio Grape Belt, and David was motivated by being an individualist there in the Ohio wine revolution.

The Lake Erie AVA, an agricultural preserve situated in proximity to Lake Erie in Ohio, Pennsylvania, and western New York, has had a reputation for grape growing and winemaking for over 150 years. Its moderate climate made it possible to grow some 40,000 acres of commercial grapes. "The climate makes Hermes Vineyards stand out most of all," says Kraus.

The Hermes Vineyards—Dahs Creek Vineyard on Route 4, planted in 2002, and Limestone Hills Vineyard on Mason Rd., planted in 2005—are located five miles from Lake Erie and three miles from northwesterly Sandusky Bay. They are perched on limestone ridges, 200 feet above Lake Erie. "There is an archaic coral reef that runs north to south from Pelee Island to North Bass Island through western Erie County,"

Hermes Vineyards. *Courtesy Phil Masturzo*

David observed being planted on eastern Long Island. His brother Michael Kraus, who graduated with a BS in agronomy from Ohio State University, managed the first vineyards. Their goal was to produce high quality wine grapes by densely planting the vines, spaced five feet between each vine, and six feet between each row, resulting in low yields of concentrated fruit with minimum irrigation and fertilization.

"We have one of the densest vineyards planted in Ohio, which contains varieties, never, or rarely ever before planted in Ohio," says Kraus. The varietals are Chardonnay, Sauvignon Blanc, Riesling, Gewürztraminer, Cabernet Sauvignon, Cabernet Franc, Merlot, Viognier, Marsanne, Mourvedre, Roussanne, Sangiovese clones from Chianti, Brunella, and Romagna, Malbec, Nebbiolo, Tempranillo, Grenache, Syrah, Petit Verdot, and Touriga.

A renovated 1800's three-bay, threshing barn with a silo at Hermes Vineyards features a great room with a tasting bar, and the entertainment center. Rudy Christian and Lindsay Graham, Ohio restoration experts, authenticated the barn. They said it was one of the oldest timber-frame barns in Ohio, built between 1815 and 1820 on one of the earliest settlements in Sandusky.

The posts and beams were handhewn as timbers from the white oak trees from the virgin forests that the

says Kraus. "The climate in the western basin of Lake Erie creates a long growing season of over 200 days. The climate is warmer than France's Bordeaux, closer to the Rhone Valley, and in Italy's Barolo. The daily highs and lows are similar. The cool lake water delays bud break in April when there is little frost. The warm lake in fall creates conditions for growing late ripening grapes."

Hermes Vineyards was modeled after modern French vineyards, which

Bringing in the vintage at Hermes Vineyards. *Courtesy Phil Masturzo*

early settlers discovered, according to David. Smaller timbers were cut by water-powered vertical saws, only used in the earliest sawmills, well before the advent of the circular saw in the 1850s. The barn still retains parts of the original polar siding, taken from virgin trees and cut in excess of two feet in width. Parts of the swinging thresher doors still remain on their original hinges.

When the barn was raised on supports to excavate the foundation, several discoveries were unearthed. Round glacial field stones were used as footers for the foundation wall with an overlay of limestone slabs. The livestock were protected from the elements by a solid limestone wall; the hay was aired and dried with construction of limestone pillars.

"Let the excellent site and clones express themselves," says Kraus, who takes a minimalist approach to winemaking. The grapes are hand harvested, then crushed, pressed, and fermented. Long maceration on the skins extracts the maximum grape flavors. The wines are pumped, racked and held in Italian stainless steel tanks. He practices minimal filtration for all wines, and only the white wines are sterile filtered. Both the white and red wines are aged in stainless steel, with minimal oak aging for the red wines.

"I was inspired by my passion to experiment with new grape types, and my confidence that this location can grow any grape type," he says. Time and the substance of Hermes Vineyards wines are a testament to David's work and intuition.

Hermes Vineyards

Directions From East or West: Take I-80, then at Exit 110/6A proceed on OH 4 North to the winery on left on Hayes Ave. Five minutes from Cedar Point and Lake Erie Islands attractions.

Hours Open daily year round; call to verify the hours

Tours Self-guided tours in and around the vineyards only

Tastings Tasting always available

Gifts Seasonal produce: raspberries, blackberries, strawberries, heirloom tomatoes, apples, peaches, pears, plums, and cherries; jellys; dessert toppings; cards; bags; jewelry; gift baskets

Highlights at Winery One of the largest premium grape vineyards in Ohio; Tasting room in old 1800s restored three-bay threshing barn with a silo

Events Wine tastings; live music, acoustic guitar, every Friday and Saturday year-round, 8:30 PM

Restaurant Light menu: imported cheeses, breads, gourmet pizzas, seasonal desserts

Prices $ 9.99–$14.99; 10 percent case discount

Brand Name Hermes Vineyards

Type of Production Minimalist

Method of Harvesting By hand

Pressing and Winemaking Long maceration on the skins to extract maximum flavors

Aging and Cooperage Italian stainless steel and minimal oak aging

Vineyards Founded 2002

County Erie

AVA Lake Erie

Acreage 30

Trellising Vertical Shoot Positioning

Waterways Lake Erie, Sandusky Bay, Pipe Creek

Climate Long and hot 200-day growing season, 2900 degree days said to be similar to Napa Valley or Bordeaux

Soil Loamy sand with limestone subsoil and bedrock

Varieties Chardonnay, Sauvignon Blanc, Riesling, Gewürztraminers, Cabernet Sauvignon, Cabernet Franc, Merlot, Viognier, Marsanne, Mourvedre, Roussanne, Sangiovese, Malbec, Nebbiolo, Tempranillio, Grenache, Syrah, Petit Verdot, Touriga

Wines All of the above varieties

Best Red Cabernet Sauvignon

Best White Viognier

Best Other Wine Chardonnay

Quote "Let the excellent clones and site express themselves."—David Kraus, MD

Nearby Places to Visit Merry-Go-Round Museum; Lake Erie Islands, Cedar Point

Hillside Winery

221 Main St.
Gilboa, OH, 45875
Tel (419) 456-3434
Fax (419) 456-3434
E-mail hillsidewine@fairpoint.net
Web site www.thehillsidewinery.com
Owners Mark and Lou Schaublin
Winemaker Mark Schaublin
Founded 2007

Hillside Winery, surrounded by great stretches of rural farmland, has long been the dream of the Schaublins, Mark, a native of Pandora and Lou, a native of Gilboa. Mark's family were established farmers growing corn, wheat, beans, pickles and tomatoes. Lou's family were seasoned merchants. The Schaublins built their farm winery on historic property once belonging to Lou's great grandparents purchased in the 1900s. The winery was dubbed for their north-sloping hillside vineyard planted in 2002; the town was named to honor an old Indian chief of the same name. Early settlers said the town referenced Mt. Gilboa, a mountain mentioned in the Bible. It is located between Stoney Ridge Winery and the Winery at Versailles.

A unique, two-story timber farmhouse built after the Civil War serves as the striking Schaublin family home, surrounded by stately maples. The Schaublins have two grown children

Greg, a son, and Melissa, a daughter. There is an imposing white barn with a standing seamless roof, an intriguing wagon shed, and a small chicken coop with tall pines at the back of the property. The barn is where the estate grapes are crushed and pressed, and the first fermentation takes place.

"The original wooden building burned to the ground in the 1920s," Mark Schaublin says, "and it was replaced with a red brick restaurant in 1926." Much later, in the 2000s, the Schaublins converted the restaurant into the winery. They freshened up the white plaster walls, the woodwork, the wooden floors, and added a cozy gas stove. A large 20-foot-long wooden cabinet top was salvaged from a hardware store and used for the tasting bar. A courtyard was designed as a peaceful place for guests to sip a glass of wine and look out on the Blanchard River, a tributary of the 95-mile long Anglaize River in northwestern Ohio.

The Schaublins got the homewine-making bug, and started making small wine batches of four and five gallons, then later six and seven gallons. The Ohio State University Wine Short Course taught them how to become winegrowers. In 2002, they purchased 33 acres of Putnam County farmland with a north-sloping hillside running to Riley Creek, and planted their vineyard east and west. The initial rootstock came from the Double A Vineyards, providers of over two million cuttings and 50 varieties, in Fredonia, New York. They started with one acre then added two more acres, cultivating Frontenac, Marechal Foch, Chardonnel, Seyval Blanc, Chambourcin, Frontenac Gris, Marquis, and Vidal Blanc in heavy loam in a temperate climate. In August 2007, an unexpected century storm caused Riley Creek to rise 11 inches, and it flooded out part of their vineyard.

"We lost our Cabernet Franc and Gewürztraminer. You could say we got our feet wet," Schaublin says. "Our first vintage in 2007 was a light crop. We did pretty well for a four year-old vineyard, and sold out of everything—65 gallons of each estate wine: Chambourcin, Chardonnel, Seyval Blanc, Marechal Foch, and Vidal Blanc."

Grapes are hand-harvested and taken to the winery for fermentation in stainless steel tanks. "I keep a constant eye on the wine—checking the tanks and sampling the wine," Schaublin says. "I ferment the reds wines on the skin for five to seven days, and then I ferment the white wines for half a day, before I press, crush, and tend the wines in the cellar."

Customers from Putnam County love the Quarry Red and Quarry White. Other customers think the Cabernet Franc is too dry, but like the semi-sweet Riesling. So far, the estate wines are getting good reviews. "We just hope everyone enjoys the wine, and likes it as well," Schaublin concludes.

Hillside Winery 🍃

Directions Take I-75 to U.S. 224 west 15 miles to Gilboa. Turn left on Pearl St., and go two blocks to the winery

Hours Thursday–Saturday: 12–6 PM

Tasting When open

Gifts Wine-related

Highlights at Winery Antique red brick winery with courtyard; Blanchard River

Events Mother's Day and Father's Day dinners

Prices $8.99 to $12.99; 10 percent case discount

Brand Name: Hillside Winery

Type of Production By hand

Pressing and Winemaking bladder press

Aging and Cooperage Stainless steel

Vineyards Founded 2003

County Putnam

Appellation Ohio

Acreage 3

Trellising Type High cordon

Waterways Riley Creek and Blanchard River

Climate Temperate climate without the snow

Soil Heavy loam

Varieties Cabernet Franc, Riesling

Wines Estate: Chardonnel, Seyval Blanc, Vidal Blanc, Marechal Foch, Frontenac, blend Chambourcin; Non-Estate: Cabernet Franc, Riesling, Quarry Red, Quarry White

Best Red Cabernet Franc

Best White Riesling

Other Best Wine Quarry Red and Quarry White

Quote "We hope everyone enjoys the wine and likes it." Mark Schaublin

Nearby Places to Visit Gilboa Quarry for scuba diving

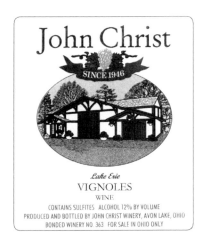

John Christ Winery

32421 Walker Road
Avon Lake, OH 44012
Tel (440) 933-9672
Fax (440) 930-0605
Web site www.johnchristwine.com
Winemaker Jack James
Founded 1946

The site of the original 23-acre Horwittel Concord and Niagara Vineyard on Walker Road in Avon Lake dates from the 1930s. These prime vineyards were part of the Lake Erie Grape Belt, which extended as far west as Michigan and as far east as western New York. Even with the repeal of Prohibition in 1933, the sale of table grapes did not prove profitable for Horwittel. In 1946, Native Macedonians Toda and John Christ breathed new life into the property when they purchased the vineyard and established the John Christ Winery.

The Christs built a simple but elegant Swiss chalet with scalloped trim. The foyer leads to a magnificent great room with a curved tasting bar, beamed ceilings, and hand-painted grapes covering the walls. The room has a warm and open welcoming atmosphere reminiscent of old Europe. A bright red pot-bellied stove with a hearth heats the room during the winter months. Banks of windows look to the vineyards and the

lawn for summer picnics. Just off the foyer, the wines are artistically displayed in a green sales room. Another door leads to the wine-production center with its lab, bottling line, tiers of Italian stainless steel tanks, and aging cellar. Informal tours are available if the staff is free.

The remaining 5-acre agricultural preserve was designed for the community, with a farmhouse, John Christ Winery, and a small vineyard framed with tall pine trees. The response by the community has been positive with almost all of the winery's sales at the wine bar.

During the late 1990s to early 2000s, the 5,000-case John Christ Winery produced handcrafted vitis vinifera wines, a time-consuming method of winemaking. West Virginian, Jack James, a retiree, had the opportunity to work with Mac McLelland to learn winemaking before he became winemaker. "He helped me out," says Jack, "as have Claudio Salvador and Lee Klingshirn."

Hand-carved and hand-painted wine barrel.
Courtesy Ohio Wine Producers Association

James buys 80 percent of the grape juice from the 1880s Firelands Vineyards, situated on the North Bass Island in the western basin of Lake Erie. This 50-acre *vitis vinifera* and *vitis labrusca* vineyard was Ohio's first official American Viticultural Area. The vineyard is one of the few island winegrowing districts in the world with its own appellation. The remaining 20 percent of grape juice is purchased from Dick Walker's New York vineyards.

"When we receive the grape juice, I take care of it. My philosophy of winemaking is to be careful and not rush the process," James says.

Once the juice has been transported to Avon Lake from Sandusky, the winemaker turns the grape juice into wine by fermenting it. The grape juice is pumped into stainless steel tanks, and yeast turns the sugar into alcohol and carbon dioxide. "I am constantly watching the wine."

Cold-stabilization plunges the red wine to near freezing, and removes all tartrate crystals during fermentation. James draws below-freezing, outside air around 32 degrees Fahrenheit into the wine production area for ten days. He lets the wine settle naturally, then racks and filters it. For the white wines, James uses bentonite, a fining agent that removes particles and leaves the wine bright and clear. "Bentonite takes out the impurities," he says.

The John Christ Winery has built its reputation by producing award-winning Gold and Silver Medal wines. They consist of Chardonnay, Pinot Grigio, Riesling, Vignoles, Cayuga, Niagara, Vidal Blanc, Vidal Blanc Ice Wine, Cabernet Sauvignon, Merlot, Ruby, Ruby Port, Claret, Labrusca, Raspberry, Blackberry, Peach, and Special Blend, a mixture of Sweet Concord and Niagara, their number one bestseller. These wines—a mixture of vinifera, hybrids, and labrusca—reflect Ohio's historic struggle to establish the region's true wine identity once and for all.

John Christ Winery 🍂

Directions From I-90, head north on State Route 83 in Avon Lake for two miles. Turn right on Walker Rd. for .5 mile to the winery

Hours Retail: Mon.–Wed., 10 AM–6 PM; Thurs., 10 AM–11 PM; Fri., 10 AM–midnight; Sat., 10 AM–midnight; Sun., 1–6 PM. Wine Bar: Thurs., 5–11 PM; Fri., 5 PM–midnight; Sat., 12 PM–midnight. Sun., 1 PM–6 PM

Tours No formal tours

Tastings Daily when open

Gifts Wine-related

Picnics Garden, lawn, backyard picnic area with tent

Highlights at winery Great place for friends to gather for wine and fun

Events Cookouts in summer and clambakes in fall, both with entertainment

Wine Bar Light fare with appetizers. May bring own food

Prices $7.49–$29.99; 10 percent case discount

Brand Names John Christ

Type of Production Handcrafted wines

Method of Harvesting By hand

Pressing and Winemaking Bladder press and non-intrusive winemaking

Aging and Cooperage Oak barrels and stainless steel tanks

Vineyards Founded Planted in late thirties; established in 1946

County Lorain

AVA Isle St. George & Ohio

Acreage Buys all grape juice

Waterway Lake Erie

Climate Long, cool, moderating lake effect, growing season

Soil Limestone bedrock, topped with silty and sandy loams

Varieties Vitis vinifera, French-American hybrids, vitis labrusca

Wines Chardonnay, Pinot Grigio, Riesling, Vignoles, Cayuga, Niagara, Vidal Blanc Ice Wine, Cabernet Sauvignon, Merlot, Ruby, Ruby Port, Claret, Labrusca, Raspberry, Blackberry, Peach, special blend

Best Red Merlot

Best White Riesling

Other Best Wine Special Blend

Quote "Be careful, and don't rush the process."—Jack James

Nearby Places to Visit Avon Lake's Sweetbriar Golf Course; Vermilion's Mill Hollow Park

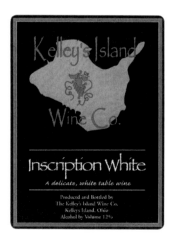

Kelley's Island Wine Company

418 Woodford Road
Kelleys Island, OH 43438
Tel (419) 746-2678
Fax (419) 746-2678
E-mail kiwineco@aol.com
Web site www.kelleysislandwine.com
Owners Kirt and Robby Zettler
Winemaker Kirt Zettler
Founded 1983

The family-owned and -operated Kelley's Island Wine Company, now the region's only wine producer, lies on the southernmost side of Kelleys Island, the largest and easternmost of Ohio's Lake Erie Islands. Brothers Datus and Irad Kelley bought the 2,888-acre island in the 1830s, and with other settlers prospered from fishing, quarrying, lumbering, and grape growing. Charles Carpenter, Datus Kelley's son-in-law, started the first commercial vineyard there in 1845, planting forty-six Isabella and forty Catawba vines. In 1850, Carpenter had an acre of grapes and pressed 100 gallons. By 1854, he had established the first wine cellar north of Cincinnati.

Around that time, a migration of German immigrants from that country's wine district settled on Kelleys Island, and they established the island as a leading winegrowing center from the late 1800s through the early 1900s, with many firms and more than one thousand acres of grapes. On the eve of Prohibition, there were but five wineries in operation; upon repeal only one reopened, and grape growing declined.

When Kirt and Robby Zettler arrived on the island in the seventies, there were a handful of growers and one winery, Sweet Valley Wine Company. Kirt had studied viticulture and enology at the University of Australia while his parents were on assignment there for the U.S. Department of State, and had continued his studies at Ohio State University upon his return. In 1979, the Zettler family purchased twenty acres of island farmland on Woodford Road for commercial vineyards. "We planted Chardonnay, Riesling, Cabernet Sauvignon, and Pinot Noir, which we thought ideal in this unique temperate microclimate," Kirt says. "We were motivated by the idea of getting $1,500 per ton, and challenged by the low yield of 2.5 tons per acre."

The Lake Erie coastline at Kelleys Island. *Courtesy Lou Gardella*

In 1983, the Zettlers bought the limestone Civil War-era house of Nicholas Smith, the stonemason for the original Kelley mansion and other grand houses. Adjacent to the vineyards, the farmhouse was first the winery, then later the bistro. "We applied for a license, opened the new Kelley's Island Wine Company (a name with a storied past that had never been trademarked), and started making wine," Kirt says. "We were convinced that the quieter island and beauty of Lake Erie would draw families, boaters, hikers, and collegians." The Zettlers also built an Australian Outback building with a sloping porch and rail fence that includes a restaurant, deli, and winery. Graced by pines and vineyards, the property has a pavilion, a picnic area, a playground, a volleyball court, and horseshoe pits.

The winery chef has created a seasonal menu of starters—smoked-chicken salad, heirloom tomato salad, and Prince Edward Island mussels—and entrees—veal chops, sauteed shrimp, and yellowfin tuna—in addition to deli appetizers, cheeses, dips, and spreads. Popular local Jimmy Buffet plays piano jazz and show tunes evenings and weekends.

After a particularly harsh winter in 1992, Kirt simplified the operation by leasing vineyards in addition to growing grapes.

With annual production at 500 gallons, the Zettlers make small batches of wine on an as-needed-basis. "I average two to three tons a day, bottling ten, twenty, or fifty cases at a time," Kirt says. He uses a basket press, variable-capacity Italian stainless steel tanks, a natural cold room for wine stabilization, hand bottling equipment, and storage.

The Kelleys Island vinifera consist of Chardonnay, Johannisberg Riesling,

Pinot Grigio, Merlot, and Cabernet Sauvignon. The blends include Inscription White, a Chardonnay and Vignoles blend; Indian Red, a Rhone-style Cabernet Sauvignon and Chancellor blend; Glacial White, a Germanic-style wine; Sunset Pink, a crisp blush blend; and Coyote, a sweet Niagara. "A good winemaker enjoys time with his friends, testing his products as well as drinking them," Kirt says.

Kelley's Island Wine Company

Directions From I-80, take exit 118 towards Sandusky. Take Ohio 2 west to 269 north (Marblehead/Lakeside exit) to Ohio 163 east, turn left on Frances Street and Kelleys Island Ferry. Travel to Kelleys Island via the ferry boat line

Hours June–Aug., Mon.–Sat., 11 AM–10 PM; Sun., 12–8 PM; Sept.–Oct. & April–May, Sat.–Sun., 12–8 PM

Tours Winery-viewing windows

Tastings Daily when open

Gifts Signature clothing, wine-related gifts, and pottery

Picnics No wine or food can be brought on property

Highlights at Winery Only winery on Kelleys Island; outdoor area featuring children's play area, volleyball, and horseshoes

Events Annual Spring Fling, first Saturday in April

Restaurant Classic and regional culinary favorites; Wine Company Bistro: pizza, pasta, and the like; Deli: imported and domestic cheeses, spreads, dips, sausages, fresh fruit, French bread, and house mustard

Prices $3.75–$4.50 by the glass; $10–$15 per bottle; 10 percent case discount; $4 off six bottle purchase

Brand Names Kelley's Island Wine Company

Type of Production Full grapes to bottle

Method of Harvesting Hand

Pressing and Winemaking Bladder and cold fermentation

Aging and Cooperage Stainless steel tanks

Vineyards Founded 1981

County Erie

AVA Lake Erie

Acreage 12

Waterway Lake Erie

Climate Temperate

Soil Limestone-based

Varieties Johannisberg Riesling, Chardonnay, Cabernet Sauvignon, Merlot, various French hybrids

Wines Chardonnay, Johannisberg Riesling, Cabernet Sauvignon, Merlot

Best Red Indian Red

Best White Chardonnay

Quote "A little vino would be keen-o!" —Kirt Zettler

Nearby Places to Visit Activities of Kelleys Island; Sandy Beach State Park

Klingshirn Winery

33050 Webber Road
Avon Lake, OH 44012-2330
Tel (440) 933-6666
E-mail info@klingshirnwine.com
Web site www.klingshirnwine.com
Owners Corporation, includes Lee
and Nancy Klingshirn
Winemaker Lee Klingshirn
Founded 1935

The story of Klingshirn Winery begins when Michael Klingshirn departed Bavaria's Wolfsig, a hamlet along the Mosel, and headed for Ohio's Avon, a farming community along Lake Erie. In 1899, Anton, the patriarch of the American branch of the family purchased a farmhouse, barn, and vineyard. Over time, Klingshirn prospered and bought farms for each of his four sons. In 1919, Antone sold the sixty-five-acre Klingshirn farm and vineyards to his son Albert R. Klingshirn. A surplus vintage in 1935 inspired Albert to establish a winery. He began to produce small batches of wine in 50-gallon wooden barrels in his home wine cellar.

By 1940, Albert, along with two brothers and a neighbor, broke ground for the two-tiered Klingshirn Winery. The all-purpose second floor was utilized for sales, bottling, and case storage. The downstairs production facility had room for two hundred 50-gallon wooden barrels. For decades, grapes were pressed at Antone's homestead.

In 1955, Albert's son Allan and his spouse, Barbara, purchased the Klingshirn Winery. Their growth strategy to invest in stainless steel tanks and large wooden barrels was timed to expand the overall product selection. "As the business grew, there was value in grapes and additional value in wine," says Lee Klingshirn, Allan's son and the current winemaker. During the next two decades, the American wine business accelerated with limitless possibilities. Ohio caught the fever, and Allan, who anticipated future growth, quadrupled the Klingshirn Winery's sales room and production center.

"In 1978, there were 20 Ohio wineries, all hit by a major market shift in the opposite direction. Customers became 'wine savvy,' and competition from foreign and domestic wine pushed our product off its base," explains Lee, who in 1986

Jim pressing the grapes at harvest. *Courtesy Klingshirn Winery*

graduated from Ohio State University with a BA in enology and viticulture. To counter this trend, his father, Allan, and several other Ohio vintners founded the Ohio Wine Producers Association.

The present Klingshirn property, an agricultural oasis of sorts, consists of the brown-shingled Klingshirn Winery and adjacent buildings, twenty-three acres of prime vineyard, and two family homes. The dramatic change in zoning laws from agriculture to residential/industrial continues to challenge the future of the Klingshirn Winery. "We plan to stay put for the long term," Lee says. "We are global thinkers-marketers, and we value the reputation of the wine industry as a whole. As the industry grows, so shall we and always maintain our quality."

The silty, clay-soiled Klingshirn Vineyards is located on a peninsula between Cleveland's west side and the Lake Erie Islands. "This is a sunbelt, not a snowbelt," Lee says. "The weather is 10

percent to 15 percent drier here. In any typical season, any given variety grown here reaches harvestable maturity ten to fourteen days earlier than the same varieties grown in northeast Pennsylvania; and for the late-season premium grapes, this is a huge advantage. Our award-winning, twenty-year-old Riesling vines continuously produce good yield and consistent quality."

The 12,000-case Klingshirn Winery—with its 30,000-gallon capacity, stainless steel tanks, and oak cooperage—markets custom wine products and even has a personalized label program. "We sell 80 percent of our production at the winery and deliver the remaining 20 percent to Lorain County beverage shops," Lee says.

Klingshirn consistently advocates practical winemaking and economic profitability. "We absolutely depend on the production of quality fruit from our vineyard. Smaller lots of premium grapes express both the character of the fruit and the nature of the vineyard. However, my energies are consumed with the production of labruscas, which continue to be the backbone of our operation," Lee says.

The Klingshirns have persevered with their age-old approach of quality with profit, and after six decades of implementing this practice, they are confident their approach works. Come visit and decide for yourself.

Klingshirn Winery

Directions I-90 west to exit 153. Go north on State Route 83 for 1.6 miles. Turn left on Webber Road. Winery is ½ mile

Hours Mon.–Sat., 10 AM–6 PM. Closed Sundays and holidays

Tours/Tasting Tours with tasting for groups (up to 25) by appointment; informal tours and tasting when staff available

Gifts Wine items

Picnics Encouraged for small groups

Highlights at Winery One of the most historic vineyards & urban wineries in Ohio

Events Summer steak cookouts

Prices $6–20; 10 percent case discount

Brand Name Klingshirn Winery

Type of Production All types of grapes and wine

Method of Harvesting Mostly mechanical, except Ice Wine

Pressing and Winemaking Bladder and screw-type presses; improvisational winemaking

Aging and Cooperage Oak for Cabernet Sauvignon and Chardonnay; stainless steel for the rest

Vineyards Founded 1899

County Lorain

AVA Lake Erie

Appellation Ohio

Acreage 20

Waterway Lake Erie

Climate Long, warm growing season

Varieties White Riesling, Chardonnay, Pinot Gris, Cabernet Sauvignon, Concord, Delaware, Chambourcin, Vidal Blanc

Wines Cabernet Sauvignon, Cabernet Franc, Chambourcin, Chardonnay, Pinot Grigio, White Riesling, Vidal Blanc, Country Blush, Catawba, Golden Chablis, Concord, Niagara, Vin Rosé, Haut Sauterne, Pink Catawba, Sweet Concord, Cherry, Delaware Ice Wine, Champagnes: Contemporary Blend, White Riesling, Traditional Blend

Best Red Cabernet Franc

Best White Riesling

Other Best White Iced Lake Erie Delaware

Quote "We are global thinkers-marketers, and we value the reputation of the wine industry as a whole."—Lee Klingshirn

Nearby Places to Visit Avon Antiques; Sunset Shores Bed & Breakfast

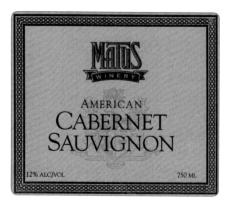

Matus Winery

15674 Gore Orphanage Rd.
Wakeman, OH, 44889
Tel (440) 774-wine (9463)
Fax (440) 774-2124
E-mail matus_winery@yahoo.com
Web site www.matuswinery.com
Owner Robert F. Matus
Winemaker Robert F. Matus
Founded 2006

Three generations of the Matus family in Wakeman in western Lorain County have lived and farmed the same 250 acres since the early twentieth century. Robert F. Matus, the present owner, expresses great deference to his father and grandfather who cultivated corn and soybeans on this land not far from Lake Erie. He followed in their footsteps until he got the inspiration to pursue the art of winemaking.

As long as Matus can remember, someone in his family was growing grapes. "I remember we had relatives in Avon Lake who grew Concord grapes for the Welch's Grape Juice Company. My uncle Marty, also a Matus, who lived across the street from us grew Concord and Niagara. I loved those grapes. I use to trim and harvest the grapes, and made a huge batch of Concord wine for about twelve years," he says.

Matus admits he was totally obsessed with making wine. He entered home winemaker contests in Ohio,

and planted more and more grapes. He started with 500 vines, and ended up with 3,000 vines. He entered still more home winemaker contests, then started to win medals for "Best of Show" in the Northern Ohio Wine Guild Competitions. "In 2003, I won the award for "Northern Ohio Winemaker," the highest recognition for home winemaking. I kept on saying to myself, why can't I do this?" he says. He trudged onward. By 2003, Matus started building the Matus Winery, founded the winery in 2006, and finished the winery in 2008.

Today, the Matus Winery is a family affair. Bob, his spouse MaryBeth, plus their two sons, Hunter and Hayden, and his parents, Bob and Germaine Matus are all actively involved. An example to future winegrowers, Bob Matus is one of the very few new winery owners who actually planted vineyards. The family's six acre, tiled, Lake Erie AVA, Matus Vineyard, planted in clay, sand and black humus consists of Marechal Foch,

Vineyard view of the winery. *Courtesy Matus Winery*

Harvesting the grapes. *Courtesy Matus Winery*

Traminette, Vidal Blanc, Charonell, Concord, Chambourcin, Cabernet Sauvignon, Riesling, and Frontenac.

"We are constantly protecting our grapes from the winter weather that comes from the unpredictable Ohio climate," he says. "Traminette and Frontenac do the best. We chose grapes that blossom late in the spring to avoid the frost. We have so many different varietals; it's like a Noah's Ark effect, a little of everything," he says.

The 3,000-gallon, modern beige, Matus Winery with the gabled green roof is designed for the easy-flow of people coming and going, with a separate wing devoted to winemaking and barrel aging. An antique 1860s oak barn belonging to a neighbor was added to their winery to increase the seating capacity to 100, and a transparent sandstone fireplace was installed for warmth.

"I rock and roll when I make wine," he says. "We use an antique basket press. I make natural wines and do no filtering. I cold stabilize the wine to clarify it. I use no chemicals, and the minimum of sulfites." The dry wines are fermented in French Alliers oak barrels, and aged for one year before bottling. The sweeter wines are fermented in stainless steel, and bottled, corked, and labeled as soon as they are ready to drink.

Matus Winery makes great fruit wines. Bob purchases pears from McDowell Orchards to make Pear wine. He and his friends harvest elderberries and blackberries from a swampy, wooded area called The Out Back, also the name of his popular Elderberry wine. He also buys grapes that he purchases for his Cabernet Sauvignon, and Riesling. "Make hay when the sun shines," he says.

Matus Winery 🍇

Directions From I-90 take the Baumhart Road exit, and proceed south to State Route 20. Go west on State Route 20, then south on Gore Orphanage Road to the first driveway and winery on the right

Hours Mon.–Wed., by appointment; Thurs., 4–10 PM; Fri.–Sat., 1 PM–midnight

Tours Self-guided, educational tour

Tastings Daily when opened

Gifts Certificates, gift baskets, and home winemaking supplies

Picnics Weather permitting, we offer grills and picnic tables under tents on the lawn

Highlights at the Winery The winery has added a new 1860s oak barn with a dual-sided sandstone fireplace

Events Steak Frys and Clambakes

Type of Production "Mushin & crushin"

Method of Harvesting Handpicked

Pressing Old basket press

Aging and Cooperage Sweet wines in stainless steel and dry wines in French oak Alliers barrels

Vineyards Founded 1998

County Lorain

Appellation American

Acreage 6

Climate Unpredictable Ohio weather

Soil clay, sand and black humus mix

Varieties Marechal Foch, Traminette, Vidal Blanc, Charonelle, Concord, Chambourcin, Cabernet sauvignon, Riesling, Frontenac

Wines Concord, Pink Catawba, Niagara, Vidal Blanc, Outback (blackberry/elderberry blend) Moonlight White (Traminette/Seyval Blanc blend), Pear, Riesling, Twilight Blush (Cabernet Sauvignon/Seyval Blanc blend) Chardonnay, Merlot, & Cabernet Sauvignon

Best Red Cabernet Sauvignon

Best White Riesling

Other Best Wine Outback

Quote "Make hay when the sun shines." —Bob Matus

Nearby Places to Visit Thomas Edison birthplace in Milan, Oberlin Art Museum, Lake Erie Islands

Mon Ami Restaurant & Historic Winery

3845 E. Wine Cellar Road
Port Clinton, OH 43452
Tel (419) 797-4445 or (800) 777-4266
Fax (419) 797-9171
E-mail info@monamiwinery.com
Web site www.monamiwinery.com
Owners Lonz Winery, includes John Kronberg and Claudio Salvador
Winemaker Claudio Salvador
Founded 1872

The most magnificent architectural treasure in the Lake Erie Islands wine country is the Mon Ami Restaurant & Historic Winery in Port Clinton. Toledo stonecutter George Loeb built the winery in 1872 as a symbol of strength. From its foundation upward, it is constructed of six-foot limestone walls sealed with limestone mortar, sand from the lake shore, and walnut from the woodlands. It stands as a testament to the generations of winemakers who inspired fine winemaking in Ohio, guided the Catawba to regional prominence, and gave rise to the vinifera revolution.

Three growers and vintners—the Neals, the Landys, and the Ellithorpes—pioneered the 130,000-gallon Catawba Island Wine Company in 1873. At the time, it was said to be one of the largest of the four existing wine cooperatives in the district. By 1937, the winery complex was purchased by the Sandusky-headquartered Mon Ami Champagne Company. Taking its name from the French words for "my friend," Mon Ami was one of a few domestic wineries producing premium champagne in America. At its present location, forty workers produced 500,000 bottles of still wine and premium champagne. During the 1940s, the Mon Ami Restaurant was established to showcase Mon Ami wines with the local Zappone family's Italian cuisine.

In 1956, Norman Mantey, third-generation owner of Mantey Vineyards (now Firelands), purchased Mon Ami. Leon Adams, author of *Wines of America*, dubbed Mantey one of the busiest winemakers in America. His vaulted underground cellars were a tourist destination, and Mantey was a leading producer until he sold both Firelands and Mon Ami to Cincinnati's Meier's Wine Cellars in 1980.

Historic winery, featuring stonework completed by George Loeb in 1872. *Courtesy Mon Ami Winery*

In 2000, John Kronberg and Claudio Salvador formed Lonz Winery, Inc. and acquired Firelands and Mon Ami. "We wanted the place to come alive," they say. Firelands was modernized for vinifera wine production and for volume grape processing. "Our goal was to enhance and distribute Firelands, Mantey, and Mon Ami well and widely," Salvador says. "Currently, we retail 30 percent of our stocks and wholesale the remaining 70 percent of our stocks in Ohio, Michigan, Illinois, Kentucky, Nebraska, and Indiana."

At Mon Ami Restaurant & Historic Winery, landscapers spruced up the grounds and gardeners planted an arbor and rose garden. The interior was redesigned to offer customers an authentic wine and food experience. The kitchen was updated to facilitate larger, more sophisticated groups of visitors. The Main dining room was furnished for comfort and decorated with elegance, and proudly features American cuisine. Mon Ami premium wines pair well with their coveted prime rib, grilled steak, rack of lamb, perch, walleye, and halibut.

Tourists come from near and far for the Saturday seafood buffet and the Sunday brunch. They are dazzled with the Mon Ami California premium line—Chardonnay, Sauvignon Blanc, Shiraz, Merlot, and Zinfandel; they taste and compare it with the broader Mon Ami Ohio premium line—barrel-fermented Proprietor's Reserve Chardonnay, fragrant Riesling, spicy Gewürztraminer, full-bodied Proprietor's Reserve Cabernet, and berry Pinot Noir. Mon Ami also hosts banquets, celebrations, and weddings.

Mon Ami Restaurant & Historic Winery

Directions Take I-90 to Ohio 2 west. Exit at Ohio 53 and head north to Catawba Island. Turn left on Township Highway 238 east to Wine Cellar Road

Hours Chalet: Mon.–Thurs., 4 PM; Fri.–Sat., 11:30 AM; Sun., 10:30 AM. Wine shop: Mon.–Thurs., 4–10 PM; Fri.–Sat., 10 AM–9 PM; Sun., 10 AM–8 PM

Tours By appointment

Tastings Daily for individuals or groups

Gifts Log Cabin Gift Shop for jellies, jams, wines, and wine-related artifacts

Highlights at Winery Wine-tasting bar, Saturday Night Seafood Buffet and Sunday Brunch

Events Fine dining, shopping, cooking classes, dancing, live entertainment, Sunday jazz on the lawn or by the fire

Restaurant American cuisine with emphasis on Mon Ami California and Mon Ami Ohio lines of wine, champagne and dessert wine; Chalet: Tuesday and Wednesday, steak; Thursday, pasta; Happy Hour, 4–7 PM

Prices $5–$50; 10 percent case discount

Brand Names Mon Ami Ohio, Mon Ami California

Type of Production Classic and innovative

Method of Harvesting Mechanical

Pressing and Winemaking Bladder press for vitis vinifera and screw press for juice

Aging and Cooperage Stainless steel, temperature-controlled fermenters and tanks, American and French oak cooperage

Vineyards Founded 1950

County Ottawa

AVA Lake Erie

Acreage 50

Waterway Lake Erie

Climate Moderating lake effect

Soil Clay loam

Varieties Chardonnay, Pinot Grigio, Riesling, Gewürztraminer, Cabernet, Merlot, Pinot Noir, Catawba, Niagara, Concord

Wines Proprietor's Reserve Chardonnay, Riesling, Pinot Grigio, Gewürztraminer, Chablis, Cellar Master White, White Catawba, Haut Sauterne, Proprietor's Reserve Cabernet, Pinot Noir, Cellar Master Red, Concord, Reserve Cuvée, Brut, Extra Dry, Pink Spumante, Pale Cream Sherry, Rare Ruby Port, Spiced Wine, and others

Best Red Proprietor's Reserve Cabernet Sauvignon

Best White Proprietor's Reserve Chardonnay

Other Best Wine Methode Champenoise Champagne

Nearby Places to Visit Great Wolf Lodge indoor water park; Cedar Point Amusement Park

Quarry Hill Winery

8403 Mason Rd.
Berlin Heights, OH 44814
Tel (419) 706-8005
Web site www.quarryhill.org
E-mail info@quarryhillwinery.com
Owners Mac McLelland & Bill Gammie
Winemaker Mac McLelland
Founded 2005

Quarry Hill Winery has the distinction of being the only vineyard-estate located at the highest point in Berlin Heights, Ohio, among the rolling foothills of Erie County. Proprietors Mac McLelland and Bill Gammie named the winery for the three sandstone quarries on the 100-acre-farm. Today, Quarry Hill is built on the historic Firelands, large tracts situated in the Western Reserve in north-central Ohio. These lands were deeded to Connecticut fire sufferers whose homes and land were destroyed by the British during the American Revolutionary War, 1776–1783.

"In the 1800s, the property was settled by descendants of fire sufferers in search of a better life," McLelland says. The quarries provided the settlers a livelihood and the sandstone from which to build a home, such as the 1835 sandstone house still in existence on the property. By the time the Scottish Gammie family acquired their farm in 1931, the land had

been divided into farmland and parkland. William G. (Bill's father), brother Alex, sister Margaret, and mother Elizabeth were fortunate to purchase one of the farms, where they planted vegetable gardens, then, later, lucrative fruit crops. As wholesalers, William G. and Alex trucked their bounty to Cleveland, where it was sold at the North Ohio Food Terminal. Bill continued as Quarry Hill Orchards until he crossed paths with his current partner.

McLelland, who garnered his career experience as the winemaker at John Christ Winery in Avon Lake, made the acquaintance of Gammie because he was one of his customers in the wine business. One conversation led to another and finally resulted in a shared wine venture. The partners started Quarry Hill, a winery, at Quarry Hill Orchard. They outfitted it for the production of grape and fruit wines. They also cultivated a three-acre, Lake Erie AVA, vertical-

Once a dream, now a blessing. *Courtesy Quarry Hill Winery*

shoot-positioned, *vitis vinifera* and French hybrid vineyard in coveted sandy loam soil. The 2007 harvest produced their very first Quarry Hill Winery estate-bottled wines.

"We grow our own fruit," he says. "Berlin Heights fruit is abundant because the grapes thrive in the good climate and good elevation that protect the vines. We are four miles inland from Lake Erie positioned at an elevation of 778 feet, with a moderating climate, frequent wind, and well-drained soils—which create a unique *terroir*." The primary grapes featured are Pinot Noir, Cabernet Franc, Riesling, Pinot Grigio, and Vidal Blanc, in addition to vast orchards that grow cherries, peaches, and apples.

In 2008, McLelland and Gammie entertained the idea of creating a rustic, all-purpose winery with a vaulted ceiling, wooden beams, lots of windows, an upper deck for viewing, and a lower patio for relaxing. The intention was to position the winery at the top of the vineyard overlooking the orchards at "the pinnacle," which boasts panoramic views of beautiful Lake Erie.

"We handcraft several thousand cases of 16 different wines annually, and target people who love wine. Half drink fruit wines and half drink grape wine," McLelland says. After they extract the fruit, utilizing a press, they commence with a cool fermentation in stainless steel tanks or oak barrels for their grape and fruit wines. He typically produces light, fruity, acidic white wines with no oak. While he prefers full-bodied reds, he recently experimented with a lighter Beaujolais style Cabernet Franc that sold out. His style of red wines depends on when the grapes are picked and what grapes are harvested. He also takes pride in producing 100 percent, pure, natural fruit wines from cherries, peaches, apples, and raspberries that express the flavor of the fruit.

"We make small batch quality wines. Each batch is uniquely crafted to one's taste. The wines may change from year to year, but the quality is always consistent," he says. The Vidal Blanc and Vidal Blanc Ice Wine are exemplary wines bearing the 2008 Ohio Quality Wine (OQW) designation, granted by a sensory analysis conducted by the Ohio Grape Industries.

Quarry Hill Winery 🍇

Directions From State Route 2, head south to Mason Rd., then proceed one mile east to the winery

Hours Seasonal, please call

Tastings When open

Gifts Wine related

Picnics Welcome

Highlights at Winery Quality wines from fruit and grapes; on-site orchard market; entertainment

Wine Prices $7–$34; 10 percent case discount

Brand Names Quarry Hill, McLelland's Reserve, Harbortown Vineyards

Type of Production Fruit and wine estate, and non-estate

Method of Harvesting By hand

Pressing and Winemaking Modern equipment

Aging and Cooperage Stainless steel and some oak barrels

Vineyards Founded 2005

County Erie

AVA Lake Erie

Acreage 3 acres; 100 acres fruit trees

Trellising Vertical shoot positioned

Waterways Lake Erie, Vermilion, and Huron rivers

Climate: Cool growing season

Soil Sandy loam

Wines Riesling, Vignoles. Pinot Grigio, McLelland's Reserve Magnolia White, Vidal Blanc, Vidal Ice Wine, McLelland's Reserve Scarlett, Cabernet Franc, Stonehouse Red, Buckeye Red, Apple, Hard Cider Frizzante, Peach, Blueberry, Red Raspberry, Strawberry-Rhubarb, and Red Raspberry Framboise

Best Red Cabernet Franc

Best White Vidal Blanc

Other Best Wine Buckeye Red

Quote "A person's best tool to evaluate wine is his or her glass." —Mac McLelland

Nearby Places to Visit Cedar Point, Edison woods, and Kalahari Indoor Water Park

Stoney Ridge Winery

107144 County Rd 16
Bryan, OH 43506
Tel (419) 636-3500
Fax (419) 636-5075
E-mail stonridg@powersupply.net
Web site www.stoneyridgewinery.com
Owners Phillip and Pamela Stotz
Winemaker Phil Stotz
Founded 2001

Among the windswept farmlands and century-old New England houses in the northwest corner of the Buckeye State lies Stoney Ridge Winery. The winery adopted its name from the district's Stoney Point Schoolhouse, built on glacial stones on the ridge of old Lake Erie.

A long gravel road bisects stanchions of well-manicured, trellised vines that take the visitor to a gabled two story, stick-built Amish winery with a loft and tower, which affords a view of an ancient Indian Trail along the beachhead of Lake Erie. Beaver Creek, the site of an 1800s flour mill, meanders east to the old flood plains, now planted in grapes and corn. The residence of Phil and Pamela Stotz, the proprietors, and their children sits to the south. Raised beds of asparagus, cabbage, peppers, blackberries, flowers, and herbs grow in front of the vineyards to the west.

The locally born and bred Stotzes met in the real estate business. Pamela expressed to Phil her interest in starting a farmer's market on their 40-acre property. One idea led to the next, and the market grew into a plan to plant a vineyard in 1996 and to found a winery. New vines have come up every year thereafter. The couple wanted to provide their customers a friendly and relaxing environment in which to learn about wine. "Wine is meant to be fun," Phil says. "Our friends and neighbors like to stop by for an afternoon. Our business consists of 65 percent locals and 35 percent tourists."

People enjoy the harvest party near the vineyard and flock to the rustic tasting room. Shoppers crowd the gift store in search of Stoney Ridge jams, jellies, sauces, wines, cheeses, pastas, crafts, and gift baskets. Customers enjoy a glass of wine huddled by the stone fireplace in winter and the pond in summer. Cooks buy fresh estate-grown or local farm-raised produce.

Stoney Ridge Vineyards consist of 27 varieties planted in well-drained

Stoney Ridge Winery, viewed through the vineyards. *Courtesy Ohio Wine Producers Association*

soils. "The silty loams are almost too productive, and minimize the grape production on the vines," Phil says. "We prune back the leafy vines and utilize two types of vine placement. We grow grapes that can withstand the cold Midwestern climate."

Come fall, the Stotzes hand-harvest their French-American hybrids, starting in late August and finishing by late September. Their Pinot Grigio, Riesling, and Cabernet Sauvignon is purchased from Firelands Vineyards on North Bass Island. Other juice is bought from growers in Erie, PA. The wines are made in the stick-built Amish-style 3,800 square feet processing building attached to the original winery. It is a modern facility with 20,000 gallon plus capacity, and a 1,000

square foot crush pad. Like the original winery, it is equipped with Italian stainless steel, variable-capacity tanks and American oak cooperage. "All told, we have over 8,000 square feet under roof. We now truly feel we are a destination of choice," he says.

Winemaker Stotz produces well-blended, ready-to-drink premium and everyday wines that undergo minimal to no aging. "We believe in the development of the right blend with the right degree of sweetness," he says. With aspirations to reach 20,000 gallons a year, Stotz turns over his white wines in 16 to 18 weeks, his red wines in 20 to 24 weeks (with the exception of Cabernet), and his sweet or fruit wines in 12 to 14 weeks.

Stoney Ridge Winery produces 25 different wines and categorizes 35 percent of its wines as dry to semi-dry. Some popular examples are Pinot Grigio, Riesling, and Cabernet Sauvignon. Some of their bestsellers include Sweet Barn Dance Red, Barn Dance Blush, semi-dry Riesling, and Cranberry Tart. "No wine drinker should apologize for their taste in wine," Stotz says. "Can it not be as varied as their taste in art?"

Stoney Ridge Winery 🍃

Directions From the Ohio turnpike, take exit 13/2, then go 5 miles south on State Route 15 and 2 miles east on Road "G." Take a left on County Road 16 to the winery entrance

Hours Monday–Saturday 11 AM–6 PM

Tours Yes

Tastings Daily when open

Gifts Farmer's market, produce, wine, Amish cheese, flowers, herbs, crafts, and gifts

Picnics Welcome at outside tables

Highlights at Winery Peaceful farm winery setting; unique country atmosphere by lakeside or fireside; circular staircase to owl's nest for view of vineyards; catered special events in upstairs loft

Events Summer Steak Fries; Lobster Boil; Chili Cook-off

Prices $8.95–$19.95; 10 percent case discount

Brand Name Stoney Ridge Winery

Type of Production Traditional

Method of Harvesting By hand

Pressing and Winemaking Four ton Bladder press

Aging and Cooperage Stainless steel with minimal American oak cooperage

Vineyards Founded 1996

County Williams

Appellation Ohio

Acreage 15

Waterway Beaver Creek

Climate Midwestern (first frost early October)

Soil Well-drained, productive silty loams

Varieties Marquette, Riesling, La Crescent, Seyval Blanc, Marechal Foch, Vignole, Frontenac, Lacrosse, Traminette, and others

Wines Riesling, Seyval Blanc, Barn Dance White, Cabernet Sauvignon, Marechal Foch, Barn Dance Red, Stormy Nights, Sweet Harvest, Golden Apple, Country Rhubarb, Blueberry Crisp, Cranberry Tart, Raspberry Patch, Vineyard Dew, Moonlight Cruise

Best White Riesling

Other Best Wine Barn Dance Blush

Quote "No wine drinker should apologize for their taste in wine. Can it not be as varied as their taste in art?" —Phillip Stotz

Nearby Places to Visit Old Indian trail on Lake Erie beachhead; Amish country (Ohio, Indiana, Michigan corner)

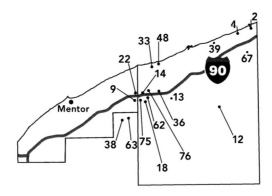

Lake Erie and Grand River Tour East

Biscotti Family Winery & Pasta

724 Whitney Road
Conneaut, OH 44030
Tel (440) 599-5555
E-mail joepro@suite224.net
Owner Nancy Biscotti
Winemaker Joe A. Biscotti
Founded 2002

Located in a charming yellow century house, the Biscotti Family Winery near Lake Erie in Conneaut is surrounded by one thousand maples and pines. This resort hamlet provides an escape from city life and a place to unwind.

Midwesterners Joe and Nancy Biscotti of Biscotti Restaurant fame left their many establishments in Greater Cleveland for a quieter lifestyle. "We thought of retiring," Joe says—but it was hard to keep Joe, a one-time PGA golf professional and instructor, idle, much less out of the kitchen where he has spent forty years as an Italian chef. And it was even more difficult to keep Nancy from her art or partnership as a woman entrepreneur.

In 1991, the Biscottis initially purchased a ten percent interest in Conneaut Shores, a golf club and restaurant. They renovated the house on the property into their family home, and converted the adjoining buildings into a small winery, a banquet facility,

a gift shop, a logo design firm, and a gift basketry studio. "We have a small café and a covered patio that seats 50. All the businesses complement each other.," says Joe Biscotti.

At the same time, the Biscottis obtained a license to make wine. "I buy fresh juice and produce 2,000 gallons on-site. We buy from different wineries to our taste in Ohio, Pennsylvania, and California and import wine from Italy." Biscotti makes wine in the old Italian style. "I am not a soulful winemaker like Arnie Esterer of Markko Vineyard, but rather a marketing winemaker," he says. After Joe purchases the fresh grape juice, he coddles the wine, adding yeast to commence fermentation, then cold stabilizing the wine, introducing basic ingredients and any residual sugars. Once properly aged, Biscotti wines are held in small cooperage in the wine cellar below the restaurant.

"Both the Sangiovese (which is aged in Hungarian oak) and the

63

Muscatel have no residual sugar. I stick-stir each wine," he says. "A 12 to 14 percent fortified wine, the Old Italian Red is wine in the style Old Italians would make." Made from Chambourcin, Tony Soprano Red, a deep red, dry wine goes well with pasta.

"I always loved to cook, make wine, and run golf courses," says Joe, who started as a chef at age twenty-one. During the nineteenth and twentieth centuries, his Italian grandparents had a mountainside restaurant with stone-carved booths in Fogia near the Adriatic Sea. His parents came to the United States in the early 1900s.

"Traditionally our family invited someone to dinner almost every night," he says. "My mom always asked my friends if they were hungry."

The Biscotti Italian culinary legacy continues to thrive. During the week, Joe crafts wine and property manages E.S. Properties. During the weekends, he cooks at Biscotti Winery & Pasta in Conneaut serving up Italian buffets—Summer Cookouts, Steak and Chicken Fry, Lake Erie Perch Fry, Rib Roast, Clam Bakes, and a Ravioli Buffet. "We serve old-fashioned Italian, Depression food—big portions of spaghetti with meatballs and great salads. Two people can have a great meal for $35," he says.

A porch with overhead pull fans and a pot-bellied stove serves as the restaurant. Dining options include cozy booths, cafe tables, a tasting bar with a fireplace, a wine cellar, intimate porch rooms, and deck tables with umbrellas on the golf course. Wine artifacts—a Biscotti stained-glass window, a basket press, a wine cask, and photographs of the Italian wine country—give character to the room. Celebrity shots of Johnny Desmond of the Glen Miller Band, baseball Hall-of-Famer Bob Feller, Chi Chi Rodriguez, Bryant Gumbel, Tim Conway, and Dean Martin highlight the picture gallery. "Come join us for an adventurous evening of friends, fun, food and good wine," says Biscotti.

Biscotti Family Winery & Pasta 🍇🍂

Directions Take I-90 to Conneaut. Go north on State Route 7 for eight miles, then left and west on State Route 531. Turn left on Whitney Road to the winery

Hours Tuesday, Wednesday, and Thursday, 12 PM–6 PM; Friday and Saturday, 12 PM–8 PM

Tours Daily

Tastings Daily

Gifts Variety of handcrafted, painted, and designed wine glasses, jellies, jams, preserves, sauces, wine gadgets, and golf items

Picnics Permitted if they buy wine, and that day the winery isn't providing food

Highlights at Winery Old World Italian atmosphere with good food and good wine; scenic golf course near Lake Erie with one thousand old-growth maples and pines

Events Monthly Italian buffets, cookouts, frys and themed events

Restaurant Family-style Italian cuisine with interesting wine list

Prices $7.50–$20

Brand Name Biscotti Family Winery

Type of Production Handcrafted old world style of winemaking from purchased grapes, rest custom-produced

Pressing and Winemaking Bladder press and old world methods

Aging and Cooperage Variety of small cooperage

AVA Lake Erie

Appellation American

Varieties Niagara, Catawba, Concord, Chambourcin, Chardonnay, Riesling, Pinot Gris, Cabernet, Merlot, Zinfandel, Sangiovese, Berry sources

Wines Niagara, Riesling, Pinot Gris, Catawba, Nancy's Blush, Pink Rosé, Tony Soprano Red, Concord, Elderberry, Peach and Strawberry

Best Red Old Italian

Best White Nancy's Blush

Other Best Wine Tony Soprano Red

Quote "Winemaking is an art similar to making love. Go slow and easy and enjoy yourselves."—Joe Biscotti

Nearby Places to Visit Charter fishing at Conneaut Marina, Railroad Museum, Casino in Erie, PA

Buccia Vineyard

518 Gore Road
Conneaut, OH 44030
Tel (440) 593-5976
E-mail bucciwin@suite224.net
Web site www.bucciavineyard.com
Owners Joanna and Fred Bucci
Winemaker Fred Bucci
Founded 1975

Just south of Lake Erie, the road to Buccia Vineyard in Conneaut takes the traveler through northeast Ohio farmlands and past the Conrail Crossing to an unexpected country getaway. Proprietors Joanna and Fred Bucci established the Buccia Vineyards in 1975 and added Buccia Bed and Breakfast in 1986.

"One stormy February night in the seventies, Fred, originally from North Kingsville, started home from AT&T and got stuck in a two-hour traffic jam. He decided it was time for a change," remembers Joanna, a native of Conneaut, who agreed wholeheartedly with her husband. They relocated to Ashtabula County.

"I was a home winemaker," Fred says. "We often tasted and talked wine with Arnie Esterer at Markko Vineyard. So, planting a vineyard and making wine as a livelihood didn't seem farfetched. I began to seriously study and

to attend winemaking conferences at Ohio State University."

By 1975, the Buccis purchased a picturesque six-acre farm with a cottage and pastureland once used for beef cattle. They reconfigured the cottage into a modern family home. A series of odd buildings was magically transformed into a gabled winery, romantically reminiscent of Italy, with a patio for picnics, pink flower baskets, a grape trellis, and a vineyard.

A hand-carved wood-and-glass door leads to a vaulted hall decorated in a festive grape motif. Visitors have many choices for a good time. A library with books, brochures, and maps provides information on what to do and where to go in the area. A gift shop sells wine, shirts, and gadgetry for the aficionado. An oak upright player piano belts out tunes from the corner. Round and square tables for tasting wine or gathering with friends fill the hall. Murals of people, life, and events at the winery cover the walls. Daily (except Sunday), guests stop by the winery to taste Joanna's delicious breads and assorted cheeses with Buccia wines.

"We offer visitors a total wine experience," Joanna says. "People book in advance over the Internet." The bed and breakfast extends from the winery's center. The rooms advertise comfy beds, hot tubs, high tech stereos and TVs, microwaves, fridges, coffeemakers, and a patio with an arbor. The loft, reached by a ladder, has one of the only waterbeds in the wine country. The honeymoon suite features its own den and fireplace, and a private patio with a fountain and hot tub.

The Buccia Vineyard, located in the Lake Erie American Viticultural Area half a mile from the water, has a long, cool growing season. Here the soils consist of four feet of sand with an underpan of twelve feet of gravel. "The soils are very well-drained," Fred says. "Our grape varieties have good color and taste." He notes the four-and-one-half-acre vineyard planted to Baco, Seyval Blanc, Steuben, and Vignoles. "We also grow Agawam, a red grape that makes a white wine. We acquired some two hundred grape cuttings from one of the last growers of Agawam in Madison, Ohio."

Buccia Vineyard has a reputation for producing wines in a classic manner with flair. "We make the best wines from the best grapes. We do the best job

Buccia Vineyard and Bed and Breakfast. *Courtesy Ohio Wine Producers Association*

possible," Fred says. The hand-harvested grapes are brought to the winery, where they are crushed and pressed in a bladder press. The white wines are cold-pressed and fermented in stainless steel, then pumped over and held in stainless steel and other cooperage. The red wines are fermented on the skins in stainless steel, then pumped over and held in stainless steel and other cooperage.

"My goal is to make wine for people to enjoy," Fred says. Fairly priced, Buccia wines are sold at the winery for $7.31 to $14.08 a bottle. Buccia Vineyard produces Baco, Seyval Blanc, Reflections, Riesling, Vignoles, Agawam, Catawba, Maiden's Blush, Terrace White, Terrace Red, Pinot Gris, and Chambourcin. "Different winemakers make different styles of wine," he says, explaining that he tries to satisfy the changing tastes and demands of his target market.

For almost two decades, the Buccis have won the hearts and minds of fiercely loyal customers. Recently,

Joanna and Fred redesigned the Buccia Vineyard and Bed and Breakfast on a somewhat grander scale. They have a stately new entrance, an outdoor patio, and an expanded tasting room with a stone floor. The Buccis eagerly await your arrival and a chance to extend their hospitality to you!

Buccia Vineyard 🍇

Directions Take I-90 east to exit 235. Proceed north on State Route 193 toward North Kingsville. Turn right on East Center Street/U.S. Route 20, then left on Poore Road, then right on Gore Road to the winery

Hours 10 AM–6 PM, Closed Sundays

Tours Upon request

Tastings Daily when open

Gifts Wine related: T-shirts, denim shirts, sweatshirts, logo wine glasses

Picnics Welcome

Highlights at Winery Relaxed and romantic getaway; fun-filled activities; good atmosphere and friendly people; unique accommodations with hot tubs

Events Steak fry; ox roast

Restaurant Homemade breads and assorted cheeses

Prices $7.31–$14.08; 10 percent case discount

Brand Name Buccia Vineyard

Type of Production Classic winery

Method of Harvesting By hand

Pressing and Winemaking Bladder press with emphasis on good winemaking

Aging and Cooperage Stainless steel and other cooperage

Vineyards Founded 1975

County Ashtabula

AVA Lake Erie

Acreage 4.5

Waterway Lake Erie

Climate Temperate, cool spring and summer, lake breezes, cold winters

Soil Sandy with underpan of gravel

Varieties Baco, Seyval Blanc, Steuben, Vignoles, Catawba, Agawam, Chambourcin, Riesling, Pinot Gris

Wines Baco, Seyval Blanc, Reflections, Riesling, Vignoles, Agawam, Catawba, Maiden's Blush, Terrace White, Terrace Red, Pinot Gris, Chambourcin

Best Red Baco

Best White Vignoles

Other Best Wine Agawam

Quote "We make good wine for people to enjoy!"—Fred Bucci

Nearby Places to Visit Conneaut Marina; covered bridges

Chalet Debonné Vineyards

7743 Doty Road
Madison, OH 44057
Tel (440) 466-3485
Fax (440) 466-6753
E-mail info@debonne.com
Web site www.debonne.com
Owners Anthony P., Anthony S., Tony J., Rose M., and Beth A. Debevc
Winemaker Edward Trebets
Founded 1971

The country road to Chalet Debonné Vineyards turns and bends, passing Mill Creek (part of the Grand River Valley Watershed) before it bursts with the beauty of emerald green vineyards and purple grape clusters.

In 1916, Anton Debevc departed Ljublana, Yugoslavia, an area rich in grapes and lumber, and migrated to West Virginia before finally settling in Madison, Ohio and establishing a farm with apples, pears, peaches, raspberries, grapes, and animals. He sold Concord and Niagara grapes to local farmers and customers in Cleveland. Anton's son, Tony J. Debevc, eventually purchased land next door and raised cattle and planted corn, wheat, and grapes.

Today, Tony P. Debevc recalls his grandfather, Anton, who entertained friends on his farm with chicken dinners and homemade wine. "During the Depression, those picnics were how he made a living," says Tony P., a 1969 Ohio State University horticulture major and pomology specialist. "An old inspector who knew Anton made wine then said my grandfather never took advantage of the situation. But that was how he fed his family and also farmed."

The heyday of Concord and Niagara grapes in northeast Ohio lasted from the mid-forties to the late sixties. The Debevcs gained name recognition and increased sales as grape growers to Smucker's and Welch's, producers of juice, jams, and jellies. In 1970, two enterprising generations of Debevcs embarked on a venture that dramatically changed their lives. Tony P., his spouse, Beth, and his parents, Tony J. and Rose M., pooled their resources and invested in Chalet Debonné Vineyards. "Our dream was to start a family-owned and -operated farm market on our vineyard estate," Tony P. says. In 1971, they crushed 5,000 gallons of their first Chalet Debonné wines. "We did well with Pink Catawba and River Rouge, hybrid blends. Our customers, many

Three generations at the winery; the three Tonys.
Courtesy Chalet Debonné Vineyards

Slovenians, preferred sweet wine. A Slovenian highball was 50 percent dry Concord and Niagara sweetened with 50 percent soda." As the customers changed, their tastes changed, and they began to buy dry wines.

The hilltop Chalet Debonné has windowed atriums accented by a red bottle pattern. A draftsman of sorts, Tony P. Debevc designed the Chalet from his own drawings. He created a warm environment and a practical, modern winery. A wooden door opens to a great room with a brick fireplace, rustic barn walls, brick floor, an oak tasting bar, and wine-gift shop. People gather for grand banquets, simple summer fare, or a mid-winter escape to taste Debonné Vineyards premium varietals or Chalet Debonné Vineyard Select house wines. An open-air pavilion for parties and dances leads to a lawn and gazebo with unrivaled vineyard views.

The Debevc family has a reputation as both growers and vintners. Tony P. attributes this to Chalet Debonné's attention to detail in the vineyard and its high standards of sanitation in the winery. "We bring quality fruit and varietal character in from the field. Because Ohio has a European climate with four distinct seasons, the quality of our grapes is consistent, but the vintages can vary from year to year."

Vineyard manager Gene Sigel oversees 130 acres of vineyards comprising twenty-one varieties. He uses John Deere tractors and a mechanical harvester to implement the latest practices, such as high-cordon trellising, irrigation, leaf removal, crop thinning, use of micronutrients, and improved drainage. Enologist Ed Trebets oversees the technical winemaking procedures in the 30,000-case, state-of-the-art wine production center. It is equipped with Bucher presses, stainless steel, temperature-controlled, jacketed fermentors and Southern Great Lakes, Demptos, Canton, and Radoux American white oak cooperage. Trebets does the crushing, pressing, processing, and wine aging.

Debonné Vineyards has won Double Gold and Gold Medals in major competitions around the world for Chambourcin, its signature Riesling Reserve, Pinot Gris, Chardonnay, Chardonnay Reserve, and Lake Erie Riesling.

Chalet Debonné Vineyards 🍃🍂

Directions Take I-90 to Madison. Take State Route 528 south. Go left on Griswold Road, left on Emerson Road, then right on Doty Road to winery

Hours Jan.: Mon.–Sat., 12–6 PM; Feb.–Dec.: Mon.–Tues., 12–6 PM; Wed. & Fri., 12–11 PM; Thurs. & Sat., 12–8 PM. April–Oct.: Sun., 1–6 PM

Tours Tuesday–Saturday 1–4 PM

Tastings Wine & beer tasting bar and wine/beer tasting trays available

Gifts Wine gifts and casual clothing

Highlights at Winery On-site brewery, umbrella tables in the wineglass overlooking estate vineyards, wood burning fireplace in hospitality room

Events July Pet Day; August Classic Car Show; and Selected Sunday JazzFest

Restaurant Grilled sandwiches, cheese plates, dips

Prices $7.99–29.99; 15 percent case discount

Brand Names Chalet Debonné; Debonné Vineyards

Type of Production Traditional

Method of Harvesting Machine-harvested; ice wine grapes by hand

Pressing and Winemaking Bucher presses

Aging and Cooperage Stainless Steel Tanks and Hungarian and American oak barrels

Vineyard Founded 1916

County Lake

AVA Grand River Valley and Lake Erie

Acreage 130 acres; in 2008 seven new acres of Chardonnay and Pinot Noir

Waterways Grand River Valley and Lake Erie

Climate Lake Erie and Great Lakes microclimate influence

Soil Clay

Varieties Chardonnay, Pinot Gris, Riesling, Cabernet Franc, Pinot Noir, Merlot, Chambourcin, Vidal Blanc, Seyval Blanc, Vincent, De Chaunac, Foch, Concord, Catawba, Niagara, Delaware

Wines Jazz White, Cab/Cab, Vidal Blanc, Chardonnay, Chardonnay Private Reserve, Pinot Gris, Riesling, Riesling Reserve, Razzberry Riesling, Vidal Blanc, Harmony, Pinot Noir Syrah, Chambourcin, Cabernet Franc, Merlot, Classic Red, Grand Bélo, Grand Dolina, Delaware, Classic Rosé, Pink Catawba, River Rouge, River Blush, and River Blanc, Ice Wine

Best Red A Cab

Best White Riesling Reserve

Other Best Wine Pinot Grigio

Quote "We bottle perfect days."—Tony P. Debevc

Nearby Places to Visit Hogback Ridge Lake Metropark, President Garfield's Mentor home

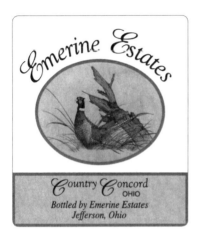

Emerine Estates Winery

5689 Loveland Rd.
Jefferson, OH, 44047
Tel (440) 293-8199
Fax (440) 293-8199
E-mail jemerine@emerineestates.com
Web site www.emerineestates.com
Owner Jason Emerine
Winemaker Jason Emerine
Founded 2006

Jason Emerine founded Emerine Estates Winery, a small handcrafted establishment producing exotic, artisanal 100 percent natural fruit wines in Jefferson, Ohio in 2006. The Cherry Valley homestead and winery originated out of the different winemaking traditions of the Emerine and Hovanic branches of the family.

During the 1930s–1940s, the Emerines, who were custom carpenters, produced unrefined wine in the cellar of their barn for their own consumption. During the 1940s, 1950s, and 1960s, the Hovanics made refined wine—reds and whites—for local Slovenian Clubs throughout Northeast Ohio. The year 2009 marked the 40th anniversary celebration of winemaking for the descendants of both the Emerine and Hovanic families.

For decades, Jefferson County prospered with its abundant production and rich harvests of vitis labrusca

wine grapes—Concord, Delaware, Catawba and Niagara. "Serious flooding during the nineties caused the roots of the vines to become prone to a surface disease," says Jason, and the vineyards were destroyed.

Currently, Emerine is in the early stages of cultivating 125 plants per plot in the first five acres of vineyard on the 65-acre farm. Emerine penetrates the tough clay soil by digging down three feet. He constructs a well that he packs with sand, pebbles and clay then the rootstock. "The deep penetration of the soil allows the vines to grow," he says. Until the vineyards and orchards get underway, Emerine purchases all the fresh fruit he uses in producing 5,000–7,500 bottles annually.

Earlier, he completed the construction of a large brown wooden building with a front porch that is both home and the winery. The 1,200 square foot hall and tasting room, called the "Outside-

In-Room," was created from a 1940s refurbished barn donated by a local farmer. It was designed so guests could experience the outside while they are inside. And it was imaginatively decorated with a white picket fence, lanterns, a string of Italian lights, and a 1920s popcorn stand. Here or on the outdoor deck and patio, the public gathers for formal and informal wine tastings, paired with light fare. A private party room is a favorite for special events.

"Wine is a form of self-expression. I believe in the old school—hard work and experimentation. I am a creator and an artist. I work on my wines for years. I do not use other people's ideas," Jason says.

This creative wine production facility, now off-limits to the public for safety considerations, combines modern stainless steel tanks with adaptations of 14th and 15th century winemaking equipment. "We are committed to the production of wholesome, 100 percent all natural, wines; we use no artificial colors, flavors, preservatives, or additional sulfites," he says. "Our wines are enriched with 11 essential vitamins and minerals for Stabilization and preservation."

Emerine uses special pressurized fermentation vats, following the destemming of the fruit, which sheds the grapes and fruit of their skins. By using this technique there is little waste during the preparation process. The grapes and fruit then go through a double fermentation stage followed by one to four years of clearing, stabilization, and aging.

Stainless steel and traditional oak barrels with a hint of red cedar seem to be aging vessels preferred by the winemaker. "There is no standard practice," he says. "We never blend our finished wine. We marry them from start to finish in order to produce a more balanced wine. "

Emerine Estates Winery has two intriguing wines made this way: Tear Drops Butter Chardonnay Reserve that pairs perfectly with seafood and poultry; and Seduction Pinot Noir Reserve that goes with lightly peppered red meat. Other wines include Chocolate Raspberry, Cherry Niagara, Harvest Peach-Apricot Chardonnay, Tropical Paradise, Strawberry Shortcake, Country Apple Riesling, Country Concord, Hunters Cranberry Wine, Razzle Dazzle Raspberry Wine, Blueberry Wine, Caramel Wine and Apple X-Cider. "By adopting traditional winemaking techniques and incorporating them with ours, we are able to produce a new generation of wines," says Jason.

Emerine Estates Winery 🍇

Directions Take OH 11 to the exit at US 6 (Chardon/Andover). Take US-6 east for 1.4 miles to a right on Loveland Rd. The winery is 0.6 miles on the right

Hours Closed Sunday. Monday–Thursday:11 AM–7 PM.; Friday & Saturday: 11 AM–midnight

Tours None at this time

Tastings Sit-down tastings, 15 wines, cheese and crackers, $10; informal tastings, $5

Gifts Wine and craft orientation

Events June 1st Anniversary Party; Steak Frys and Fish Frys with live music; Halloween and Christmas Parties

Picnics Outdoor designated area

Highlights at Winery Cherry Valley, home of exotic, 100 percent natural fruit wines; old-fashioned 14th and 15th century-type equipment

Restaurant Simple fare

Prices $19.50; 10 percent case discount

Brand Name Emerine Estates

Type of Production Ancient winemaking practices

Pressing and Winemaking By hand

Aging and Cooperage Stainless steel tanks with red cedar and local oak accents

County Ashtabula

AVAs Grand River Valley, Lake Erie

Appellation Californian and American

Acreage Five of 65 under development

Trellising Vertical Shoot Positioning

Climate Northeast Ohio (warm-humid summers; cold winters, four seasons)

Soil Platea silt loam

Varieties Concord, Niagara, Delaware and Vidal Blanc

Wines Chocolate Raspberry, Cherry Niagara, Harvest Peach-Apricot Chardonnay, Blackberry-Cabernet, Tropical Paradise, Strawberry Shortcake, Country Apple Riesling, Country Concord, Hunters Cranberry Wine, Razzle Dazzle Raspberry Wine, Blueberry Wine, Caramel Apple Wine, Apple X-Cider, Seduction, Déjà vu, Tear Drops, and Pinot Noir

Best Red Country Concord

Best White Harvest Peach-Apricot Chardonnay

Best Other Wine Seduction

Quote "Our wines are in a class that stand alone when winemaking is a passion and not a profession." –Jason Emerine

Nearby Places to Visit Cherry Valley Furniture Store, Andover, Covered Bridges of Ashtabula County

Farinacci Winery

3951 West State Route 307
Austinburg, OH 44010
Tel (440) 275-2300
Fax (440) 275-1255
E-mail farinacciwinery@aol.com
Web site www.farinacciwinery.com
Owners Michael and Dawn Farinacci
Winemaker Michael Farinacci
Founded 2002

The Farinacci Winery, on thirty-eight acres of farmland, was named for generations of Farinaccis who made wine in their native Gildone, Italy, by the Adriatic Sea before migrating to Canada, Venezuela, and America.

Antonio Farinacci brought the family tradition of winemaking to Cleveland's Little Italy, where he settled in 1912. He later passed the practice on to his son Dominic. In 2004, Antonio's grandson, Michael, and his spouse, Dawn, broke ground for the first commercial Farinacci Winery in the country. The name "Farinacci," which means "miller of wheat" in Italian, recognizes not only their family's name but also their interest in agriculture.

As a boy, Michael Farinacci often accompanied his grandfather Antonio to the flat, fertile vineyards along Lake Erie. "They would bring home fresh grape juice," recalls Dawn, whose Eastern European family introduced

her to wine. "Michael kept a five-gallon container for wine in the kitchen. One day when it was ready to drink, his father asked him, 'How is that wine?' Michael never realized his father knew he was secretly making wine."

Michael's grandfather and father made wine and vinegar. "They made wine from whatever grapes they purchased. There were no commercial wine yeasts for fermentation," he says. "They all were strict traditionalists with limited knowledge of wine chemistry. The wine was predicated on sugar content of grape juice in that particular year. If the sugar was high, it was wine. If the sugar was low, the wine was unstable."

Michael and Dawn purchased an Ohio farm with a house and barn on 38 acres, located along scenic State Route 307 in the heart of the Grand River Valley. The Farinaccis converted the barn into a modern winery. The interior has a warm and bright Italian décor

Crushing the grapes. *Courtesy Farinacci Winery*

Harvesting by hand. *Courtesy Farinacci Winery*

with a great room and a tasting bar. The main room, which was designed for wine tastings and live music performances, is illuminated by candlelight and furnished with comfortable chairs and tables for guests and patrons.

"We wanted to create a place where our customers can relax, kick-back, enjoy the wines, and good conversation," says Dawn. "The atmosphere at Farinacci Winery is traditional, quiet, and easy-going. Our niche market share is best described as low-key."

In 2005, the Farinaccis established a three-acre Grand River Valley AVA estate-vineyard planted with Vidal Blanc and Landot Noir. The grapes are hand-harvested, then taken to the winery where they are de-stemmed, crushed and pressed, then fermented

and held in stainless steel or oak barrels depending on the varietal. "We want to offer our customers a cross-section of different types and styles of wine," says Michael. "We concentrate on wine," says Dawn, the office manager. The winery markets home winemaking supplies and kits, wine casks, and a premium line of Farinacci wines.

Farinacci Winery sources grapes from Italy, British Columbia, Washington, Oregon, and California. "The whole world is our vineyard," says Michael, a traditional winemaker. The grapes will eventually come from his estate vineyard. The juice is blended, balanced, and held in stainless steel tanks to which oak chips and staves are added for complexity. "We like our wines to be consistent."

Farinacci Winery 🍇

Directions From I-90 exit at State Route 534 and proceed south to State Route 307, and turn left. The winery is located approximately two miles on the left side

Hours Saturday: 1–8 PM; please call for extended hours and winter hours

Tours None at this time

Tastings When open

Gifts Wine and gift items

Events Light jazz and easy listening music

Highlights Bucolic location in the Grand River Valley; outdoor patio with wine country views; quiet conversational winery with excellent wine

Prices $9.99–$19.99; 10 percent case discount; modest food prices

Brand Name Farinacci Winery, Ltd

Type of Production Traditional

Aging and Cooperage 100 percent stainless steel

County Ashtabula

AVA Grand River Valley

Appellation American

Acreage 3

Waterways Grand River Valley and Lake Erie

Climate Long, cool, growing season

Varieties Landot Noir, Cabernet Sauvignon, Merlot, Chardonnay, Riesling, Muscat, Vidal Blanc

Wines Landot Noir Estate Cabernet Sauvignon, Merlot, Chardonnay, Matrice White, Vidal Blanc, Riesling, Gewürztraminer, and Ice Wine

Best Red Cabernet Sauvignon

Best White Riesling

Best Other Wine Chardonnay

Quote "People with great minds drink great wines."—Michael Farinacci

Nearby Places to Visit Geneva State Park in Austinburg; Shandy Hall in Unionville

Ferrante Winery & Ristorante

5585 State Route 307
Geneva, OH 44041
Tel (440) 466-8466
Fax (440) 466-7370
E-mail info@FerranteWinery.com
Web site www.FerranteWinery.com
Owner Peter Ferrante
Winemaker Nick Ferrante
Founded 1937

The imposing Ferrante Winery & Ristorante in Harpersfield Township has a stone entrance with French doors, a peaked roofline with a cupola, and a garden and wrought-iron fence. A back terrace with gazebos is lit by lanterns for entertaining. The original farmhouse remains, and the barns are used for winemaking. Rows of well-tended emerald vineyards surround the property as far as one can see.

In 1937, Nick and Anna Ferrante, whose families sailed from Italy to the United States, lived in Cleveland's Collinwood district. Nick was a tailor by day and a winemaker by night at the Ferrante Winery. Anna saved their money and invested in land in South Euclid and Harpersfield Township. On weekends, the Ferrantes, accompanied by their sons, Peter and Anthony, drove to their Ashtabula country retreat—a farmhouse and barn where they also had gardens and vineyards. In 1955, Peter married a woman named Josephine, and

they relocated to Mentor. In 1957 Nick Ferrante died, followed in 1958 by Anna. This marked the end of an era.

Peter was both a carpenter and a winemaker. On weekends, the Ferrantes packed their car and their eight children and motored to Harpersfield Township. In 1973, the Ferrante Winery in Collinwood formally closed. Peter, with the help of his brother, Anthony, hand-built the wood-and-stone Ferrante Winery, which opened in Harpersfield Township in 1979. Peter's daughter, Mary Jo Ferrante, recalls the operation: "My father made four different wines: Russo, Bianco, Concord, and Niagara. We also built a small Italian ristorante, where he made pizza to go with his Italian wines." A key decision maker in the family business, Mary Jo handles winery and restaurant finances and, with her sister Carmel, oversees public relations and marketing.

Through the eighties, Peter and his son, Nick, expanded the winery. They

Ferrante Winery; Nick Ferrante sampling a glass. *Courtesy Ashtabula County Visitors Bureau*

purchased new equipment and planted new vineyards. "Then, the winery and restaurant were run as a small business," Mary Jo says. "By 1989, the family opened a full-service Italian restaurant and featured Josephine Ferrante's original recipes—wonderful lasagna, rolled meatballs, and spaghetti." The younger Ferrante women assumed increasingly more responsible executive positions in running the wine venture; the men managed the vineyard and winemaking.

In November 1994, a horrific fire gutted the restaurant but not the wine-production center or aging cellars. Undaunted, the Ferrantes redefined their life's dream. They hired Willoughby architect Joe Meyers to design a wine complex and Geneva contractor Raymond Builders to implement it. "We showcased Italian wine and food in a place with an Italian Old World feel. We wanted an open and airy restaurant with spectacular vineyard views and needed a functional winery," Mary Jo says.

Since 1995, when the Ferrante Winery & Ristorante reopened, business has boomed. The wine gift shop is crammed with merchandise and jammed with buyers. The fireside café with a wine bar and outdoor patio attract customers year-round. The more formal dining room, with its floor-to-ceiling brick fireplace and overhanging balcony, boasts views from almost any table.

The Ferrante Winery produces classic vinifera and labrusca wines from its excellent 47 vineyard acres. "We emphasize practical winemaking," Mary Jo says. "We do minimum filtering and fining. Forty percent of the wines are sold off-premises, and 60 percent of the wines are sold in the restaurant or at the winery."

A winery of distinction, Ferrante is known for its Cabernet Franc and Cabernet Sauvignon, its Pinot Grigio, and its signature Grand River Valley Riesling. Generations of customers return, sold on the Ferrantes' commitment to quality wine and service to their customers.

Ferrante Winery & Ristorante 🍇

Directions Take I-90 to Geneva. Go south on State Route 534, then go right on State Route 307 to winery

Hours Monday–Tuesday 10 AM–5 PM; Wednesday–Thursday 10 AM–8 PM; Friday–Saturday 10 AM–10 PM; Sunday 1–6 PM

Tours Guided educational and historic tour; tour and tasting, $4 per person

Tastings Daily when open

Gifts Extensive gift shop

Highlights at Winery Great wine, great food, Great Lakes!

Restaurant Full-service Italian cuisine

Prices Wine $14–$42; 10 percent case discount (carry-out only)

Brand Name Ferrante

Type of Production Vitis vinifera

Method of Harvesting Mechanical

Pressing and Winemaking Bladder press and traditional winemaking

Aging and Cooperage Stainless steel and French ,and American white oak

Vineyards Founded 1937

County Ashtabula

AVA Grand River Valley

Acreage 47

Waterways Grand River and Lake Erie

Climate: Long, cool growing season

Soil Clay

Varieties Chardonnay, Riesling, Pinot Gris, Cabernet Franc, Cabernet Sauvignon, Merlot, Catawba, Concord, Niagara, Vidal Blanc, Gewürztraminer

Wines Grand River Valley Chardonnay, Pinot Grigio Gewurzt, Golden Bunches, Grand River Valley Riesling, Grand River Valley Vidal Blanc, Bianco, White Catawba, Rosato, Jester's Blush, Pink Catawba, Pinot Noir, Reserve Red, Grand River Valley Cabernet Franc, Long Island Merlot, Vino Della Casa, Rosso, Celebration Spice, Vidal Blanc Ice Wine, Cabernet Franc Ice Wine

Best Reds Pinot Noir & Cabernet Franc

Best White Golden Bunches (dry white) and Pinot Grigio

Other Best Wine Grand River Riesling

Quote "We showcase Italian food and wine."—Mary Jo Ferrante

Nearby Places to Visit Ashtabula County rivers, lakes, parks, and covered bridges

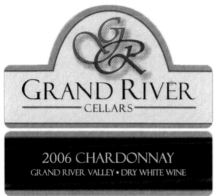

Grand River Cellars Winery & Restaurant

5750 Madison Road (Rt. 528)
Madison, OH 44057
Tel (440) 298-9838
Web site www.grandrivercellars.com
E-mail grcinfo@grandrivercellars.com
Owners Cindy & Jeff Lindberg, Tony &
Beth Debevc, Tony Rego, Ed Trebets
Winemaker Ed Trebets
Founded December 2005

The Grand River Cellars Winery & Restaurant, nestled at the back of a deeply wooded forest in Madison, was named for the region's famous scenic waterway and the appellation of the same name, the Grand River. Founders Bill and Carol Worthy established the first Grand River Winery in 1978 as one of the earliest Ohio producers of fine wine.

Four wine colleagues Bill Worthy, Arnie Esterer, Joseph Gruber, and Bill Pile made a pilgrimage to visit Dr. Konstantine Frank, a New York wine expert. He advised them to plant vitis vinifera grapes. Worthy planted a vitis vinifera and French hybrid vineyard, Esterer cultivated vitis vinifera, and Gruber and Pile chose French hybrids. Over twenty years, the Worthys developed a reputation for innovation and quality. The winery was sold in 1998.

In 2005 Madison Wine Cellars, a partnership consisting of three Ohio wine families—Jeff and Cindy Lindberg, Tony and Beth Debevc, and

Tony Rego—purchased the 53-acre wine estate and started to renovate the buildings and grounds. Their objective was to create an enhanced wine experience.

"Our goal is to provide our customers a wonderful time. We celebrate life. We want to be one of the wineries instrumental in growing the Grand River Valley as a respectable wine region," says Cindy Lindberg, the daily operations manager.

Grand River was transformed into an inviting destination winery and gathering place. A long driveway lined with black wrought-iron lanterns passes through a gateway made of wrought iron and Coshocton stone, flanked on either side by Vidal Blanc vineyards. A sweeping walkway landscaped with flowers and foliage leads to the wooden winery and an outdoor patio for entertainment. French doors open to a hallway that leads to the Great Room. The sea-green hall with painted murals is centered around a blazing fireplace surrounded by

Grand River Cellars. *Courtesy Grand River Cellars*

comfy chairs and couches. The soothing colors are repeated in the chairs and tables and contrasted by the pale grey and blue tile floors. The busy grille features lunch and dinner, with a large tasting bar, light rock, rock and roll, Motown, or rockin' blues, and smooth jazz.

"We want to be known for great wine, great food, and outstanding music," says Lindberg, a psychologist and former Debonné Vineyards event coordinator.

A Pennsylvania chef, Chris Gilmour, turns out popular entrees—homemade winter soups, beef fillets in Cabernet sauce, and scallops steamed in Chardonnay—that fill the house. "People come to eat and drink, and by Wednesday most reservations are booked." The winery has the capacity to seat 160. The private dining room with vineyard views seats 50 and is booked for showers, reunions, birthdays, anniversaries, and parties.

The vertical shoot positioned vineyards are planted in clay and come from the Lake Erie and Grand River Valley AVAs. Lake Erie's moderating effect on the climate and the growing season result in quality wine grapes. There are four acres of Vidal Blanc at the winery, and the remaining 90 percent are acquired locally. These include Seyval Blanc, De Chaunac, Chardonnay, Riesling, Pinot Grigio, Cabernet Franc, Merlot, Chambourcin, and Niagara.

Once the grapes are machine-harvested (with the exception of the grapes handpicked for the ice wine), they are taken to nearby Chalet Debonné Vineyards. There Tony Debevc, partner, oversees traditional wine production, and Ed Trebets, the winemaker, crafts the wine. The wine is then aged in stainless steel tanks and American oak cooperage at Grand River until bottling. "We are noted for our unusual blends and award-winning wines," says Lindberg, "Ed has a reputation for being consistent. There is something for everyone from dry to sweet."

Grand River Cellars produces a rich, full-bodied slightly sweet Chardonnay, a bright, green appley Riesling, an earthy, medium-bodied Cabernet Franc, and a fresh, citrusy Pinot Grigio. The 2006 Vidal Blanc Ice Wine won the award for the Ohio Department of Agriculture Best Dessert Wine in the State. Austin's Red and Austin's White are made in honor of a friend's son who has autism, and the proceeds go toward autism research.

Grand River Cellars 🍂

Directions Exactly three miles south of Interstate 90 on Route. 528

Hours Jan.–April, Wed., 12–6 PM; Thurs., 12–8 PM; Fri.–Sat., 12–11 PM; Sun. 1–8 PM. May–Dec., Wed.–Thurs., 12–8 PM; Fri.–Sat., 12–11 PM; Sun. 1–8 PM. Memorial Day–Labor Day, Mon.–Tues., 12–6 PM

Tours Tours of the cellar anytime before 6 PM, just ask

Tastings A tasting welcomes all customers. Tasting trays are available for a more leisurely visit

Gifts Wine related items and t-shirts

Highlights at Winery Beautiful outdoor deck nestled in woods. Rock on Friday evenings; Rock-n-roll, Motown, or rockin' blues on Sat. evenings, and smooth jazz on Sun.

Events Winery Margarita Party in June, July, and August. Progressive Dinners in February, March, October, & November visiting Chalet Debonné Vineyards and South River Vineyard. Check Web site

Restaurant Specializing in appetizers, grilled sandwiches, three different steaks, chicken, ribs, shrimp and lobster

Wine Prices From $8.99 to $14.99; 10 percent case discount

Brand Names Grand River Cellars

Type of Production Traditional

Method of Harvesting Machine harvested; handpicked ice wine grapes

Pressing and winemaking Bucher press and traditional

Aging and Cooperage Stainless steel and American oak cooperage

Vineyards Founded 1976 by Bill Worthy as Grand River Winery

County Lake

AVAs Grand River and Lake Erie

Acreage 4

Trellising Vertical Shoot Position

Waterways Grand River and Lake Erie

Climate Impacted by moderating effect of Lake Erie and Great Lakes

Soil Clay

Varieties Vidal Blanc, Seyval Blanc, De Chaunac, Chardonnay, Riesling, Pinot Grigio, Cabernet Franc, Merlot, Chambourcin, Concord, & Niagara

Wines Pinot Grigio, Chardonnay, Riesling, Cabernet Franc, Merlot; Austin's Red, Austin's White, Vidal Blanc Ice Wine, Grand White, Grand Red, White Fox, Winehound Red, Grand Blush

Best Red Cabernet Franc

Best White Chardonnay

Other Best Wine Vidal Blanc Ice Wine

Quote "People come here to enjoy wine and celebrate life."—Cindy Lindberg

Nearby Places to Visit Geneva-on-the-Lake, Grand River for fishing & hiking, Covered Bridges, Golf courses, Lake Farmpark

Harpersfield Vineyard

6387 Route 307
Geneva, OH 44041
Tel (440) 466-4739
Fax (440) 466-4896
E-mail harpersfieldwine@aol.com
Web site www.harpersfield.com
Owners Patricia and Adolf Ribic
Winemaker Wes Gerlosky
Founded 1979

The back country roads in Geneva roll past meadows, hayfields, tree farms, and a century-old village before they reach Harpersfield Vineyard in the heart of the Grand River Valley. A gravel driveway, which passes through rows of tended vineyards brilliant with mustard, statis, and clover, turns left at the bend toward an imposing stucco mission with wooden doors, a tower with a purple fleur-de-lis, and extensive grounds. Inside the large hall with beautiful hand-hewn beams and wrought iron chandeliers lies a seating area that faces the lighted sandstone hearth and brick il fornaio. Here people relax by the fire as they taste wine paired with international cheeses and served with flatbread pizza.

"La vie est bonne," booms Wes Gerlosky, a big man whose hair stands upright. He makes a sweeping gesture with his hand. Originally, this picturesque apple farm, orchard, and press house was the retirement home of Gerlosky's father. But unbeknownst to Wes, his wife, Meg, and his father had conspired otherwise. They convinced Wes the farm was the ideal place for home and family.

The younger Gerloskys purchased the property from Wes's father in 1979. Their introduction to fine French wine—Chablis and Chassagne Montrachet—by their tasting partner David Skiba inspired them to found a vineyard estate that same year. "We planted Chardonnay and Riesling, made wine, and sold grapes to vintners," Gerlosky says. "I made wine in the house until my wife said it was time to construct a building."

In 1985, with shovels in hand, Gerlosky and a friend used their architectural imagination and sweat equity to build a two-story winery. The upstairs consists of a system for bottling and corking by hand and case storage; the downstairs houses an underground stone cellar with tiers of American oak puncheons for winemaking and aging. Presently Patricia and Adolf Ribic are the sole owners of Harpersfield Vineyard. Mystic Hill, their newest seven-acre vineyard, is planted to Chardonnay, Gewürztraminer, Pinot Gris, and Pinot Noir.

Harpersfield has a bucolic atmosphere and a French outlook. "We have a distinct vision to make quality-oriented, estate-bottled wines from grapes reflective of the *terroir*—the characteristics of the land, the soil, the climate, and the grapes. The wines are magical and mysterious. We are both iconoclastic and slightly insouciant," Gerlosky says.

At harvest, the grapes are hand-picked into 25-pound lug boxes. Grapes are lightly pressed using a low-tech Howard Rotapress, fermented in Canton Cooperage American oak and/or stainless steel, then aged in small oak barrels. "We are non-interventionists," Gerlosky says. Of its annual 4,000 cases, 75 percent of the wines are sold at the winery and 25 percent at wholesale only in Ohio.

Noted for his outstanding Burgundian-like Pinot Noir, Gerlosky follows traditional practices, fermenting the grapes 100 percent on the stems in big open stainless steel fermentors. Then the wine is held in American oak barrels. The cherry Pinot Noir, Clos Mes Amis, tastes of raspberries and cranberries, with medium tannin and a silky acidity. The deep garnet Pinot

Simply charming! *Courtesy Harpersfield Vineyards*

Noir, Clos Mes Amis Reserve Cuvée, is deep garnet with a rich, berry aroma and full spiciness.

Chardonnay St. Vincent, named for the patron saint of winegrowers, is rich, opulent, and full-bodied with intense perfume and fruit flavors. Named for Joseph the carpenter-father, the Chardonnay St. Joseph is a fresh, delicate, grassy blend, leaner in style and austere, with good acidity. A smoky blend with fruit flavors, Chardonnay Isidore, noted patron of gardens, has pronounced personality and acidity. Elegant richness, Chardonnay St. Vincent "Le Coeur du Cote" originated from grapes along the heart of the slope. Other Alsatian powerhouses include the Riesling, the Gewürztraminer, and the Pinot Gris. The newest blockbusters are Chardonnay "Les Reeves," Rosé of Pinot Noir, and Musette Red.

"I am not a renegade," says Gerlosky says. "I am a traditionalist making wines from vinifera grapes that have grown around the world for centuries. If one works, it is a miracle what one gets in return," quips this extraordinary winemaker.

Harpersfield Vineyard 🍇

Directions Take I-90 to Geneva. Go south on Route 528, then left and east for four miles on Route 307

Hours Mon.–Tues., closed; Wed.–Thurs., 12–8 PM; Fri.–Sat., 12–11 PM; Sun. 12–6 PM

Tours By appointment

Tasting When open, 12–6 PM

Highlights at winery High-quality, estate-bottled vinifera wines; bucolic atmosphere; sustainable viticulture practices

Events Call for special events

Restaurant Gourmet flatbread pizzas and selection of international cheeses

Prices $17–$35; 10 percent case discount

Brand Names Harpersfield Vineyard

Type of Production Vinifera grapes

Method of Harvesting By hand

Pressing and Winemaking Light pressing and non-intervention

Aging and Cooperage American oak and stainless steel

Vineyards Founded 1979

County Ashtabula

AVA Grand River Valley

Acreage 18

Waterway Grand River

Climate Cool growing region, moderated by Lake Erie

Soil Platea silt loam

Varieties Chardonnay, Pinot Noir, Pinot Gris, Gewürztraminer, Cabernet Franc, Riesling, Gruner Veltliner, Muscat Ottonell, Kerner

Best Red Pinot Noir

Best White Chardonnay and/or Riesling

Other Best Wine Pinot Gris and/or Cabernet Franc

Nearby Places to Visit Canoeing on the Grand River; Shandy Hall, home of Alexander Harper

The Lakehouse Inn Winery

5653 Lake Road
Geneva-on-the-Lake, OH 44041
Tel (440) 466-8668
Fax (440) 466-2556
E-mail inquiries@thelakehouseinn.com
Web site www.thelakehouseinn.com
Owners Fagnilli family
Winemakers Sam Fagnilli & Lance Bushweiler
Founded 2002

State Route 534 travels north through the red-brick town of Geneva (an antique collector's dream), past its clock tower on Main Street and through a residential area before the road bends past small cottages and tall condominiums. It is here in Geneva-on-the-Lake where the white of the sun and the blue of the sky meet the gray-blue of Lake Erie. And it is here that The Lakehouse Inn Winery was situated to capture one of the most spectacular, breathtaking views—especially at sunset—in all of northeast Ohio.

Since 2000, proprietors Karen and Sam Fagnilli and their children, Andrea and Nathan, have envisioned this wine-country escape. Karen, who updates their picturesque Web site daily, says, "The majority of our bookings come over the Internet. We tried to appeal to people who cherish the leisure of reading a book or the quiet of their surroundings."

During the spring, summer, and fall, guests flock to this old-fashioned resort community, where they can relax as they pair good wine with delightful fare. During the winter, visitors nest by the warm fire to taste wine with hors d'oeuvres or homemade pizza and listen to classical music. Families enjoy swimming, fishing, boating, cycling, walking to nearby attractions, touring wineries and covered bridges, playing bocce ball and croquet, or taking in sunset bonfires at the beach.

The Fagnilli family renovated and furnished the 1940s Collinger Hotel and cottages in New England green and white. Andrea, who manages the inn, artistically decorated and furnished the guest rooms, suites, beach house, and cottages. The suites and beach house feature Jacuzzis and lake views. The great room doubles as a living room and dining room. The special-occasion dinners—pork or beef tenderloin and

Beauty to behold. *Courtesy Ashtabula County Visitors Bureau*

grilled salmon—and the hot breakfasts have great appeal for the guests.

The beach house, an atelier of sorts, consists of a luxury cottage upstairs and a winery, cellars, a tasting room, and a deck downstairs. The tree-lined lawns—dotted with red cascading geraniums, picnic tables, viewing benches, and flower gardens—sweep to the beach. "We are open to the public as a year-round bed and breakfast. People tour the wine country with us, taste our wine and food, and stay the weekend," says Sam, who also is the winemaker.

A self-taught enologist, Sam regularly attends winemaking classes at Ohio State University and Purdue. He names Arnie Esterer of Markko Vineyards as his mentor. The first year, 2001, the Fagnillis purchased finished juice, which they blended and bottled. Ready for 2002, the first wines released included Lakehouse Inn Winery Grand River Valley AVA Riesling, Cayuga, and

Chambourcin. They also continue to purchase grapes from Chalet Debonné and other vineyards. "We try to purchase mostly Grand River Valley AVA or Lake Erie AVA grapes, but due to the supply and demand, we also purchase some California and Oregon grapes," Sam says.

Once the grapes arrive at the winery, they are crushed and fermented. The Chardonnay, for example, is barrel-fermented in small, 60-gallon French Nadalie oak barrels, and the Pinot Grigio and Riesling are fermented in stainless steel. The Merlot, Pinot Noir, and Cabernet Franc, however, are fermented in stainless steel and barrel-aged. The Chardonnay and Cabernet Franc are aged in barrel for eighteen to twenty-four months before additional aging in bottle. Similarly, the Riesling is held in stainless steel tanks for up to twelve months, with additional bottle age. Typically, the Merlot is oak-aged for eight months in barrel, then the balance held in stainless steel tanks. "Less is more," Sam says of his approach to winemaking. "Patience is my teacher. Sometimes a wine will taste good, and sometimes it will taste off. With patience, the wine usually improves."

The Lakehouse Inn Winery attracts customers from as far away as Columbus and Cincinnati. Of course, southern Clevelanders are their big supporters. Patrons' tastes vary from dry to semi-dry to sweet. "They typically order a Pinot Grigio or Riesling followed by a Cabernet Franc."

The Lakehouse Inn Winery 🍇

Directions Take I-90 to Geneva, then head north on State Route 534 (becomes State Route 531) for 6 miles to winery

Hours Memorial Day thru Labor Day: Mon.–Tues., 12–6 PM, Wed.–Thurs., 12–8 PM, Fri.–Sun., 12–9 PM; Sept.: Wed.–Thurs., 12–8 PM, Fri.–Sun., 12–9 PM; May & Oct.: Thurs., 1–6 PM, Fri.–Sat., 12–8 PM, Sun., 12–7 PM; Nov.–April: (closed Jan.) Thurs., 1–5 PM, Fri.–Sat., 1–8 PM, Sun., 1–6 PM

Tours Educational tours of local wineries by appointment

Tastings $1 per taste, $5 for five tastes and a complimentary glass

Gifts Small gift area

Picnics Snack menu available

Highlights at Winery Spectacular views and sunsets of Lake Erie; small family-owned and -operated; comfortable bed and breakfast and cottages on Lake Erie

Events November Vino Novello Italian Dinner celebrates the new Harvest wines; May Bacchus Festival features barrel tasting with Italian cuisine and hors d'oeuvres

Restaurant Casual Lakefront setting, featuring Lake Erie perch, steaks, pork chops, chicken, homemade pizza

Prices $15–$24 per bottle; $2 off for carryout

Brand Name The Lakehouse Inn Winery

Production Traditional but drinkable

Method of Harvesting Mechanical

Winemaking Minimal

Aging and Cooperage French Nadalie small oak barrels and stainless steel tanks

Vineyards Purchased grapes from local vineyards

County Ashtabula County for Lake Erie grapes; Lake County Grand River grapes

AVAs Lake Erie and Grand River

Waterways Lake Erie

Climate Long, cool growing season

Soil Mixture of sandy topsoil and rocky clay in Lake Erie; sandy loam in Grand River

Wines Chardonnay, Riesling, Pinot Grigio, Cabernet Franc, Merlot, Pinot Noir, Chambourcin, Red Sky

Best Red Pinot Noir

Best White Riesling

Other Best Wine Red Sky

Quote "Less is more."—Sam Fagnilli

Nearby places to visit Geneva State Park and Marina; Ashtabula Harbor

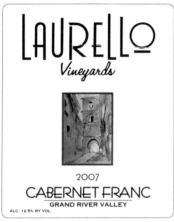

Laurello Vineyards

4573 State Route 307 East
Geneva, OH 44041
Tel (440) 415-0661
E-mail wineabite@laurellovineyards.com
Web site www.laurellovineyards.com
Owners Larry and Kim Laurello
Winemaker Larry Laurello
Founded 2002

Named in honor of the Laurello Family, Laurello Vineyards in Geneva is derived from the Italian word meaning "laurel tree." As the tradition goes, Olympians were honored by their peers and crowned with laurel wreaths. In that same spirit, the Laurello family pays homage to their guests and visitors by inviting them to share in the authentic Laurello wine experience.

"The secret to a good life is passion, hard work, and the love of family," say Larry and Kim Laurello, proprietors, who established the winery in 2002.

In 1944, Larry's grandfather, Cosmo Laurello, ran a small winery in Ashtabula. Decades later, when Larry and Cosmo were driving past a vineyard along I-90, he asked his grandson to stop for some grapes for them to share. Serendipitously, when that same 86-acre Burkholder Orchard and Vineyard came up for sale in the nineties, the family bid on the property and won.

"Our goal is to make people feel welcome and part of our family," Kim says. For starters, the Laurellos turned the Burkholder open-air market into a Tuscan-style mission reminiscent of Italy. A grand hall with Bryant gold walls, tiled floors, and a terra-cotta ceiling features a painting of the island of Capri above the bandstand. On the weekends, live music fills the room. "Our clients like to listen to music or share a conversation and enjoy good food and wine," Kim says. Other guests patronize the tasting bar, small gift shop or admire the wall of photos. The family makes homemade pizza in their outside Italian il fornaio. Homemade panini sandwiches and appetizers are also available. Private wine cellar parties are held in the renovated fruit market coolers.

"Friends and family have donated their time and creativity," Kim says. "Multiple generations have given of

Even the sign looks relaxing. *Courtesy Laurello Vineyards*

themselves in the tradition of being a family." Her mother-in-law designed the swags and banners, and her children and their friends painted the winery.

Laurello Vineyards has five acres of newly planted estate-grown Chardonnay. Vidal Blanc for ice wine and Riesling and Chambourcin. The remainder of the grape varietals are sourced from Foxhollow Vineyards, which Kim & Larry partially own, along with John Carlo Calicchia and Tara & Matt Meineke, both farmers in the Grand River Valley, and Nancy and David Genger in Conneaut, Ohio.

A separate building at the back of the property serves as the wine production center. Laurello takes a minimalist, somewhat eclectic approach to fine winemaking. Here the grapes are crushed and pressed in a vertical Italian press, then fermented in stainless steel and/ or small oak cooperage. The maturing wines are held and aged in either stainless steel or in American, French or Hungarian oak barrels with additional time in bottle. The renovated 100-year-old barn has been redesigned as a unique gathering place for private functions.

Customers find the outdoor covered patio with its refreshing views and comfortable furniture, surrounded by Kim's herbal and perennial gardens, a welcomed relaxation spot. They gather in the open air or under the canopy to taste the Laurello Vineyards Cabernet Sauvignon, Cabernet Franc, Pinot Noir, Cosmo and Rodavi, Chardonnay, Pinot Grigio, Riesling, Muscat Blanc, Viognier, and Vidal Ice Wine.

Larry produces the popular Cosmo, a Chianti blend made from California Sangiovese and Merlot, named out of respect for his grandfather. Josephine, made from Grand River Valley white varietals reflects his grandmother's sharp personality. Sweet Genevieve, a Vidal ice wine, is dubbed for Kim's mother. Every Easter, Kim's father gave his spouse, Genevieve and his daughters a gardenia. "My mother loved this fragrant flower and this memory continues through the gardenia on the label of this precious wine."

Laurello Vineyards

Directions Take I-90 east to exit 218. Go south on State Route 534 and left on State Route 307 east for 1.5 miles; winery on left

Hours Mon.–Tues., open for private functions only; Wed., 12–6 PM; Thurs., 12–8 PM; Fri.–Sat., 12–10 PM; Sun., 1–6 PM

Tours Educational tours of the wine-production center by reservation only

Tastings Daily and scheduled in advance for groups of 10 and above

Picnics Backyard patio and lawn suitable for picnics

Highlights at Winery Authentic Italian cuisine; high-quality dry wines; top entertainment

Events Laurello Vineyard–Lakehouse Inn and Winery, Spring "Bacchus Fest" & Fall Winery progressive tasting, "Vino Novello"

Prices $8–$35; 10 percent case discount

Brand Name Laurello Vineyards

Type of Production Vinifera & French hybrids

Method of Harvesting By hand

Pressing and Winemaking Traditional

Aging and Cooperage American, Hungarian, and French oak

Vineyards Founded circa 1930s

County Ashtabula

AVA Grand River Valley & Conneaut Lake

Acreage 18 (Laurello Vineyard 5 acre estate, 8 acre Foxhollow estate, and 5 acre Southridge vineyard)

Waterways Lake Erie and Grand River

Climate Long, cool growing season

Soil Clay

Varieties Cabernet Sauvignon, Cabernet Franc, Pinot Noir, Chambourcin, Chardonnay, Pinot Grigio, Riesling, Vidal, Muscat, Viognier, Gewürztraminer

Wines Chardonnay, Pinot Grigio, Riesling, Muscat Blanc, Viognier, Vidal Ice Wine Cabernet Sauvignon, Cabernet Franc, Pinot Noir, Cosmo, and Rodavi

Best Red Cabernet Franc GRV

Best White Pinot Grigio

Other Best Wine Pinot Noir GRV

Quote "The secret to a good life is passion, hard work, and the love of family."—Larry Laurello

Nearby Places to Visit 17 covered bridges; Geneva-on-the-Lake

Maple Ridge Vineyard

6326 Dewey Road
Madison, OH 44057
Tel (440) 829-8783
E-mail mrvllc1@windstream.net
Web site www.mapleridgevineyard.com
Owners Jim and Patti Iubelt
Winemaker Patti Iubelt
Founded 1994 (bonded winery: 2001)

The road to Maple Ridge Vineyard in Thompson is a paradise for people who love animals, farms, and a natural lifestyle. Come spring or fall, visitors who stop by this charming vineyard estate are greeted by horses, Navajo Churro sheep, Italian honey bees, Rhode Island Red and Bard Rock Hens, and Wolf Hounds who freely roam the grounds.

A beige farmhouse with green trim, accentuated with purple and yellow flowers, adjoins a patio with a green umbrella and café tables and chairs, the tasting room, and winery. A red barn looms in the distance. This is as ecologically as pure a home as owners Patti and Jim Iubelt could create for their children—Jessica, Tricia, and Jim.

A registered nurse in pediatrics and critical care/open heart, Patti descended from several generations of agriculturists. Her father, an organic farmer and an advocate of the Rodale Press, taught her how to farm cool climate conditions. An applications engineer and marketing guru, Jim has toured small world class wineries and vineyards, passionately reading about and tasting wine. Their paths crossed over a mutual love of wine, and they settled in the Ohio wine country.

The Iubelts built a totally self sustainable wine farm in the old European tradition. "Maple Ridge is a small farm, practicing sustainable agriculture and biodiversity following organic practices and processes. The farm depends on the synergistic environment where all the farm activities contribute to the entire operation," says Jim. Friends and visitors were invited to buy their farm products (in season)—wine, fruits, vegetables, honey, vinegar, poultry, and lamb.

In 1994, the Iubelts purchased 20 acres of farmland in the Lake Erie American Viticultural Area, 45 miles from Cleveland and eight miles from the lake. Here the distinguishing features that make this growing area unique are the topography, the climate, and the soil, excellent for vitis vinifera varieties.

Harvest time, Maple Ridge. *Courtesy Ohio Wine Producers Association*

The countryside consists of gently rolling hills and valleys. In the south-ernmost part of the appellation, Maple Ridge Vineyard stands at 1,200 feet above sea level, the highest altitude of any vineyard in Ohio. Along the top of the property a treeline breaks the wind off the lake, recirculates it, and results in warmer temperatures over the vineyard. Mean temperatures equal Burgundy and Bordeaux, averaging 2300 mean day degree days. The soil consists of six feet of packed clay, with a base of shale. This winning combination adds soil nutri-ents and amplifies grape flavors.

The Iubelts consulted with Herman Amberg, a viticulturist active in the wine education at Cornell University,

on the preparation of their slightly north-westerly sloped three acre vine-yard. At the onset, Gold Seal Winery imported the plants from France, and the cuttings were sent to Amberg, who grafted them onto 3309 root-stock, which he sold to Maple Ridge Vineyard. Clonal blocks were planted to Chardonnay, Riesling, Pinot Gris, Cabernet Franc and Pinot Noir. The vines are trellised at a height of 36 inch-es, then shoots are positioned vertically. This creates a higher fruit zone for grape maturation and increases the survival of the vine during the harsh winters.

Maple Ridge Vineyards utilizes a tractor with a mechanical grape hoe to weed around surrounding vines. The Iubelts fertilize the vines with seaweed, kelp, humic acid, mined rock powders and manure. "We strive for the perfect nutrients," explains Patti, who manages the vineyard operations. As a recipient of a Sustainable Agricultural Research and Education grant, Patti studies the impact of a natural compost tea and its benefits on their vineyard, Markko and Tarsitano. Every seven to ten days dur-ing the growing season, a Bordeaux mix of copper and lime or sulfur is sprayed on the vines to control the fungus.

Since 1999, the highest organic winemaking practices are followed. By October, the last grapes are hand-har-vested into lug boxes with a yield of two tons per acre. All the wine fermentation and barrel aging takes place in a com-bination of Italian stainless steel and

French oak cooperage. Once blended both the red and white wines are bottled unfiltered and given up to one year additional time in bottle. The popular Cabernet Franc, comes in three styles: a berry flavor wine and two reserves wines, one a French Pomerol style and the other a French Bordeaux style (with lamb orders only), starting at $25. The exquisite Chardonnays include two reserve wines, one a White Burgundy style and one a French Montrachet style, a library reserve, French Chablis style wine, and a Sauterne, from $21 to $35. The best Chardonnays are barrel-fermented in 60 gallon or 120 gallon French Allier oak barrels, then blended, bottled and aged.

As a 400-case producer of small lots of high quality organic wines, Maple Ridge has carved out an excellent reputation. "Our wines are made in the vineyard, therefore, we are concentrating on caring for the life in our soil, which allows our wines to exhibit their true varietal characteristics," they say with pride.

Maple Ridge Vineyard 🍁

Directions Take I-90 toward Madison. Go south on State Route 528 for 4 miles, west on Mosley Rd, south on Dewey Rd., third drive on right

Hours Call for appointment

Tours Guided, organic farm with sheep, goats, horses, and chickens

Tastings During hours when open

Gifts Produce, honey, vinegar, and wine

Picnics Bring your own

Highlights at Winery Small, organic farm making European-style wines

Events Wines & Vines Trail Tastings

Prices Call or E-mail to request

Brand Names Maple Ridge Vineyard

Type of Production 20 case lots; very limited

Method of Harvesting By hand

Pressing and winemaking Bladder press; some French oak barrel and some Italian stainless steel fermentation

Aging and Cooperage Some French Allier and Nevers oak barrel-aging and Italian stainless steel; additional bottle age

Vineyards Founded 1996

AVA Lake Erie

Acreage 3

Trellising Vertical shoot positioning

Climate Cool climate

Soil Clay & Sandstone

Varieties Cabernet Franc, Chardonnay, Pinot Gris, Pinot Noir, Riesling

Best Red Cabernet Franc

Best White Chardonnay

Other Best Wine Pinot Gris

Quote "Wines are made in the vineyard; we concentrate on caring for the life in our soil, this allows our wines to exhibit their true varietal characteristic."—Patti Iubelt

Nearby Places to Visit Pioneer Waterland, Geneva State Park, Geneva-on-the-Lake

Markko Vineyard

4500 South Ridge Road
Conneaut, OH 44030
Tel (440) 593-3197 or (800) 252-3197
Fax (440) 599-7022
E-mail markko@suite224.net
Web site www.markko.com
Owner Arnie Esterer
Winemakers Arnie Esterer and Linda
Frisbie
Founded 1968

As you wind your way off I-90 in Kingsville and head north, a turn on South Ridge Road leads to a jewel of a winery. Here the road passes through a splendor of woodlands, interspersed among century-old farmhouses with green pastures and leafy vineyards. Just as South Ridge becomes a country dirt road, stone pillars mark the entrance to Markko Vineyard.

The rustic winery founded in 1968 by Arnie Esterer and Tim Hubbard was named for its original Finnish dairy owners. Markko was the first Ohio winery to pioneer vitis vinifera varieties: Chardonnay, Cabernet, and Riesling. For more than 40 years, this 2000 case producer has championed these classic, estate-bottled, vintage-dated wines.

Wine grapes have grown in this historic wine district called the Lake Erie American Viticultural Area for more than 150 years. The cold winters on Lake Erie are one of struggle and survival for

Markko Vineyard. The vines often face ten-below-zero temperatures that test the life of the vine and the vigor of the budwood. Markko Vineyard reflects the *terroir,* a French expression that defines all physical aspects that influence the personality of the wine.

The fourteen-acre Markko Vineyard sits atop a ridge with a three-mile view to Lake Erie. Markko trellising is characterized by five-foot-high wire cordon, which creates great exposure to sunlight and thus better fruit and an improved grape climate. "How we manage the trellis system and the cultivation process is very important in maximizing the quality of the fruit," Esterer says. The low crop yield imparts a distinct character to the wine—one of depth, complexity, and intrigue. "Each wine speaks for itself, and the aroma, flavor, and body vary from harvest to harvest."

How did Esterer learn to produce a world-class Chardonnay? He exchanged his time for the tutelage of one legendary wine figure, New York wine expert Dr. Konstantin Frank. Esterer was also inspired by Maryland's Boordy Vineyard winemaker Philip Wagner, a red wine specialist, and California winemaker Andre Tchelistcheff of Georges de Latour fame. But it was Dr. Frank who most influenced Esterer's philosophy.

"Quality in wine, grapes, and soil with honest winemaking practices are the classic components that Dr. Frank emphasized," Esterer says. Applying this approach, he established a demonstration vineyard consisting of Chardonnay, Cabernet, Riesling, Pinot Noir, and Pinot Gris. "Chardonnays from different vintages produce a rainbow of wine with no preconceived style," he says. Dr. Frank advocated three marriages for a vineyard to be successful: the soil with the rootstock, the rootstock with the scion, and the scion with the climate. Markko Vineyard's Homage Chardonnay was made as a tribute to Dr. Frank.

Wagner believed that red wine grapes produced better wines when blended. Tchelistcheff emphasized that the earlier one made the marriage of grapes in red wine, the better the marriage. "It is this unity that gives wine its personality," Esterer says.

All winemaking and barrel aging at Markko take place below ground in a Burgundian environment, including a heavy cellar mold brought from France. Esterer and vineyard manager Linda Frisbie work as a team to make the wine. The Chardonnay is barrel-fermented and aged in fifty-nine-gallon, lightly toasted, air-dried, American white oak barrels. The Cabernet and Pinot Noir are fermented in stainless steel, then aged for two years in similar American white oak barrels. The Riesling is fermented and held in stainless steel for aging. "The lighter toast provides more expression in the wine, and the taste of the fruit comes forward," Esterer says.

The late Leon D. Adams, author of *Wines of America,* told the American Wine Society Conference that Esterer made the finest Johannisberg Riesling in North America in 1972. Adams wasn't sure if the winemaker could repeat it. In 1997, the American Wine Society presented the Award of Merit, its highest honor, to Esterer.

Markko Vineyard 🍇

Directions From I-90 at exit 235, head one-half mile north on State Route 193 to traffic light in Kingsville, then right for three miles on South Ridge Rd. to winery driveway

Hours Monday–Saturday 11 AM–6 PM; closed Sunday

Tours Self-guided

Tastings Daily when open

Gifts Wine-related

Picnics Welcome

Highlights at Winery Lovely wooded setting; outdoor tasting deck; great destination for dog-lovers; earthy experience tasting some of Ohio's best vitis viniferas

Events Blessing of the Vines, third Saturday in May; Odds & Ends Sale, third Saturday in September

Prices $12–$66; 10 percent case discount

Brand Name Markko Vineyard; Covered Bridge; Excelsior Champagne

Type of Production Traditional

Method of Harvesting: Hand-harvested into cart-mounted lug boxes; two to three tons per acre

Pressing and Winemaking Wilmes 10HL press and Burgundian winemaking

Fermentation Barrel-fermented Chardonnay in American oak casks, stainless steel, temperature-controlled, fermented Cabernet, Pinot Noir, and Riesling

Aging and Cooperage Traditional, 59-gallon American, oak-aged Chardonnay, surlees; Pinot Noir and Cabernet also American oak-aged for two years; Riesling held in stainless steel

Vineyards Founded 1968

County Ashtabula

AVA Lake Erie

Acreage 14

Waterway Lake Erie

Climate Temperate growing season, cool spring and summer, lake breezes just right for wine production; cold winters one of struggle and survival

Soil Plateau silt loam

Varieties Chardonnay, Riesling, Pinot Gris, Cabernet, Pinot Noir

Wines Excelsior Brut Methode champenoise Champagne, Chardonnay, Riesling, Cabernet, Pinot Noir

Quote "Each wine speaks for itself."— Arnie Esterer

Nearby Places to Visit Covered bridges at Creek Road, State Road, and Middle Road, including the Smolen-Gulf Covered Bridge

Lake Erie
SEYVAL BLANC
A Semi-Dry Table Wine

Old Firehouse Winery

5499 Lake Road
Geneva-on-the-Lake, OH 44041
Tel 1-800-UNCORK-1
E-mail contact@oldfirehousewinery.com
Web site www.oldfirehousewinery.com
Owner C. Joyce Morgan
Winemaker Don "Woody" Woodward
Founded 1988

Situated in the resort town of Geneva-on-the-Lake, the Old Firehouse Winery captures the imaginations of guests and visitors who long for a taste of nostalgia. The red-shingled winery, once the town's first fire station, and "Old Betsy," the 1924 Graham Brothers fire truck, are an invitation to experience life along the Lake Erie shore.

What enticed David Otto, Joyce Morgan, and Don Woodward to start a wine venture? They loved the rambling nineteenth-century firehouse with a big red barn and open space. The town had a storied reputation as a fashionable 1920s resort, and the region had a legacy for producing fine wine. "We only make wines we like, and we only make what sells," says Don Woodward, an advocate for quality grapes from the Lake Erie AVA.

The story of the Old Firehouse Winery is deeply linked to the history of the town's first firehouse. Woodward's grandfather, "Pop" Pera, was one of seven businessmen who formed the Geneva-on-the-Lake Fire Department in 1924. "After fruitlessly battling blazes with a bucket brigade, the seven businessmen purchased a 1924 Graham Brothers fire truck," says Don, a third-generation volunteer firefighter, EMT, and former assistant fire chief.

With the arrival of the fire truck, the firemen needed a barn and a chief. So, one Emory Tyler, a fireman, happily donated his barn, which became the fire station. By 1987, the story had come full circle, when Dave Otto, Joyce Morgan, and Don Woodward purchased an old red barn and a rusty fire truck. "We had the formula for the Old Firehouse Winery!" Woodward says.

Old Firehouse customers come from near and far to reach this favorite outpost, where there is something for everyone—especially families with children. They often escape to adjacent Erieview

Old Firehouse Winery. *Courtesy Ashtabula County Visitor's Bureau*

Park, with its rides, slides, roller coaster, train tour, video arcade, and billiard parlor. Shoppers head for Nature's Touch, which offers an assortment of novelties and gifts. But most guests begin their visit with a good meal accompanied by Old Firehouse wines and a tour.

Set amongst a stand of tall pines, the winery and restaurant consist of a series of decks, patios, a gazebo, and walkways. A bandstand features live music throughout the summer. Small and large groups sit at tables in the open, under red and white tents, in the latticed gazebo, or under green umbrellas. "The atmosphere is both informal and friendly, a place for fun and relaxation," Woodward says. Distinguished by variety and price, the full-service restaurant features Mexican and American cuisine

on the outdoor grill, as well as appetizers, barbequed chicken and ribs, healthy salads, and hearty sandwiches.

As winemaker, Woodward follows three cardinal rules handed down by Tony Carlucci, the winemaker who made the winery's first six wines. "He said there is no mystery in making wine. Use sound grapes, clean premises, and watch for light and air," he says. The Old Firehouse and Firehouse Cellars brands consist of 45 percent vitis vinifera grapes and 30 percent vitis labrusca grapes and other fruit. "Close to 70 percent of the grapes come from Tony Debevc, a local grower, and 30 percent of the grapes and fruit come from New York," Woodward says. "Ninety percent of the wine is made at the eight-thousand-gallon Geneva-on-the-Lake Winery, and all the wine is sold in Ohio."

During harvest, the white grape juice is bought outright and then finished and held in stainless and oak barrels. Some red grapes are crushed, pressed, and fermented on the premises and held in stainless and oak barrels. Select wines, such as The Firehouse Cellars Chardonnay and the Firehouse Cellars Cabernet Sauvignon, are crafted and bottled by hand at the winery. So, the next time you visit Geneva-on-the-Lake, be sure to experience the "heart of it all" at the Old Firehouse Winery.

Old Firehouse Winery 🍃

Directions Take I-90 to Exit 218 toward Geneva/Geneva-on-the Lake. Go north on State Route 534 for seven miles. When State Route 534 deadends into State Route 31, turn right on State Route 531 for 2/10 of a mile to winery on left

Hours Memorial Day–Labor Day, 12 PM–1 AM; Labor Day–January 1st, Sunday–Thursday, 12 PM–10 PM, Friday–Saturday, 12 PM–midnight; January–April, Saturday & Sunday, 12 PM–7 PM

Tours For groups of 15 or more

Tastings Group tastings; individual tastings by wine or sampler tray

Gifts Fire and wine oriented

Highlights at Winery Lovely decks, patio and gazebo overlooking Lake Erie; largest lake front winery on the Great Lakes; live music seven nights a week during summer

Events Northeast Polka Fest (second week in June); ethnic menu; music 12 PM–midnight, Irish-Scottish Celtic Feis (weekend before Labor Day); ethnic menu, music 12 PM–midnight

Restaurant American Continental; 22 wines

Prices $7.99–$31.07; 10 percent case discount

Brand Names Old Firehouse and Firehouse Cellars

Type of Production Handcrafted

Method of Harvesting Machine-harvested, and some hand-harvested

Pressing and Winemaking Hot press reds on skin

Aging and Cooperate American oak cooperage for Chardonnay, Cabernet Sauvignon and Merlot

County Ashtabula

AVA Lake Erie

Varieties Vitis vinifera, vitis labrusca, French hybrids, fruit wines, ice wines

Wines Sweet Concord, Pink Catawba, Grape Jamboree, Spiced Apple, Frosty Peach, Lighthouse Niagara, Firehouse White Catawba, Firehouse Red, Sunset Blush, Reflections of Lake Erie, Seyval Blanc, Vidal Ice, Spumante Champagne, Lake Erie Riesling, Gewürztraminer, Cabernet Sauvignon, Chardonnay, Merlot, Chambourcin, and Port- Eli #5 Dessert Wine

Best Red Merlot

Best White Reflections of Lake Erie

Other Best Wine Vidal Ice

Quote "If you want to play hard, learn to work hard."—Don Woodward

Nearby Places to Visit Go to www.visitgenevaonthelake.com, eclectic amusements, golf course, restaurants, nightlife, cottages, motels, lodge, camping, outdoor recreation, boating, 100 attractions

South River Vineyard

6062 South River Road
Geneva, OH 44041
Tel (440) 466-6676
E-mail southriverwinery@windstream.net
Web site www.southrivervineyard.com
Owners Gene and Heather Sigel
Founded 2000

The elegant simplicity of this tall white stark chapel surrounded by beautiful well-tended vineyards on South River Road in Geneva stirs the soul. This church, more than a century old, marks the site of one of the most spectacular views in the Grand River Valley, where the quiet of the moment magically transports the first-time visitor to an earlier time in the history of Ohio viticulture.

Proprietors Gene and Heather Sigel met while they were employed at Chalet Debonné Vineyards, Gene managing the vineyards and Heather working the tasting room. They married and merged their talents. "We were growing grapes and selling wine, so we decided to make wine for ourselves," Heather says.

The Sigels leased a small two-acre vineyard in 1995, and purchased their present 35-acre estate primarily in 1998. They dubbed it South River Vineyard, and tore out the Concord vines and rejuvenated the land. The tight, heavy clay soils were bulldozed and tile-drained every nine feet in preparation for a vitis vinifera vineyard. High cordon trellises were installed to promote vertical shoot positioning. The vineyard is planted to Chardonnay, Riesling, Pinot Grigio, Semillon, Cabernet Franc, Pinot Noir, and Merlot. The dense, cool-climate plot reflected Sigels modern farming practices: fertilization, draining, and canopy management. "Our strategy is to create low yields of intense and concentrated fruit," he says.

The Sigels learned about an abandoned 1892 Victorian chapel situated in nearby Portage County, and they thought it would be a perfect home for their winery. In early 2000, the Sigels began the artful process of dismantling the chapel one nail at a time. Each piece of the building was identified and packed for the fifty-mile road trip back to Geneva. "The reconstruction was a labor of love; we did most of the work ourselves," Heather says. The vaulted

The striking Victorian, dressed in winter white. *Courtesy South River Vineyard*

ceilings create space and light, contrasted by stained glass windows and rows of
chestnut pews and small tables grouped
for tastings. Outside, a lovely summer
pavilion with comfortable Adirondack
chairs overlooks the vineyards.

South River Vineyards opened in
2000 as a small artisan winery with an
emphasis on quality vineyards. A metic-
ulously detail-oriented farmer and consultant, Gene spends most days outside
maintaining the vineyards. "Our wines
are made in the vineyard," says Gene,
an economist with a PhD from the
University of Massachusetts. "We thin
the fruit, select the best, and harvest by
hand." The Sigels lease the tractors and
their equipment from Chalet Debonné
Vineyards, where Gene is still the vineyard manager. He received his formal

viticultural training under the tutelage
of its owners, the Debevc family, which
began growing grapes in the Grand
River Valley in 1916. Gene oversees
one hundred acres of prime vineyards
for South River Vineyards and Chalet
Debonné Vineyards combined.

Gene describes himself as a
minimalist winemaker. "Our wines are
lightly filtered, pressed, matured, aged
in American Demptos and Canton oak
cooperage and oak chips, then served,"
he says. "I produce 200 gallons to 300
gallons, sometimes 800 gallons, of a
specific variety at a time. Our goal is
become known for our special lots of
fine wines."

South River Vineyards attracts educated consumers and sophisticated devo-
tees who like a taste challenge. These

include a buttery-vanilla Chardonnay; a lemon-citrus Dry Riesling; a Pinot Grigio; a Cabernet Franc; a jammy-plumy Exodus; Trinity, a proprietary blend of Cabernet Franc, Chambourcin and Pinot Noir; Karma, a Merlot and Cabernet blend; Pinot Noir; Temptation, a strawberry-lilac rosé; Creation, a Chardonnay and Pinot Grigio blend; Sweet Riesling, a silky-peachy-apricot; Concord Ice and Blush Ice. This is the Ohio wine country at its best!

South River Vineyard 🍂

Directions I-90 east to Geneva. Go south on State Route 528, take a left on Griswold Road, and turn left again on Emerson Road. Turn right on Doty Road, which turns into South River Road and leads to the winery on the right

Hours Monday–Thursday: 2–6 PM; Friday 12–11 PM; Saturday: 12–11 PM

Tours By appointment

Tastings Daily when open. Three tastes for a $1

Gifts Imprinted wine glasses and wine

Picnics Bring one. Be modest—no grills or beer

Highlights at Winery Views of Lake Erie sunset from back veranda. Belly dancers every summer

Events See web site

Prices $6 by the glass; $16–$18 per bottle; $154 by the case; Ice wines $25–$29 by the bottle; $130–$150 by the case

Brand Names South River Vineyards

Type of Production Classic

Method of Harvesting Machine usually at night

Pressing and Winemaking Basket press for reds; membrane press for whites

Aging and Cooperage Demptos, American oak; Hungarian oak for Chardonnay

Vineyards Founded 1998

County Ashtabula

AVA Grand River Valley

Acreage 45

Waterways Grand River Valley watershed and Lake Erie

Climate Long, cool growing season

Soils Heavy clay

Varieties Riesling, Chardonnay, Pinot Grigio, Semillon, Pinot Noir, and Merlot

Best Red Karma

Best White Sweet Riesling

Other Best Wine Blush Ice wine

Quote "Our wines are made in the vineyard."—Gene Sigel

Nearby Places to Visit Covered Bridge at Harpersfield Park, Steelhead fishing, Grand River

St. Joseph Vineyard

6060 Madison Road
Thompson, OH 44086
Tel (440) 298-3709
E-mail stjosephvineyard@windstream.net
Web site www.saintjosephvineyard.com

Pinot Vista Tasting Room
4900 County Line Road
Thompson, OH 44086
(Use 307/Warner Road entrance)

Owners Art and Doreen Pietrzyk
Winemaker Art Pietrzyk
Founded 1987

The Grand River Valley has a reputation for being one of Ohio's finest viticultural districts for growing vitis vinifera grapes. After experimenting with winegrowing at other locations, Clevelanders Art and Doreen Pietrzyk came to this prestigious sub-appellation to plant St. Joseph Vineyard, named after their son Joseph. Their objective was to create nothing less than the best vineyard possible.

The Pietrzyk family has a history of winegrowing in the region that dates from 1972. Their appreciation for fine wine began in the eighties when they began to take it seriously. "Then my wine never met my expectations, says Art, an engineer. "We realized we needed to start with quality grapes." By 1982, the Pietrzyks invested in Bill Worthy's Grand River Winery. They experimented with a Pekin Road vineyard, 50 percent French hybrids and 50 percent vinifera, but ran into frost problems every third year. "We grew grapes, we made wine, and we were passionate for certain wines, especially Pinot Noirs," they say.

Through their research at Ohio State University, the Pietrzyks learned that the Lake Erie AVA was a premiere winegrowing district. They consulted with Arnie Esterer of Markko Vineyard, who in 1968 planted Ohio's first cold-climate vinifera grapes. They talked with Doug Moorehead, proprietor of Presque Isle Winery, one of the first to grow vinifera in Pennsylvania. With the Lake Erie Tasting Group, the Pietrzyks tasted Grand Cru Pinot Noirs from France's most highly rated vineyards and vintages. At La Tache, they observed, there were no great winemakers, just generations of agriculturists committed to maintaining great vineyards, from which came great wines.

By 1986, the Pietrzyks had purchased twenty acres of farmland along Madison Road in Thompson. A curving road meanders past the lush, rolling vineyards to the family home and pole barn. From April to October, it isn't unusual to see Art tending vines. At the back of the property stands the winery, built in 1999, showcasing a colorful stained-glass window of the vineyard. Upstairs in the cedar tasting room with its displays of wines and medals, Doreen, an accountant, oversees the wine education, taking visitors through flights of St. Joseph Vineyard wines. Outside, the terrace offers comfortable places to gather or picnic next to the gorgeous open spaces. "We start tasting dry whites, dry reds, then finish with sweet wine," she says. Downstairs, the winery consists of the fermentation center, the bottling room, and the aging cellar.

The St. Joseph Vineyard philosophy parallels Matthew 7:16: "Where-fore ye shall know them by their fruits. The good vine bears good wine." High quality is the emphasis here. "We bring intensity and complexity to our wines. There is vibrance in the vineyard, in the winery, and in the wines," Art says. His vineyard differentiates itself by offering its patrons a heightened wine experience, where they are encouraged to arrive with curiosity and leave with knowledge.

Education begins in the vineyard with those natural characteristics that give St. Joseph wines their sense of place, which the French call *terroir*. The wines are the combination of the parts: the cultivar, the gravel and sandstone with its sandy topsoil, the warm mornings and cool evenings that moderate the long growing season, the classic viticultural practices, and the traditional winemaking.

The vineyards comprise seven acres of wine grapes in Thompson's Grand River Valley AVA that include Chardonnay, Riesling, Sauvignon Blanc, Shiraz, Merlot, and Pinot Noir. Their newer 12-acre vineyard on Route 307 on the north side of the Grand River is planted with Riesling, Pinot Gris, Pinot Noir, Shiraz, and experimental Italian varieties.

"St. Joseph Vineyards are located in a unique microclimate in the Grand River Valley AVA which benefits from both the proximity to a large body of water and its moderating effects and elevation which promote good air and water drainage. With the longest growing season in the region, the grapes ripen to perfection during warm sunny days and cool breezy nights," says Art.

"Some of the varieties we grow include the Dijon Pinot Noir clones including 113, 114, 115, Pommard, 777, 677, 2A, 13 and others to broaden the flavors and nuances. Other red varieties include Merlot, Shiraz, Petite Shiraz, Sangiovese, and Cabernet. White varieties are Riesling, Sauvignon Blanc, Vidal Blanc and Pinot Gris."

Typically the white and red wines are fermented and held in Italian (with a variable–top tank) and American stainless steel, with time in bottle. Both the Chardonnay and the Pinot Noir are aged in 60-gallon French Nevers oak barrels, with time in bottle.

St Joseph Vineyards' premium wines have garnered national and international commendation of increasing significance. Their Pinot Noir received a Gold Medal at the Grand Harvest Awards in Santa Rosa, CA., and a Gold Medal at the Riverside International Wine Competition in Riverside, CA. Their Riesling was awarded a Gold Medal at the Finger Lakes International in New York, and a Gold Medal at the Tasters Guild Internal Wine Competition in Grand Rapids, MI. Their Ice Wine won a Gold Medal at the Tasters Guild International as well as awards for their Merlot and Pinot Gris. "Since entering recent competitions, our Pinot Noir has consistently won medals in national and international competitions, and may prove to be the red wine that puts the Grand River Valley on the map as a great region," Art says.

St. Joseph Vineyard 🍃

Directions Take I-90 east toward Madison. Go south on Route 528 for four miles to the winery

Hours Friday 3–7 PM; Saturday 1–7 PM

Tours By appointment

Tasting Daily during above hours

Gifts Hats, T-shirts, glasses, cork pullers, and wine-related items

Picnics Bring from home

Highlights at winery Internationally and nationally recognized wines; wine quality at boutique winery; personal attention; wine education

Restaurant Light fare—selection of cheese, crackers, and fruit

Prices $8.99–$34.99

Brand Names St. Joseph Vineyard

Type of Production Vinifera grapes and one French hybrid

Method of Harvesting By hand into 25-pound lug boxes

Winemaking and Pressing Traditional

Aging and Cooperage French Nevers oak barrels

Vineyards Founded 1986

County Geauga

AVA Grand River Valley

Acreage 19

Waterway Farm pond

Climate Cool, long growing season

Soil Rock and gravel

Varieties Chardonnay, Riesling, Pinot Blanc, Pinot Gris, Sauvignon Blanc, Pinot Noir, Merlot, Shiraz, Cabernet Sauvignon, Vidal Blanc, and Sangiovese

Best Red Pinot Noir

Best White Riesling

Other Best Wine Sauvignon Blanc

Quote "You will know us by our fruit." —Doreen Pietrzyk

Nearby Places to Visit Geneva-on-the-Lake; Shandy Hall

Pinot Vista Tasting Room 🍃

Directions Rt. 307, 2 miles east of Rt 528 near the Intersection of Rt. 307 & County Line Rd

Hours Friday and Saturday, 1–7

Tarsitano Winery

4871 Hatches Corners Road
Conneaut, OH 44030
Tel (440) 224-2444
E-mail ken@tarsitanowinery.com
Web site www.tarsitanowinery.com
Owner Kenneth Tarsitano
Winemaker Kenneth Tarsitano
Founded 2001

Conneaut's Tarsitano Winery, a gabled, cedar-sided building with French doors, stands atop a knoll overlooking rolling vineyards. The Conneaut River lies to the north, and Bear Creek flows to the south. The winery, established in 2001 by Ken Tarsitano, symbolizes the will of two branches of the family: the Finnish Ahos and the Italian Tarsitanos.

"The farm is a gathering place. When we all get together, we are very strong-willed," Ken says. "We have connected the land with the history of a traditional farm that grows, develops, and produces an end product."

The family's belief in these lands as a premiere growing district began almost a century ago. Ken narrates the story of Issac Aho, his great-grandfather, who migrated from Finland to northeast Ohio. There, he established a successful dairy farm that lasted until the 1980s. Every summer, Aho's grandchildren, Marsha and Tim, visited from Parma, Ohio, to partake in the ritual of baling hay. From the onset, the farm had a magnetic pull on the family and each successive generation. When Marsha married Ralph Tarsitano, they shared the same custom with their children, Ken and Michele.

"I followed in the same tradition," affirms Ken, the one-time advertising executive and computer whiz. A career change in the mid-nineties inspired him to tap his creative muses and explore his world. With his camera in tow, Ken set off to photograph life in China for three months. Upon his return, he took to the open road to hike the Appalachian Trail from Maine to Georgia. In his absence, the family farm remained vacant for seven long years.

Once Tarsitano returned home to Conneaut, he divided his time pursuing two separate but parallel career paths. He worked both for the Ohio State University Grape Research Center in

Kingsville and as an organic farmer on his property. "On fifteen acres, I farmed seventy-two different fruits, nuts, and vegetables, which I sold directly to the Community Sponsored Agricultural Programs, to the North Union Farmer's Market, and to the Willoughby Farmer's Market. Mother Nature knew she wanted to grow grapes," he says. So, he took the first step in that direction.

By the late nineties, Tarsitano had talked to vinifera guru Arnie Esterer from Markko Vineyards and French hybrid advocates Joe Biscotti of Biscotti Family Winery, Fred Bucci of Buccia Vineyards, and Nick Ferrante of Ferrante Vineyards. "I asked questions and listened," he says.

Tarsitano chose the vitis vinifera route, planting two acres of Chardonnay; Bianca, a Hungarian hybrid; and Lemberger, a Blaufrankish vinifera (from the same town that produces Limburger cheese). "Our reasoning was practical," he says, explaining that the Bianca tolerates cold and the Lemberger resists disease.

Tarsitano Winery produces hard-to-find specialty wines with unique tastes and flavors. "We are showcasing the land," says Ken, the principal, CEO, and winemaker of this small artisan winery. The diversity of the grapes is highlighted by meticulous field-blending and artful barrel blending, which makes wines of depth and complexity.

"We pick, crush, and press by hand, we ferment both our white and red grapes in oak, and we craft our wines with care."

Great variety in Ken's line of premium Chardonnays is a source of pride. "With this variety, we emphasize the clonal mix and vintage expressions. Some of the wines are made *surlees*, filtered, unfiltered, lightly oaked, or heavily oaked. Of the many wines we produce, we age in French, German, American, and Hungarian oak," he says.

Over the years as Tarsitano Winery grew, so did Ken's passion for Ohio regional cuisine. Since opening the cafe in 2004, Ken and Kelly, his wife, have made their own pastas, ravioli, cavitelli, and fresh bread daily. Their diverse menu now includes entrees such as chipotle ravioli, stuffed with smoked gouda, Moroccan steak with Tarsitano's wide cut pasta in a saffron cream sauce, and an overstuffed chicken breast with fresh mixed green salad.

Continuing the tradition of maintaining a working family farm and winery, Ken and Kelly have added three new vineyard workers to the Tarsitano clan, two daughters, Isabella and Mia, and a son, Brant. Hurrah!

"Our motto is by sharing, we learn," says Ken, who envisions a second phase of his dream that includes building a new winery and tasting room with a bed and breakfast.

Tarsitano Winery 🍂

Directions From Erie, take I-90 to Conneaut. Take State Route 7 south and turn right on Hatches Corners Road to the winery. From Cleveland, take I-90 to State Route 193 and continue straight ahead. Proceed east on State Route 84 for 2.9 miles, left on Ohio Road for 1.5 miles, then right on Hatches Corners Road to the winery

Hours Open year round; please visit web site for winery and café hours

Tours By appointment only

Tastings Daily when open

Gifts Wine accessories and gift certificates

Highlights at Winery Beautiful location with terrace views of the vineyards and farmlands; a small boutique winery and regional café

Events Cooking Classes, Specialty Tastings, Club Member Events

Restaurant Ken's homemade pastas and ravioli, paired with his special sauces, specialty steaks and chicken, and fresh-baked breads and desserts. See Web site for restaurant hours

Prices $10–$50; 10 percent case discount

Brand Name Tarsitano Winery

Type of Production Interpreting wine, mixing artistic and natural elements

Method of Harvesting Hand-harvested into lug boxes

Pressing and Winemaking Ferment primary and secondary reds; some whites in oak barrels

Aging and Cooperage New and used American, French, Hungarian, and German oak

Vineyards Founded Since 1998 certified organic

County Ashtabula

AVA Lake Erie

Acreage 17

Waterways Lake Erie, Conneaut River, and Bear Creek

Climate Long, cool growing season on north-facing slopes called Pinnacles; influenced by three water sources that create cool spring and warm fall

Soil Heavy platea loam

Varieties Chardonnay, Riesling, Gewürztraminer, Pinot Gris, Auxerrois, Lemberger, Cabernet Sauvignon, Pinot Noir and other vinifera

Wines Chardonnay, Riesling, Pinot Gris, Inaugural, Lemberger, Auxerrois, Lemberger, Cabernet Sauvignon, Cabernet Franc, Pinot Noir, and Bear Creek Red

Best Red Cabernet Sauvignon

Best White Chardonnay

Other Best Wine Auxerrois

PEACH
Peach Fruit Wine

The Winery at Spring Hill

6062 South Ridge West, P.O. Box 47
Geneva, OH, 44041
Tel (440) 466-0626
E-mail info@thewineryatspringhill.com
Web site www.thewineryatspringhill.com
Owners Jim Pearson, Tom Swank, Rick
Trice, & Cindy Swank
Winemakers Tom Swank & Jim Pearson
Founded 2008

The Winery at Spring Hill in Geneva evolved spontaneously out of an idea that Tom Swank, vice president of operations and co-winemaker, shared with Jim Pearson, president and co-winemaker, at the 2006 Christmas Party of the Geneva Chamber of Commerce. The concept snowballed.

In early 2007, the now foursome, Tom Swank, Jim Pearson, Rick Trice (vice president of finance/treasurer), and Cindy Swank (vice president of food service/secretary), planned how to start the venture. That year, they wrote the business plan, found financing, and worked toward the 2008 launch of The Winery at Spring Hill. "Our business slogan was born—'Our heritage is fruit, our legacy fine wines,'" says Tom Swank.

Their farm's history began years ago when the Swank's grandfather Tom White, a 1917 OSU horticulture graduate, pioneered the fruit business

near Mentor, Ohio. During the thirties, he purchased land west of Chardon and founded Tom White's Geauga Orchards. He later added orchards in Windsor, Ohio, in Ashtabula County.

White successfully sold fruit at retail and wholesale—shipping product to Marietta, Cincinnati, and Cleveland. He was also one of the founders of the East Cleveland Farmers Market at Coit and Woodworth. For over fifty years, his family has maintained a fruit stand at the Geauga County Fair.

In 1953 White acquired and planted a 200-acre farm in Harpersfield Township, which was called Spring Hill for the numerous natural springs on the property. In 1980, White's daughter and son-in-law, Lillian and Chester Swank returned to Ohio with their family to expand the fruit business. Lillian was an OSU home economics major; Chester, also an OSU graduate, had worked for the U.S. Department of Agriculture

The tasting room fireplace. *Courtesy Spring Hill*

The Winery at Spring Hill. *Courtesy Spring Hill*

in marketing. They built a farm market and cider mill with a sales room with a stone fireplace, oak walls, family antiques, and decorations. In 1984, Tom Swank, an OSU horticulture graduate, joined the business, representing the third generation. In 1990, his sister Cindy Swank, an OSU hospitality management graduate, was hired to renew the bakery.

During the renovations, the Winery at Spring Hill added a second stone fireplace and a wine bar. The expanded bakery serves baked breads, pies, pizzas, pastries, cheesecakes, and other sweet temptations. The kitchen features cheeses, breads, appetizers, pizzas, seasonal menus, specialty coffees, and desserts to be paired with Spring Hill wines.

Grapes are sourced from the six acre vitis vinifera and vitis labrusca vineyards, first established in 1990, in the Grand River Valley AVA and the Lake Erie AVA, or purchased from local winegrowers. The varietals include Cabernet Franc, Riesling, Vidal Blanc and other labrusca wine grapes. "We want to make the best wines out of locally grown grapes and fruit and showcase the Lake Erie and Grand River Valley appellations," he says.

The winery has three different labels. Their Spring Hill premium label—vinifera and French-American hybrids—consists of Cabernet Sauvignon, Merlot, Chambourcin, Chardonnay, Riesling, and Vidal Blanc. Their Covered Bridge label—vitis labrusca grapes—includes Covered Bridge Red, Blush, White, Pink Catawba, and Niagara. Their fruit labels—100 percent fruit wines—are Apple, Spiced Apple, Cherry, Peach, Blackberry, Blueberry, Raspberry, and Sangria. According to Swank, their emphasis is on fresh, succulent, high end fruit used to produce small quantities of quality wine.

The Winery at Spring Hill 🍃

Directions From I-90, take State Route 534 north, then go west on State Route 84 for 1.5 miles to winery on the left

Hours Check Web site or call winery

Tastings Daily when opened

Gifts Wine-related

Picnics Food available for purchase

Highlights at Winery Great atmosphere; everyone welcome; great wine and food pairings

Restaurant Hot and cold appetizers, pizzas, soup of the day, specialty coffees, desserts, and beverages.

Prices $9.95–$19.95; 10 percent case discount

Brand Name The Winery at Spring Hill

Type of Production Traditional

Method of Harvesting Handpicked

Pressing and Winemaking Basket press and traditional winemaking methods

Aging and Cooperage Stainless steel tanks and oak barrels

Vineyards Founded 1990

County Ashtabula

AVA Grand River Valley and Lake Erie

Acreage 6

Trellising Vertical Shoot Positioning & Geneva Double Curtain

Waterways Lake Erie and Grand River

Climate Unpredictable Ohio weather

Soil Sandy and gravelly

Varieties Riesling, Cabernet Franc, Vidal Blanc, and various vitis labrusca

Wines Cabernet Sauvignon, Merlot, Chardonnay, Riesling, Chambourcin, Vidal Blanc, Catawba, Niagara, Fredonia, Steuben, Delaware, Apple, Spiced Apple, Blackberry, Blueberry, Cherry, Peach, Raspberry, and Sangria

Best Red Merlot

Best White Riesling

Best Other Wine Covered Bridge Fredonia

Quote "Our heritage is fruit, our legacy is fine wines."—Tom Swank

Nearby Places to Visit Geneva State Park Lodge, Wines & Vines Wine Trail, Ashtabula Harbor

Arnie Esterer pruning vines at Markko Vineyard.
Photo by Phil Masturzo

Hermes Winery.
Photo by Phil Masturzo

Charles Virant uncorks a bottle.
Photo by Phil Masturzo

Vineyards at dawn in Wooster.
*Courtesy of the Ohio State University/Ohio
Agricultural Research and Development Center*

Historic Mon Ami Cellars.
Photo by Phil Masturzo

Peter Ferrante.
Photo by Phil Masturzo

Big purply-rose grape clusters.
*Photo by John Waraksa, Sapphire Falls
Web Design. Courtesy Harpersfield Vineyard*

South River Vineyard at night.
Photo by Phil Masturzo

Virant Family Winery

541 Atkins Road
Geneva, OH 44041
Tel (440) 466-6279
E-mail winemaker@windstream.net
Web site www.virantfamilywinery.com
Owners Virant family
Winemakers Frank and Charlie Virant
Founded 1998

The view at sunset over the rolling hillside vineyards at the Virant Family Winery in Cork is unrivaled. The winery sits atop a knoll within sight of one of Ohio's oldest Slovenian agricultural communities. Two farmsteads, one new and one old, are nestled into the verdant vineyards, home to five generations of the Virant family who have made agriculture their livelihood.

At the turn of the twentieth century, Lewis Virant immigrated to the United States from Slovenia, where winemaking began some 2,400 years ago with the Celtic and Illyrian tribes of northeastern Slovenia before the Romans arrived in the first century AD. During the 1930s, employment was scarce in Cleveland, so Virant moved his family east to the countryside and established a farm with his son Frank. From sunrise to sunset, the family ran the farm with its vineyards, orchards, gardens, cattle, and chickens. "We made milk, butter, meat, and poultry. We produced wine for fun for our

friends and neighbors," says Frank's son, third-generation Charles Virant.

In 1962, Frank and Charles planted an eleven-acre vineyard left of the present Virant Family Winery. A year later, Charles and Martha Virant purchased an eight-acre vineyard opposite the former Claire's Grand River Wine Company in Thompson. Charles and his son, also named Frank, the fourth generation, grew up managing these Lake Erie AVA vineyards. They were selected for their excellent location and growing conditions between the north ridge (State Route 20) and the south ridge (State Route 84) of old Lake Erie, their clay soils, and their warmer temperatures than areas farther south.

"Along this corridor, there were flower nurseries and truck farms," Charles says. "Farmers grew grapes, peaches, apples, melons, corn, tomatoes, and blackberries." By 1998, Charles and Frank purchased the vineyards they had managed next to the Virant Family

Charles Virant toasts his family's vineyard. *Courtesy Phil Masturzo*

Winery. Concord and Niagara, dominant varieties at both sites, are used to produce the Virant wines or are sold to the Welch's Grape Juice Company.

The opening of the Virant Family Winery, also in 1998, drew on the family's rich Slovenian heritage. They emphasized traditions, inclusiveness, delicious food, and good wines with music and entertainment in a beautiful setting. "We appeal to ordinary people who want to taste wine and enjoy food. We treat everyone like family members," Charles says.

The Virant Family Winery produces a collection of dry, berry, and medium-sweet wines. The fresh, sweet Red Velvet, the best-seller, has won many awards. At the Ohio State University Wine Competition in Wooster, it won a Gold

Medal as Best American Red out of 238 wines. At the Los Angeles State Fair, an international competition with 778 wineries featuring 3,000 entries, it won a Bronze Medal. And the dry, red Midnight Chambourcin, with its peppery, plum flavor and oak nuances, won a commendation at the Ohio State University Wine Competition. The Virants now feature a Riesling and a Cabernet Franc.

Banks of purple and pink petunias interspersed with milk cans and oak cooperage flank the entrance to the peaked brick Virant Family Winery. Upstairs is a large open room with photos and memorabilia for tasting, dining, buying gifts, and listening to music. Spacious windows bring the gorgeous vistas indoors like a painting. An outdoor dining area and tented picnic area overlook the vineyards. Downstairs, the winery houses fermentation equipment, a bottling line, and a variety of cooperage for the production and aging of wine.

The winery hosts monthly events: pig and beef roasts, clambakes, and ribs and steak cookouts with jazz, polka, or light rock. The annual celebration "Christmas in July," with holiday music, Christmas trees, wreaths, food, wine, and Santa Claus, attracts crowds. The Virants invite you to visit throughout the year to meet the family and join the fun!

Virant Family Winery 🍇

Directions Take I-90 toward Geneva. Go south on State Route 534. Turn right on Cold Cork Springs Road, then right onto Atkins Road to the winery

Hours Summer: Wednesday & Thursday: 2–5 PM; Friday: 2–10 PM; Saturday; 1–10 PM; Entertainment 7–10 PM Sunday 1–5 PM; closed Sundays in January and February

Tastings Daily when open

Gifts Wine-related articles and gifts

Highlights at Winery Everyone treated like family; good wine, good food, and good service

Events Clambakes, pig roasts, steak and rib dinners with jazz, polka, or light rock

Restaurant Light fare—Steaks, ribs, and chicken dinners Fridays & Saturdays: 5–8 PM

Prices $9–$14; 15 percent case discount, except for berry wines

Brand Names Virant Family

Type of Production Innovative and adaptive

Method of Harvesting Mechanical harvesting

Pressing and Winemaking Normal

Aging and Cooperage Two to three years

Vineyards Founded 1962 and 1963 respectively

County Ashtabula County

AVA Lake Erie and Grand River Valley

Acreage 19

Waterway Grand River

Climate Long, cool growing season

Soil Clay

Varieties Concord and Niagara

Wines Midnight Chambourcin, Cabernet Franc, Mya's Majesty, Riesling, Red Velvet, White Silk, Chiffon, Delightfully Delaware, Pink Delight, Chantilly Blush, Blazzin Blackberry, and Rippling Raspberry

Best Red Red Velvet

Best White Chiffon

Other Best Wine White Silk

Quote "Treat people like you like to be treated."—Charlie Virant

Nearby Places to Visit Lake Erie and Grand River; covered bridges

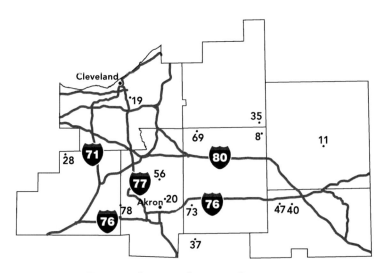

Canal and Lock Tour

Candlelight Winery

11325 Center Road
Garrettsville, OH 44231
Tel (330) 527-4118
Fax (330) 527-5912
E-mail info@candlelightwinery.com
Web site www.candlelightwinery.com
Owners Chris and Amanda Conkol
Winemaker Chris Conkol
Founded 2002

Candlelight Winery along Tinkers Creek, located in the gently rolling hamlet of Garrettsville, is one of the town's greatest features. From the time of the town's first Silver Creek grist-sawmill in 1805, this corner of the Western Reserve has appealed to farmers, artists, writers, poets, entrepreneurs, and winemakers. Chris and Amanda Conkol founded Candlelight in 2002. "Our goal is to educate, entertain, and enrich the lives of anyone who enjoys a glass of wine," Chris says. In the nineties, Chris was completing a BA at Kent State University's School of Architecture while Amanda, his high school sweetheart, was finishing a BS in computer science at Bowling Green State University. "I went to Italy, where I studied wine more than I did architecture," Chris says. Upon his return, Chris and Amanda married, and she became an Information Technology manager while he became an architect.

But Chris pursued his interest in wine, taking winemaking classes at Viking Vineyards and Portage Hills Winery. The first year, he made wine from a concentrated Chianti blend. The second year, he made wines from Concord, Niagara, and Marechal Foch juice from a winery. The third year, he made both dry and sweet wines from fresh grapes.

Chris started making wine in his apartment, later in his house, and finally in his garage. "I had a five-gallon wine container in the bedroom, and my wife told me that it was time I did something about it," he says. In 2002, the Conkols purchased fifteen acres of land, part of an old farm, with a road and site for a creek-side winery in the backcountry of Portage County. Earlier that year, they had planted a two- to three-acre vineyards in between Burton and Chesterland in Geauga County.

While maintaining their regular jobs, the Conkols hand-built their winery themselves. Chris designed a two-story modified pole barn with a great room with French doors that opened onto a deck overlooking a field by Tinkers Creek. He installed stainless steel, jacketed fermentors with variable capacity and other new equipment.

The inside of Candlelight Winery mirrors the Conkols' good taste in art and wine. The captivating great room has laminated wooden floors contrasted with a midnight-blue ceiling dotted with twinkling stars that light up, and a fireplace surrounded by wood-stained wine racks. "Wine just isn't grapes; it is the atmosphere or mood of what's going on when one drinks it," Chris says. "Wine tastes different under candlelight." A tasting bar features the newest Candlelight wines and light fare. A hallway counter and wine rack display a calendar of events, including a list of live musicians that play at the winery every Saturday evening, the Candlelight Cove Light Show schedule, and other charity events that are hosted at the winery throughout the year.

In addition to the Geauga County vineyards, the Conkols planted a one-acre vineyard on their Garrettsville property in 2002. On the edge of the snowbelt, the vineyards are planted in sandy clay soil to Vidal Blanc, Marechal Foch, Chambourcin, Niagara, Concord, and Riesling. Candlelight Winery features over fifteen wines to please any palette. Their most popular wines include

The tasting room at Candlelight Winery. *Courtesy Candlelight Winery*

Pink Pug, a sweet blush, a dry Riesling, and the owners favorite, a Sangiovese.

Chris takes a traditional approach to winemaking, using a bladder press to process the grapes. He checks the wine frequently and lets the sediment settle out before he commences with the fermentation. The reds are typically fermented on the skins while the whites are not. "We let the wine run its course, and check it daily for any adjustments," Chris says.

So, the next time you want a romantic evening and a place to share a lovely bottle of wine with a friend, stop by Candlelight Winery!

Candlelight Winery

Directions Take U.S. 422 to State Route 88 south to Garrettsville. Go left and east on State Route 82 in Garrettsville 500 feet, then turn left (north) on Center Road for two miles to the winery on the left

Hours Tues.–Fri., 3–9 PM; Sat., 1–10 PM

Tours By request

Tastings Daily when open

Gifts Wine-related gifts

Picnics Bring your own food; a variety of flatbreads including Roasted Red Pepper, BBQ Chicken, and Pepperoni; a cheese sampler plate with a variety of cheeses, crackers, and pepperoni

Highlights at Winery Romantic atmosphere and personalized ambiance; stars light up on dark blue ceiling

Events Live music, Annual Charity event for Ohio Pug Rescue, Candlelight Cove Light Show

Restaurant Light fare, including a variety of flatbreads and a cheese sampler tray

Prices $10–$20; 10 percent discount on case of wine

Brand Names Candlelight Winery

Type of Production Traditional

Method of Harvesting By hand

Aging and Cooperage Stainless steel, variable-capacity tanks, American oak barrels

Vineyards Founded 2001, Burton and Chesterland; 2002, Garrettsville

Counties: Geauga and Portage

Appellation American and Ohio

Acreage (in ground) 5–6, overall 15

Waterway Tinkers Creek

Climate Harsh winters on edge of snowbelt

Soil Heavy clay

Varieties Vidal Blanc, Marechal Foch, Chambourcin, Niagara, Concord, Riesling

Wines Over fifteen wines, including Chardonnay, Riesling, Niagara, Sangiovese, Cabernet Franc, Chambourcin, Pink Catawba, and Cranberry

Best Red Wine Sangiovese

Best White Wine Chardonnay

Other Best Wine Pink Pug

Quote "Wine isn't just grapes. It is the atmosphere and the mood of what is going on when one drinks it. Wine tastes different under candlelight than fluorescent."—Chris Conkol

Nearby Places to Visit Garrettsville clock tower; Hiram College; James A. Garfield Historical Society; Nelson Ledges State Park

Cortland Wine Cellar

5292 State Route 5
Cortland, OH 44410
Tel (330) 638-0000
E-mail info@cortlandwinecellar.com
Web site www.cortlandwinecellar.com
Owners Deborah Beltz & Sheila Fisher
Winemakers Deborah Beltz and Sheila
Fisher
Founded 2008

Cortland Wine Cellar is located in Trumbull County, not far from the Mosquito Reservoir and State Park, in a metal shipping warehouse at the corner of State Routes 11 and 55. Owners Deborah Beltz and Sheila Fisher, friends whose families have shared memorable experiences for 25 years, say "Open the doors and you will be pleasantly surprised."

In the early 1980s, Beltz and Fisher met at the Warren YWCA, an organization that empowers women and girls to advocate for critical social issues. They developed their professional skills—Sheila as manager and personal trainer and Deb as an instructor—at the Cortland Fitness Studio, which emphasized workouts and good health. Their joint company, Unified Shipping Services, encouraged merchants to grow their businesses, while they handled storage and shipping.

In 2005, Beltz returned from the Grand Bahama Islands, where she met an Ohio couple who ran a wine supply company. Beltz rang up Fisher and asked if she would be interested in starting a home winemaking store with her. "Sheila just laughed and said, okay, sounds like another great adventure," she recalls.

The possibilities were endless. As a wine educator, bartender, and home winemaker, Beltz had produced wine every fall with her relatives. Fisher had attended wine seminars, and encouraged the development of a Cortland taste and style of wine. Besides seminars, they had gotten instruction from several other winemakers.

For three years, Deborah and Sheila planned and sourced juice from Ohio, Pennsylvania, New York, California, and Chile. "We plan to produce wine from a local family, who has a vineyard," Deborah says. During the next two years, they are planting their own vines. As an operational winery, they ferment in stainless steel and flex tanks. Though they filter when necessary, they prefer to use gravity racking and transfer the wine from one tank to the next to eliminate any sediment.

Beltz and Fisher have focused on the service and experiential aspect of their winery. The Homemade Winemaking Center teaches their customers to make wine from kits or fresh juice, which they purchase from them. Customers can either purchase labels to make at home, or visit web sites to create their own labels. "Customers are instructed from start to finish," she says. "They start, stir, rack, taste, stop the yeast process, bottle, cork, and label their own wine. We encourage learning and building confidence."

Today, Cortland Wine Cellars produces eleven wines by type and style. "Are you a sweetie?" says Beltz. Then try their Summer Passion, Raz-Mi, or Mysterious Woman. "Or do you like your wine just a little tart?" she continues. Then try Angels Kiss or Fall in Love. "Or do you like your wine a little on the dry side?" Then you might like Goddess of Gold, Bold Lady, or Preferred Taste.

Beltz, Fisher, and their wine dogs, Gracie Alen and Maggie May, agree they have successfully created a place where "fun and wine meet." On Therapy Thursdays Evenings, Wine Down with some chocolate and massage therapy. "Does it get any better?" they say. On Fridays, they feature Game Nite with indoor cornhole, chess, ping pong, or cards. On Saturdays, which is Entertainment Nite, local performers play guitar, jazz, country, classic or dance music.

"We are not your typical winery. Sheila and I love to have fun, meet each person, and talk while getting to know our customers and their life story. We have been blessed to meet some unique and wonderful people," she says. "People say, 'This is so relaxing and fun. Who would have thought this was inside a warehouse. We'll be back!'"

Cortland Wine Cellar 🍇

Directions From I-80, take State Route 11 north and exit at State Route 5 & 88. Cellar in the warehouse at State Route 5 & corner of 11. From I-90, take State Route 11 south and exit at State Route 5 & 88. Cellar in warehouse at State Route 5 & corner of 11

Hours Year-round, Thurs.–Fri., 5–10 PM, Sat., 2–10 PM. Open by appointment for parties, tastings, and carryout all week long, including Sunday

Tours Self-guided, educational, and historic. Guided wine production tour.

Tastings Daily when opened; private tastings and parties by appointment Tuesday–Saturday

Gifts Locally made gifts only. Hand-painted glass gifts, hand-carved wooden bowls, handmade natural soaps, handcrafted wine bags

Picnics Year-round monthly cookouts

Highlights at Winery A positive wine experience and a chance to make your own wine

Events Chefs in the Cellar: regional chefs pair locally-sourced and prepared foods with Cortland wines on premise. Gather & Give: Cortland Wine Cellar supports the local fundraisers and missions

Restaurant Appetizers—cheese and crackers, warm breads with olive oil, herbs, and parmesan cheese, mixed peppers, olive tapenade, spinach and artichoke dip, bruschetta bread with herbs, cheese, and tomato, or sandwiches. Dinner events

Prices $10–$19; 10 percent case discount

Brand Name Cortland Wine Cellar

AVA Lake Erie

Appellation Ohio, Pennsylvania, New York

Wines Summer Passion, Raz-Mi, Mysterious Woman, Angel Kiss, Fall in Love, Goddess of Gold, Bold Lady, Preferred Taste

Best Red Preferred Taste

Best White Goddess of Gold

Best Other Wine Mysterious Woman

Quote "Don't leave any good wine for your children to inherit. Gather your friends and drink it now." Deborah Beltz & Sheila Fisher

Nearby Places to Visit Mosquito Lake, Camp Grounds & State Park; Packard Park & Museum; Cortland Master Gardeners Education & Research Garden

Grande Wine Cellars

4653 Warner Road
Garfield Heights, OH 44125
Tel (216) 441-4439
Owner/Winemaker Paul Grande
Founded 1999

The Grande Wine Cellars in Garfield Heights is one of a handful of small family-owned and urban-operated wineries in Greater Cleveland. Located in one of the city's early Italian-Polish neighborhoods, the winery was established by Ohioans Paul and Linda Grande and their dentist son, Paul S. Grande, in 1999 as a natural outgrowth of their shared Italian heritage.

"We take pride in being a small winery and making wine and food for our family and friends," Paul Sr., now semi-retired, says. "If I invite you over, it is the same as inviting you to my house. I expect you to be respectful."

The Grandes were both born into Italian families that possessed a legacy of winemaking passed down from one generation to the next. "As a boy I grew up in the Collinwood district," Paul Sr. says. "I would sneak down to the basement cellars of my friends' parents and watch them make wine. Almost forty years ago, I started to make my first

wine." Linda's parents owned a restaurant across the street from the winery. "Both my grandfathers made wine," she says. Continuing in that tradition, the Grandes purchased twin red brick buildings close to the Ohio Canal District. One was for the winery; the other was for the tasting room.

The Grandes designed the tasting room for small groups of people. "Our thought was to create a small, cozy, friendly place with lots of ambiance," says Linda, also a Cleveland Clinic registrar. The décor, lit by lanterns, has an Italian flair, with a dash of 1920s Hollywood thrown in. Straw fiaschi wine bottles from Chianti Classico, lovely Italian scenes, photos of famous movie stars, and artifacts decorate the walls. The wooden bar, mirror, and stools, all handcrafted by Paul Sr., are the focal point of the room. Tables, covered with red-and-white checkered tablecloths, and wooden chairs add to the ambiance.

Experience Italian flair and 1920s Hollywood. *Courtesy Grande Wine Cellars*

The Grandes make and sell authentic Italian foodstuffs. Paul Sr. follows old family recipes, which use ingredients characteristic of another era. "I prepare dried Italian sausage; Italian prosciutto, a dried, banjo-shaped, whole leg of ham; dried capicollo, a loin of ham; and red pasta sauces, made with pork neck bones. For me, this is a hobby—a true pleasure," Paul Sr. says.

The winery emphasizes the value of working with handpicked varietals of the best quality. "I buy my wine grapes from the very best winegrowers in the Buckeye state." He mentions Tony Debevc of Chalet Debonné. "If I don't like something, I send it back. My Zinfandel is the only wine grape I purchase from California," Paul Sr. says.

Paul Sr. frankly admits that he has tried just about everything when it comes to winemaking. "I started out making all dry wines. It was suggested I add sweet wines to the list," he says. The sweeter wines have done well, especially the winery's bestselling Lake Erie White and Lake Erie Red.

Paul Sr. has enjoyed how the whole process of winemaking has changed. Demand has caused him to introduce new practices and different wine styles. Typically, the wine grapes are crushed and pressed in a bladder, basket press. The juice is fermented in stainless steel, pumped over, racked, and held in either stainless steel or oak. The whites are kept in stainless steel or oak, and the reds are aged in American or Hungarian oak barrels. "I make small batches of European-style wine with a French and Italian influence."

Today Grande Wine Cellars produces just under 5,000 gallons annually of Ohio Chardonnay, Riesling,

Cabernet Sauvignon, Merlot, Pinot Noir, Shiraz, Lake Erie White, Lake Erie Red, and California Zinfandel.

"If a wine doesn't meet my standards, I won't sell it," says Paul Sr.

Grande Wine Cellars

Directions From I-77, exit at 157 toward Ohio 17/Granger Road. Proceed right and east on Granger Road/Ohio 17. Go left on Warner Road to winery

Hours Friday–Saturday 12–10 PM

Tours None

Tastings Daily when open

Gifts Wine baskets

Picnics City winery, small outdoor patio

Highlights at Winery Best wines under $10 a bottle; small, friendly tasting room with lots of ambiance

Events Christmas Eve Feast of the Seven Fishes (traditional Italian meal including seven different fish courses); clambakes

Restaurant Limited Italian fare: cheese, crackers, antipasto, and sandwiches

Prices $6–$10 wines; $6–$10 food; 10 percent case discount

Brand Names Grande Wine Cellars

Type of Production European-style wines with a French and Italian emphasis; also vitis viniferas

Method of Harvesting Purchase only handpicked grapes of the best quality

Pressing and Winemaking Bladder, basket press

Aging and Cooperage American and Hungarian oak barrels

Appellation Ohio and California

Varieties Chardonnay, Riesling, Niagara, Concord, Cabernet Sauvignon, Merlot, Pinot Noir, Merlot, Shiraz, Zinfandel, Lake Erie White, Lake Erie Red

Wines Chardonnay, Cabernet Franc, Pinot Noir, Merlot, Burgundy, Shiraz, Lake Erie White, Lake Erie Red

Best Red Cabernet Sauvignon

Best White Chardonnay

Other Best Wine Zinfandel

Quote "If a wine doesn't meet my standards, I won't sell it."—Paul Grande Sr

Nearby places to visit Cleveland Ports and Harbor, Rock and Roll Hall of Fame; Great Lakes Science Center

Grape & Granary

915 Home Ave.
Akron, OH., 44310
Tel (330) 633-7223
Fax (330) 633-6794
E-mail mary@grapeandgranary
Web site www.grapeandgranary.com
Owner Jim & Mary Pastor
Winemaker Jim, Mary, Jimmy & Mike Pastor
Founded 1992

In 1909, the gregarious Leonardo Mazzarella, and his family left Italy's Greci, a town in the High Cervaro Valley in the region of Campania and emigrated to the United States' Canton, Ohio. With him, he brought a heritage of winemaking and $26. Decades later, the Grape & Granary in Akron was established in 1992 by Jim and Mary Pastor, in honor of Mary's grandfather, Leonardo Mazzarella, who believed it is what one brings to the experience, not what one takes away that makes it meaningful. "We are energetic and out-going people" she says with feeling. "We love people. We try to make them happy. If our customers are happy, that makes us happy, and they come back!" she says.

This closely-knit Italian family—Jim, Sr., (who comes from a family of Romanian descent), Mary Esther, and their three sons John, Jimmy, and Mike—built the Grape & Granary for

customers who share their passion for the highly revered, artisanal arts of making wine, crafting beer, tending cheeses, and roasting coffee.

The Pastors—all talented winemakers each with a particular specialty—take great pride in the Grape & Granary Winery, and their Renaissance Wine Cellars premium wines sold by the bottle. This year, these include Chardonnay, Cabernet Sauvignon, Merlot, Sangiovese, Zinfandel, and North Hill Rosso. Once a year in September, the Pastors get supplies from California—some twenty red and white grapes or pressed juice in a bucket for their customers or family's use. "We make our wine the old world way—nine months in stainless tanks and one year in oak barrel before bottling," she says.

Most importantly, the Pastors are committed to serving one's home winemaking needs through their skilled and practiced team of professionals. "We all work together as a family unit," she says. Jim, Sr., oversees the management of the retail wine and beer supplies. Mary conducts the wine tastings, and makes California, Australian, Italian and New Zealand wines from kits complete with grape concentrate and flavor components.

The Grape & Granary is popular with hobbyists, who come to master home winemaking. A staff member consults with the client about the basics of making one's own wine. After tasting wines together, the client makes a decision. The process gets underway when the client adds the appropriate starter yeast to activate the fermentation. Over four weeks, a condensed time frame in which to make wine, the staff member shepherds the wine through racking, clarifying, and filtering the juice. The client returns to the winery to bottle, cork, and label the wine. Many people design and personalize their own labels with artwork, photos or text, or use ready-made design templates. The process is extremely satisfying, and the end product very rewarding!

The Pastors sell wines at various price points. They include the juice, corks, capsules, labels and all taxes. Prices are broken down per bottle and per batch. The Winexpert Estate Series, for example, runs $180 per batch, and features eight wines: Columbia Valley Riesling, New Zealand Sauvignon Blanc, Pinot Gris, Sonoma Valley Chardonnay, Cabernet Franc/Merlot, Napa Valley Merlot, Old Vine Zinfandel, and Ranch 11 Cabernet Sauvignon. "Too much is never enough," says Jim Pastor, Sr. "Come as a customer, leave as *famiglia* (family)!" Mary concludes.

Grape & Granary 🍇

Directions From North, take I-271 south to State Route 8 south, and exit at East Tallmadge Ave., and go right and east. Proceed right on Home Ave. for ½ mile to winery. From South, Take I-77 north to State Route 8 north, and exit at East Tallmadge and go right and east. Proceed right on Home Ave., and south for ½ mile to the winery

Hours Monday–Friday: 10 AM–7 PM; Saturday: 10 AM–5 PM

Tours Guided tour

Tastings Daily; never on Sunday; groups call (330) 633-7223

Highlights at Winery International Wine Competition consisting of 500 wines with ninety people tasting wine at winery

Restaurant Light Italian fare: breads, oils, spices

Prices $9.95; Wine Kits $13.95 using California grapes

Brand Name Renaissance Wine Cellars; Grape and Granary

Type of Production Handcrafted

Method of Harvesting Hand-pick Ohio grapes

Winemaking: Traditional

Aging and Cooperage Oak barrels

Vineyards Founded 2002

Counties Stark and Summit

Appellation American

Acreage 300 vines

Climate Unpredictable Ohio

Soil Clay

Varieties Traminette, Merlot

Wines See Web site list

Best Red Merlot

Best White Traminette

Other Best Wine Spiced Green Apple Riesling

Quote "Too much is never enough!"— Jim Pastor

Nearby Places to Visit Canal Park, Metropolitan Park, Ninni's Italian Bakery, DeVitis Deli

Jilbert Winery

1496 Columbia Road
Valley City, OH 44280
Tel (216) 781-4120/ (330) 483-5909
E-mail dbjilbert@aol.com
Web site www.OhioHoneyWine.com
Owners David and Lisa Jilbert
Winemaker David Jilbert
Founded 1999

The stone fence and picturesque farm along Columbia Road in Valley City is the home of Jilbert Winery. It is one of Ohio's rare finds. The gorgeous ten-acre winery, with its tall timbers and elegant pines, has the distinction of being the first pure meadery in the Buckeye State, and was recently expanded into a working wine estate, to include grape-based wine manufacturing.

Lisa and Dave Jilbert discovered a 1905 wooden dairy barn with a sandstone foundation, a stately 1913 bluegray farmhouse with red shutters, and a small carriage house that backs up to the Rocky River, which divides their property. They purchased the property in the 1990s and settled there with their children.

Downstairs, the barn became the Jhelbare (the French translation for their surname) meadery and winery, complete with tasting room, gift shop, fermentation room, bottling line, aging cellar and case storage. A summer patio was added and dubbed The Grill at Jhelbare, which features sandwiches, burgers, strip steak, beef brochettes, chicken, other fare, desserts, and beverages.

Upstairs, the barn was made into a dining room with polished hardwood floors, new pine walls, stone fireplaces, draped tables and chairs, antique carriages and old wooden wheels. Named The Chef's Table, the restaurant offers an ever-changing menu, every week—typically a red and white meat, a choice of starch, vegetable, salad, rolls, dessert and beverages.

The winery has its own chef, who specializes in fresh Ohio cuisine. The Jilberts source food from nearby purveyors such as grain-fed beef, free-range chicken, pork, fresh fish, locally-grown fruits and vegetables, and glazed sauces infused with Jhelbare wines.

As a child growing up Dave Jilbert's

father, then a marketer of wine-crafting products, gave his son a beehive. "Because of this, I knew making mead was possible," he says.

But it was the role of the queen bee and the labor of the worker bees to build combs that captivated him. "We have learned to make something out of nothing," he says. Lisa's sentiments are similar: "Making mead and our other wines is a labor of love."

The Honey House, once a carriage house, is where the bee operations are kept. "We are beekeepers who produce pure honey as a farm commodity," he says. "We then value add that commodity (honey) to a retail product (wine)." The Jilberts make honey wine, also called mead, from wildflower honey gathered from beehives on the farm and around Medina County. Dave extracts honey from the combs by hand and centrifuge. He racks the golden honey mash into fifty-pound plastic containers and hauls it to the winery for fermentation. "Our method filters out bacteria, molds, pollens and waxes prior to fermentation," he says.

The long shelf life of honey allows the Jilberts to manufacture it year-round. After filtering a honey-water mixture to a one hundredth of a micron, the mixture is considered sterile. After filtration, a golden liquid remains to be fermented. This method ensures consistent production of honey wine/mead from batch to batch, fermentation

The Chef's Table at Jilbert Winery. *Courtesy Jilbert Winery*

within ten days, no bitter aftertaste, and no protein hazing. Jilbert Winery uses state-of-the-art equipment, stainless steel floating lid fermentation tanks, hand bottling and labeling.

The Jhelbare Summer Solstice Honey Wine and the Jhelbare Midsummer Moon Mead are two names of the same wine. The bright golden, 11-percent alcohol honey wine/mead has a floral bouquet, a clean taste, low eight percent residual sugar, and a lively citrus finish. The more recent Jhelbare wine offerings include Concord, Niagara, Lisa's Promise, Cardinal Sin, Pink Catawba, Rosé Classic, and Sarah's Blush.

Jilbert Winery 🍇

Directions Take I-71 to Route 303 west to Route 252; turn left, and look for the winery sign on the right

Hours Check Web site for hours. Mar.–May, Sat., 12–10 PM; June–Sept, Fri., 6–10 PM, Sat., 12–10 PM; Oct.–Dec., Sat., 12–10 PM; Closed January & February

Tours When open, educational and historical

Tastings Daily when open

Gifts Jam packed with honey, jams, jellies, mead, honey wine, wines, and other accessories and giftware

Highlights at Winery Wine and Dine Experience; Weddings & Banquets

Prices $8–$10; 10 percent case discount

Brand Name Jhelbare

Type of Production Honey wine/mead manufacturing; grape-based winemaking

Pressing and Winemaking Cornell University winemaking techniques

County Medina

Acreage 10.5

Waterway West Branch of the Rocky River

Wines Jhelbare Midsummer Moon Mead, Summer Solstice Honey Wine, Concord, Niagara, Lisa's Promise, Cardinal Sin, Pink Catawba, Rosé Classic, and Sarah's Blush

Quote "We are a winery that serves great food, has a beautiful dining room, and serves great Ohio wines."—Dave Jilbert

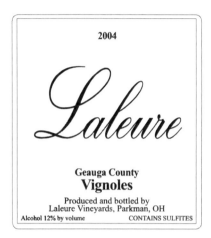

2004

Laleure

Geauga County
Vignoles
Produced and bottled by
Laleure Vineyards, Parkman, OH
Alcohol 12% by volume   CONTAINS SULFITES

Laleure Vineyards

17335 Nash Road
P.O. Box 738
Parkman, OH 44080
Tel (440) 548-5120
E-mail rich@laleurevineyards.com
Web site www.laleurevineyards.com
Owners Richard and Betsy Hill
Winemaker Richard Hill
Founded 1997

Laleure Vineyards in Parkman, with its gently rolling vineyards and thickly wooded forests, conjures up visions of farming in the heart of Amish Country in times gone by. Proprietors Richard and Betsy Hill lovingly named their wine estate for their grandmother, Jeanne Marie Laleure Hill, a native of France's Loire Valley. A woman with great *joie de vivre,* she inspired them to choose a quieter family lifestyle centered around a farm winery.

In 1997, they purchased the thirty-acre 1860s Stoll dairy farm. They were intrigued by the century farmhouse, the milking barn, and the acres of pastureland. In the spring of that year, they broke ground for a small vineyard. "I dug the first 250 holes in clay, twelve inches wide and sixteen inches deep," recalls Rich, a technical director. Thus, the Betsy-West Vineyards were christened in honor of his partner, Betsy, once owner of Ohio and New York cookware stores.

The Hills reinvented themselves as farmers. They attended courses at Ohio State University Agricultural School and Grape Extension, consulted with the Ohio Wine Growers Association, and read lots of wine books. "We were advised by our grape vendor to experiment with hardy, winter-resistant varieties because we were inland of Lake Erie. We planted grapes such as Vignoles, Bianca, Chardonnay, and Pinot Noir," Rich says.

Encouraged by the results of their initial experiment, the Hills harvested a small quantity of quality grapes in 1999. Next, they expanded their Geauga appellation hillside vineyards, noted for their excellent air circulation and frost protection, and added two acres of Riesling, Cabernet Franc, Chardonnay, and Chambourcin. They called it Jeanne-East Vineyards in tribute to their daughter and her namesake, Rich's grandmother. "We grow grapes

Where education, interest, conversation and tasting meld. *Courtesy Laleure Winery*

with tender loving care, and we are particular," Rich says. In 2002, Laleure Vineyards opened their tasting room to the public.

A 500-case Ohio artisan producer, Laleure Vineyards practices a classic style of farming and winemaking. "We believe that good fruit makes good wine," Rich says, "and we strive to make wines we like. Winters can be cold—as low as -10 degrees Fahrenheit—because we are not on the lake. In summer we get more heat because we are not cooled by the lake. Our Chardonnay grapes, for example, get more heat value, producing fruit with higher sugars and more intensity."

The grapes are hand-harvested, then crushed and pressed in a basket press, followed by a traditional fermentation in stainless steel. The wines are racked four to five times with little or no fining or filtering, with the exception of one plate-frame filtering just before bottling and a sterile filter for some of the white wines. All the wines remain in stainless steel with the exception of the Reserve wines, which are aged in American and French oak barrels. "Our wines are dry, simple, straightforward, and well balanced. The taste of the fruit comes through in our wines," he says.

Guests and visitors who travel to Parkman are struck by the natural beauty of the setting, and the warm welcome by Markko dogs, Chardonnay, Riesel, and Merlin. The Hills have renovated their home, a New England cedar farm-house with open porches. A gravel driveway leads past a huge dairy barn with a tall silo to the former milk house, now a charming tasting room. The white-washed interior has a pine tasting bar and high wicker chairs, oriental rugs, photos, a picture of the Alps, and an iron stove. A gift shop displays wine-related items. "We've greatly expanded our tasting room in addition to our original one. This allows us to have entertainment once in a while," says Rich.

The wines from Laleure Vineyards offer the consumer a step up in the quality department. The Hills are committed to making dry wines, and they find that fewer consumers are requesting sweet ones. "We see a very interested and educated group of people stopping by," says Betsy, who oversees the wine tasting room on any given weekend. The room's intimate nature allows for good wine discussion.

The Chardonnay Reserve, by far their best wine, has big, pronounced Chardonnay flavors, with fourteen months in small, American oak barrels before bottling. The aromatic Chardonnay, also of note, has a great bouquet and overall gusto. The Vignoles bursts with bright color and fresh, slightly tart, captivating taste. Their Pinot Noir has ranked among the top three in Ohio. "We are dedicated to producing high-quality wines from our top-quality fruit and simple processes," Rich says. "We also continue to win medals for our wines in the Ohio Wine Competition."

Laleure Vineyards 🍃

Directions From the west, take I-480 east to U.S. Route 422 east. After State Route 44, cross La Due Reservoir and continue 5 miles to Parkman. Go north on State Route 528 for 1 mile. Take a right onto State Route 88. Winery is 1.9 miles on the right. From the east, take U.S. 422 west to Parkman. Go north on State Route 528 for 1 mile. Take a right onto State Route 88. Winery is 1.9 miles on the right

Hours Friday 5–9 PM; Saturday 11 AM–5 PM; also by appointment

Tours Educational

Tasting On weekends or by appointment

Gifts Wine accessories

Picnics Encouraged to bring picnics

Highlights at Winery Dry, high-quality wines; beautiful country setting

Prices $9–$26

Brand Names Laleure Vineyards; Parkman Hill

Type of Production Traditional

Method of Harvesting By hand

Pressing and Winemaking Light pressing and stainless steel tanks

Aging and Cooperage American and French oak cooperage

Vineyard Founded 1997

County: Geauga

Appellation Geauga County

Acreage 3

Waterways Streams on property lead to Grand River

Climate Typical northeast Ohio, but more heat value in summer than wineries on Lake Erie, which is an advantage. Hillside vineyard location provides good air circulation and frost protection

Soil Clay

Varieties Chardonnay, Vignoles, Pinot Noir, Riesling, Bianca, Cabernet Franc, Chambourcin

Wines Chardonnay, Vignoles, Pinot Noir, Riesling, Bianca, Cabernet Franc, Three Dog White, Three Dog Red, Chambourcin Rosé, Chambourcin

Best Red Pinot Noir

Best White Reserve Chardonnay

Quote "We are dedicated to producing high-quality wines from our top-quality fruit and simple processes."—Richard Hill

Nearby Places to Visit Geauga County Swine Creek Park; Middlefield Cheese Factory

Maize Valley Winery

6193 Edison Street NE
Hartville, OH 44632
Tel (330) 877-8344
Fax (330) 877-0915
E-mail mr.maze@maizevalley.com
Web site www.maizevalley.com
Owners Kay & Donna Vaughan,
Michelle & Bill Bakan, & Todd Vaughan
Winemaker Todd Vaughan, Michelle
Bakan, assistant winemaker
Founded 2004

The Maize Valley Farm & Winery in Marlboro Township rests near the original 1800s land grant deeded to pioneer Joseph Vaughan, a teacher and farmer, signed by then President James Monroe. Vaughan's great-great-great-grandson Kay Vaughan and his wife, Donna, along with fifth-generation grandson Todd Vaughan, granddaughter Michelle Bakan, and her husband, Bill, established the Maize Valley Winery in 2004 as a tribute to their forbearers.

"Earlier generations understood reality," Bill Bakan says. "Joseph is said to have put up bear skins across the doorway of the original farmstead to keep it warm during winter. He carved out a subsistence lifestyle growing fruits and vegetables and raising livestock, which was traded for basic essentials such as food, clothing, and shelter." Succeeding generations of Vaughans and Bakans have worked hard to build a strong foundation that melded tradition with modernity.

After graduation from Ohio State University, Michelle, a dairy science major, and Bill, an education and an agribusiness major, married. They returned to Marlboro Township in 1985 and lived on the Vaughan family farm, which consisted of 120 parcels totaling 3,000 acres of corn, wheat, and soy beans; 150 registered Holstein milking cows and fifteen registered prove bulls; a grain elevator; an agriculture supply business; and a trucking business.

"Suddenly, we were impacted by global competition. To succeed in commodity crops, we needed to be low-cost producers," Bakan says. Kay Vaughan, Bill's father-in-law, planted twelve rows of sweet corn as a trial in the early 1990s; he wholesaled the corn for sixty cents a dozen, but it retailed for as high as four dollars a dozen. "We started doing direct marketing in 1997. We set up a roadside fruit and vegetable stand and realized its potential."

Where wine and food marry. *Courtesy Maize Valley Winery*

A pathway leads to the tan antique barn with the sloping green roof and enclosed front porch. A 200-seat pavilion at the back features farm views. Outside, there are Native American wildflower gardens, hanging baskets, and potted plants in pinks, purples, and yellows that surround a brick patio perfect for picnics. Inside the entry are displays of grapes, apples, peaches, pears, and local cabbages, lettuces, tomatoes, carrots, broccoli, asparagus, and other produce. The corridor opens to the barn with its sandstone and oak walls; beech, oak, and chestnut hand-hewn cross beams; tiled floor; and upright posts. The great room houses a bistro and tasting bar with tables and chairs, a fancy deli showcasing Holmes County cheeses and meats, gourmet foods, and a bakery.

Todd Vaughan, manager and winemaker, and his sister, Michele, sales manager and assistant winemaker, oversee the Maize Valley Winery. When Todd and Michele started out—they purchased juice and harvested grapes by hand. The first year they did some crushing and used a wooden basket press. They started on a small scale the first year, with considerable growth by their third year in business. "Today we are a 15,000 gallon wine operation with plans for expansion on the way," says Michele. "Eighty-five percent of our wine sales are made at the winery with the remaining wine sold through our distributor."

Since 2004, the original wooden winery has nearly tripled in size. It was enlarged to accommodate a crusher and destemmer, a bladder press, large capacity, Italian stainless steel fermentors, an oak barrel aging cellar, an improvised bottling area, and case storage. "Our emphasis is quality in the wine grapes and in the winemaking process," says Bakan, Michele's husband.

Ten acres of vines are now planted with grapes such as Chardonnay, Riesling, Traminette, Chambourcin, Concord, Vignoles, New York 73, French American hybrids, and strawberries, red raspberries, cherries, blueberries, and peaches.

"We are a farm market and winery taking a simple approach, not a sophisticated one, to all we do," says Bakan. White wines are fermented racked then held in stainless steel, red wines are fermented, racked and held in new 60-gallon French and 60-gallon American oak barrels. The wines are all carefully filtered and fined.

Today the award-winning Maize Valley wines are recognized for both their sweet white wines and dry red wines.

The proprietors invite everyone to experience an Ohio farm winery. Activities they host include wine and food pairings, wagon rides, balloon liftoffs, helicopter rides, classic car festivals, corn and haunted mazes, seasonal greenhouses, petting pasture and pumpkin picking. "We focus on the farm, families, and fun," says Bakan.

Maize Valley Winery 🌿

Directions State Route 224 (76) to State Route 44 south to State Route 619 west for 1 mile to winery on north side

Hours Seasonal, Mon.–Sat., 10 AM–6 PM, Sun., 10 AM–5 PM

Tours Group tours by appointment

Tastings By the glass or bottle, seating inside or on porch and patio

Gifts wine-oriented gifts; seasonal gifts

Picnics Yes

Highlights at Winery Live music Fri. & Sat.; farm market: fine wines, meats, cheeses, salsas, dips, jams, jellies, honeys, fresh fruits & vegetables, baked goods, and seasonal flowers

Events Balloon liftoffs, helicopter rides, May Days, October harvest happenings, campfires, wagon rides, kids' play area, petting pasture, greenhouse, corn maze, haunted maze, pumpkin picking

Restaurant Menu varies, steaks to sandwiches, with periodic hog roasts

Prices $12–$25; 10 percent case discount

Brand Names Maize Valley Winery

Type of Production Grape, fruit wines

Method of Harvesting By hand

Aging & Cooperage Limited, more as time progresses

Vineyards Founded 2004

County Stark

Acreage 10 acres of vineyards; more than 700 acres of farmland

Waterways Schwartz's Ditch & Minishellin Creek

Climate Moderate

Soil Sandy hilltops to high organic mulch

Varieties Chardonnay, Riesling, Traminette, Chambourcin, Concord, Vignoles, New York 73, French and American hybrids, in addition to fruit

Wines Chardonnay, Riesling, Sinfully White, Hanky Panky, Mad Cow, White Wedding, Chambourcin, Big Red Pecker, Sinfully Red, Fredonia, Red Neck Red, Little Red Pecker, Summer Fling, Apple, Strawberry, Cherry, Peach, Blackberry, Raspberry, Cranberry

Best Red Big Red Pecker

Best White Mad Cow

Other Best Wine Sinfully White

Nearby Places to Visit Professional Football Hall of Fame, McKinley Museum

Mastropietro Winery

14558 Ellsworth Rd.
Berlin Center, OH, 44401
Tel (330) 547-2151
Fax (330) 547-2393
E-mail MastropietroWinery@earthlink.net
Web site www.MastropietroWinery.com
Owners Daniel, Marianne, and Cathy
Mastropietro
Winemaker Daniel Mastropietro
Founded 2005

Named out of esteem for the Mastropietro family, Mastropietro Winery in Berlin Center, is a Southern Italian compound name, a title of respect formed from maestro, 'master craftsman,' and the personal name Pietro meaning Peter in Italian. As the story goes, Joseph Mastropietro, grandparent of the founders Daniel, an electrician, Marianne, a purchasing agent, and Cathy Mastropietro, a PhD. in anesthesiology, produced classic dry red Italian wine. Since the early 1970s, Daniel has continued this same family tradition. He purchased California Cabernet Sauvignon and Merlot grapes from which he also made dry Italian red wine, then bottled and labeled by name and vintage.

"We started to enter our wines in amateur wine competitions and won medals. Friends encouraged us to bottle and sell the wine," he says. When Daniel won the Bronze Medal for their

Zinfandel in the *Winemaker Magazine* International Wine Competition, he and his wife Marianne researched winegrowing and visited wineries of interest. Gradually, they moved forward and became the first 52-acre destination winery in Mahoning County southwest of Youngstown.

An Ohio State University consultant from Wooster's OARDC recommended that the Mastropietros cultivate a three-acre, north-south facing, high cordon, tile-drained clay vineyard planted with French-American hybrids—Chambourcin, Vidal Blanc, and Frontenac. "Marianne is the vineyard and business manager, Cathy does the marketing, and I do the winemaking," he says. "For a young vineyard, the grapes are coming along and we have had some very nice harvests."

A long driveway with sweeping vineyards on either side leads to the stately, split-face block Mastropietro

A stately structure with amazing ambiance. *Courtesy Mastropietro Winery*

Winery, situated on a beautiful lake with sunset views. "My wife and I designed the winery building, and Cathy laid out and decorated it," he says. Glass doors open to a 50 seat-tasting room or a 50-seat banquet room. A curved tile floor and earth tone carpet, offset by beige and olive green stucco walls with gold accentuates the Tuscan interior. Large windows draped with grapevines look to the gazebo and the 80-person lakeside pavilion. There are fire rings on three patios that offer a relaxing setting for pairing wine and food.

When the winery first opened, the back of the winery contained the crushing area, the production center, the fermentation room, the aging cellar, and case storage area. Now, there is a larger, dedicated winemaking facility on grounds; the case storage is at the back of the original building. "I make wine in the old style," he says. "Our wines are close to 12 percent alcohol. I try to balance the acid to give the wine better mouth-feel. Originally I made dry wine, and we sold more sweet wine. Every person is different. We teach that wine is fun. Those who started sweet, now drink dry wines because their palate has changed," he concedes.

The Mastropietros get satisfaction from their new winery family—enthusiastic volunteers who get together the first Sunday of every month and bring an appetizer or dish for a shared meal. "Although no one knew each other before we built the winery, our friends come rain or shine to harvest, press or bottle the wine," he says. But our immediate family gets the most enjoyment from observing our customers. "After people come to the tasting room and sit down, it is a wonderful feeling to see them smile, listen to the music, and say, 'This is really good wine!'" Come see for yourself!

Mastropietro Winery 🍇

Directions Take I-76 to State Route 534. Go south on State Route 534 for four miles to Ellsworth Road. Go left on Ellsworth Road for 1.25 miles

Hours Thursday: 4–9 PM; Friday: 4–11 PM; Saturday 1–11 PM; and Sunday: 1–5 PM

Tastings When open

Picnics Picnic baskets area permitted on Thursdays and Sundays only

Highlights Beautiful country setting, eloquent tasting and banquet rooms, creative gift boutique, outdoor seating and entertainment, fabulous sunsets, and great wines

Events Early summer starts with fireworks, followed by a Jimmy Buffett Bash, Hot Air Balloon Festival, Rib Fest, and a Clam Bake. Live entertainment every Friday and Saturday; check the listing on the Web site "Events" page. Outdoor weddings

Restaurant Appetizers, light fare: Friday & Saturday evenings

Prices $11– $19 per bottle; 10 percent case discount

Production Handcrafted wines. French American hybrid rooted vines

Method of Harvesting By hand

Pressing & Winemaking Light bladder press. Select grapes with traditional techniques

Aging & Cooperage Stainless steel. Oak staves

Vineyards Founded 2004

County Mahoning

Appellation American

Acreage 3

Trellising High Cordon

Climate Typical Midwestern

Soil Clay

Wines Chardonnay, Riesling, Sauvignon Blanc, Cabernet Sauvignon, Mastromiscela, Merlot, White Merlot, Zinfandel, Chambourcin, Dolce Bianco, Dolce Rosso, Grandpa's Best, Sangiovese, Sunset, Valley Red

Best Red Mastromiscela

Best White Riesling

Best Other Wine Valley Red

Nearby Places to Visit Arms Family Museum of Local History, Butler Institute of American Art, Fellows Riverside Gardens, Mill Creek Park

Myrddin Winery

3020 Scenic Ave.
Berlin Center, OH, 44401
Tel (330) 654-9181
E-mail info@myrddinwine.com
Web site myrddinwine.com
Owner Kristofer & Evelyn Sperry
Winemaker Kristofer Sperry
Founded 2004

Myrddin Winery sits high on a wooded hillside fifty feet above Lake Milton in a 1990s prairie-style house in Berlin Center. Founders, Kristofer and Evelyn Sperry named their winery "Myrddin" after the pagan god of high places, who is also known as Merlin, the late sixth century prophetic wild man and wizard who conceived Arthur and then featured himself in the Arthurian legend.

The Sperrys were introduced to English novelist Mary Florence Elinor Stuart, best known for her series about Merlin. In the *Crystal Cave*, Merlin lives in a cave on a mountain-top. "We liked the concept and adapted it for our winery story and used the names in it for our wines. Merlin was a natural person—so we created a slogan for our wine labels that reflected that attitude—'wine, water, woods and wildlife,'" he says.

Kris was a graduate of the Kent State University School of Architecture, and now principal of Kristofer Sperry,

Architect. "My specialty is designing wineries," he says. Evelyn, also a graduate of Kent State University, was a former designer for Union Metals Corporation, one of America's leading streetlight manufacturers. "My wife is now the office manager."

Kris designed his mother a two-storey house with low horizontal lines and open interior spaces that blends in with the natural, landscape. The downstairs of the house proved to be the perfect micro-setting for a *garagista*-innovative style of winemaking. "We wanted to produce a small, handcrafted product that we would enjoy making and selling," he says. "Today we make 1,000 gallons of wine, an equivalent of 300 cases."

The Sperrys buy and grow their own wine grapes. They own a one-and-three-quarter-acre Mahoning County, high cordon Vidal Blanc vineyard on the wine estate above Lake Milton. They also share crop another two-acre

The patio at Myrddin Winery overlooking Lake Milton. *Courtesy Myrddin Winery*

vineyard with the farmer across the street consisting of Concord, Seyval Blanc, Buffalo, Syrah, Noriet, Zweigelt, and raspberries. Although Kris and his best friend find it a challenge to source raw materials like wine grapes, they enjoy going all over to get two truckloads of the choicest grapes.

The Sperrys are a proud, family-owned and operated winery. Kris makes the wine; Evelyn brands and markets it; and his mother sells it. Their mission statement speaks about creating a wine lifestyle that they share with their friends and customers. "We found ourselves welcomed as a high-end producer. Our customers say, 'We love your wines and they are the best.' It is rare to go to a winery today, and like all the wines. It is very satisfying to us," he says.

Kris and Evelyn both believe that wine makes itself in its own time. They love what they do, and are most willing to share their wine knowledge with people who patronize the winery. They want to educate their customers, and provide them a personal wine experience.

Myrddin Winery 🍇

Directions Take 1-76 to the south on State Route 534 for about two miles to Ellsworth Road. Turn right and west on Ellsworth Road for .5 miles. Turn on the first road right and north, Southeast River Road for .25 miles. Turn left on Republic Ave. (Look for white farmhouse with green trim on right with vineyard, Republic Road is opposite the farmhouse.) Turn to the right at the mailboxes onto the gravel road and follow it around the bend to the parking lot. Take the garden walk up to the lakeside to our front door

Hours Tues.–Thurs., 3–9 PM; Fri., 3–10 PM; Sat., 12–10 PM; Sun., 1–6 PM

Tours By appointment or by chance

Tastings When opened, full tasting

Gifts Fancy baskets, clothing gift items

Picnics Bring one, or order food from Italian restaurant

Highlights at Winery Peaceful & beautiful, overlooking Lake Milton

Events Evelyn's Wood and Food Pairing Nights; Special Ice Wine Tasting

Prices $14–$38; 10 percent case discount

Brand Names Myrddin Winery

Type of Production Red, whites, and fruit wines

Method of Harvesting By Hand

Pressing and Winemaking Individual procedures for each batch

Aging and Cooperage Variety of French and American oak

Vineyards Founded 2005

County Mahoning

Acreage 1.75 acres

Trellising High Cordon

Waterways Lake Milton

Climate Unpredictable Ohio

Soil Heavy clay

Varieties Vidal Blanc, Concord, Seyval Blanc, Buffalo, Syrah, Noriet, Zweigelt

Wines Lady of the Lake, Titania, Myrddin Wyllt, Myrddin Emerys, Taliesin, Pendragon, Morgaine, Black Enchantment, Sparkling Strawberry, Oren, Ice wine, Port, Riesling, Chardonnay, Reserve Chardonnay

Best Red "We don't put out something we aren't proud of."

Best White Same as above

Other Best Wine Same as above

Quote "Each year the grapes have something special to offer. My job as a winemaker is to bring that out in it's most expressive way. We don't really 'make' the wine. We just allow it to be its best."—Kristofer Sperry

Nearby Places to Visit Lake Milton State Park for swimming and sunning. Craig Beach, Berlin Lake, and Noah's Lost Ark, a large game animal reserve

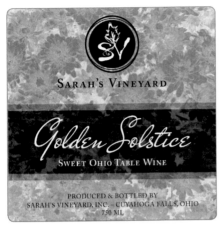

Sarah's Vineyard

1204 West Steels Corners Road
Cuyahoga Falls, OH 44223
Tel (330) 929-8057
Web site www.sarahsvineyardwinery.com
Owners Margaret and Mike Lytz
Winemaker Mike Lytz
Founded 2001

Sarah's Vineyard—a hybrid of a winery and art gallery that opened in May of 2007—is tucked in the gently rolling hills on 68-acres in the beautiful Cuyahoga Valley National Park. Proprietors Mike and Margaret Lytz named the site for their late daughter, Sarah Katherine Bertsch.

Mike, a retired teacher, and Margaret, a retired nurse, have long pursued their avocations. Mike, a home winemaker for twenty-five years, dabbles with his grandfather Miguel Archangelo Cerrone's recipe for dry Muscat, Aligante, and other wines. Margaret, a ceramicist, designs pottery and mosaic tiles.

For years, the Lytzes dreamed of a business that combined their loves of wine and art. "We envisioned a place in northeast Ohio where people could stop by and we could sell our wine," says Mike, "but the high price of land forced us to temporarily put our dream on hold."

One day, the Lytzes learned of the Cuyahoga Valley Countryside Initiative in the *Akron Beacon Journal*. It was a program to bring small farmsteads (which the government had purchased at the outset) to the Cuyahoga Valley to preserve its rural landscape. Cuyahoga Valley National Park Superintendent John Debo had studied the English agricultural practices. He learned that the British government owned 80 percent of the farms in the United Kingdom and leased them back to the farmers.

"We pursued this idea, wrote a competitive proposal, and won the bid," Mike says. "We emphasized sustainable agriculture using limited chemicals and fertilizers, mechanical weeding, integrated pest management, organic fungus control, and no application of herbicides or insecticides."

In 2002, the Lytzes moved into the original white farmhouse, accentuated by tall stands of trees. The property had no barn or significant out-buildings. They built a structure to house farm machinery, which they used to cultivate

The winery at Sarah's Vineyard. *Courtesy Sarah's Vineyard*

their hillsides. In 2003, they planted a small, silty loam, temperate climate Summit County vineyard not far from the Cuyahoga River. It is planted to Vidal Blanc, Seyval Blanc, Traminette, Cayuga, Cabernet Franc, Frontenac, Chambourcin, Niagara, and Rubiana. Their production features three white wines, four red wines, and several fruit wines. "We believe good fruit makes good wine," Mike says. "We researched the possibilities with viticulturists and winegrowers."

"We settled on 9 varieties," Margaret says, "with 2005 being our first vintage."

A sign along West Steel Corners Road reads "Sarah's Vineyard." The driveway leads to an antique, three-story, timber-framed building situated in a beautiful meadow with views of the vineyards. The winery was designed as a gathering place for friends and neighbors.

A large doorway opens to a vestibule, which leads to a 2,400-square-foot high-ceilinged art gallery and overhead loft. Colorful works—pottery, paintings, textiles, photography, and mosaics by local and regional artists—are displayed throughout the facility. The wine tasting bar introduces patrons to the winery's selections.

Customers leisurely sip wine as they stroll through the art gallery, around the garden filled with butterflies and humming birds, deck and patio to the vineyard. It is often the site of a seasonal art shows and grape harvests.

A staircase leads down to the 2,400-square-foot wine center and aging cellar. Sarah's Vineyard produces wines that appeal to everyone, from dry to sweet to semi-sweet. Their approach blends tradition and innovation.

Sarah's Vineyard 🍇

Directions From Cleveland take 77 south 20 miles to exit 143, Ohio 176. Turn left on Wheatley Road, becomes Everett Road. Turn right on River View Road, then left on Ira Road. Turn right on Akron-Peninsula Road. Turn left on Steels Corners Road. Travel 1 mile. Sarah's Vineyard on the right. From State Route 8 exit at Steel Corners Road and go west for 3.8 miles. Sarah's Vineyard is just west of the Blossom Music Center on the opposite side of the road. From I-271, exit at State Route 303, Richfield-Peninsula and go east three miles through Peninsula. Turn right and south on Akron-Peninsula Road. Turn left on Steels Corners Road to Sarah's Vineyard

Hours Wed.–Thurs., 11 AM–9 PM; Fri.–Sat., 11 AM–11 PM; Sun., 1–8 PM; Closed Mon.–Tues

Tours By appointment only

Gifts Functional and decorative

Picnics Will provide light fare, or bring your own food

Highlights at Winery Winery in park; high-quality art and fine wines; beautiful, enjoyable, and educational experience; personalized customer service

Events Sarah's Vineyard Summer Solstice Art Show, Wine Tasting & Blue's Festival, June Lobster and Clambakes, September and October

Restaurant Appetizers, sandwiches, desserts

Prices $12–$18; 10 percent case discount

Brand Names Sarah's Vineyard

Type of Production Both traditional and innovative

Method of Harvesting By hand

Pressing and Winemaking Natural

Aging and Cooperage Oak barrels and stainless steel

Vineyards Founded 2003

County Summit

Appellation American

Acreage 2.5

Waterway Cuyahoga River

Climate Temperate

Soil Silty loam

Varieties Vidal Blanc, Cabernet Franc, Frontenac, Chambourcin, Traminette, Niagara, Rubiana, Seyval Blanc, Cayuga

Best Red Wine Cuyahoga Valley Reserve Zinfandel

Best White Wine Painted Lady Riesling

Other Best Wine Sarah's Secret Red Table wine

Quote "We produce distinctive high quality wine." Mike Lytz

Nearby Places to Visit Ohio & Erie Canal Towpath Trail; Hale Farm & Village

ThornCreek Winery & Gardens

155 Treat Rd.
Aurora, OH, 44202
Tel (330) 562-9245
E-mail info@thorncreekwinery.com
Web site www.thorncreekwinery.com
Owner David Thorn
Winemaker Benny Bucci
Founded 2006

Two brick pillars with illuminated wrought iron lanterns above, surrounded by lush flowers in yellows, pinks, purples and greens, lead up a gravel driveway to the stately seven acre ThornCreek Winery and Gardens in Aurora, Ohio. Located at the nexus of Cuyahoga, Geauga, Portage, and Summit counties, the winery and garden venture was established in 2006 by Ohioan David Thorn.

"My father had a very large vegetable and flower garden and loved to grow things. I learned the patience of growing plants from him, and fortunately inherited his natural creative talents," he says. "Our yard was my palate, and I brought plants in from the woods, dug ponds by hand, and created many gardens." After a semester studying pre-med at Alderson Broaddeus College in Philippi, W.Va., he transferred to Bowling Green State University to pursue architecture and horticulture. In 1989, he graduated with a B.S. in architectural environmental design from the College of Technology.

Thorn began his career working at K.A. Architects in Cleveland designing shopping malls and office towers sites. "An opportunity came along to work at the Breezewood Gardens as a landscape designer," he says. The owner Richard Kay made him an offer he couldn't refuse. So, Thorn practiced landscape architecture in the residential arena for several years. In 1995, he bought the landscape design division of their company and renamed it.

DTR Associates, located at the winery site, is a nationally recognized landscape design firm that reinvented the concept of the modern day wine experience. "We are 'outdoor visionaries,'" he says. Thorn made an old Tudor winery beautiful again by painting it soft shades of tan, with brick wainscoting, double-paned wooden doors and windows, a

ThornCreek Winery and Gardens is absolutely gorgeous! *Courtesy ThornCreek*

gabled brown roofline, accentuated by birch, fruit and pine trees, and shrubs and flowers in gold, green and rose. A winding pathway that passes a fountain cascading with fresh flowers leads to the inner office sanctum, then onto the winery.

"I gave the tasting room a warm, Old World feel with stucco beams and burnt orange Tuscan walls." he says. Outside, there is an Italian- influenced brick terrace strung with light bulbs,

wrought iron tables and chairs, white lit pines trees, gorgeous herbs, organic produce, and blooming perennials and annuals. "I wanted to combine my love of wine and landscape architecture into a unique experience that differed from any other winery or restaurant in the region. From the moment guests turn into our driveway, we want them to feel as if they are magically transported to a small winery in the Tuscan wine country," he says.

ThornCreek's vast landscaped grounds can hold up to 500 people and are the perfect backdrop for any unique special event. All the food prepared at ThornCreek is stylized towards nature and has an organic twist, using fresh herbs, berries, and vegetables harvested from the on-site, artfully-designed kitchen garden.

Thorn's strengths have made his winery a huge success. "I have a good palate for wine and an understanding of what my clients like and don't like. They appreciate and understand fine food, wines and gardens," he says. To satisfy customers' tastes, ThornCreek Winery sources its wine juice from California's and Ohio's top AVAS. He buys Chardonnay from the Carneros District and Merlot in the Napa Valley. He purchases Cabernet Sauvignon from Sonoma's Alexander Valley and Riesling from the Lake Erie AVA. "We use the highest quality juice for wine," he says. In 2008, Ashtabula native Benny Bucci, was hired as the winemaker. "My winemaking skills were developed through practical experience rather than the textbook, and I learned technique,

chemistry, and lab analysis from the enologist at Ohio State University," he says. "My objective is to bring in high end juice from Napa and Sonoma to produce award winning wines that are elegant to drink." In response Thorn says, "In 2008, our ThornCreek Winery Cabernet Sauvignon and ThornCreek Winery Riesling both won Gold Medals in our first Ohio Wine Competition."

Bucci describes his red winemaking process. Once the juice has been fermented, he filters the wine several times prior to bottling. He uses fining agents such as bentonite to clarify the wines. Their Cabernet Sauvignon and Merlot are aged in French oak barrels for 10–12 months to add oak flavor to the wine. It is then finished in stainless steel before bottled.

ThornCreek Winery produces Aurora Cream, which is their biggest seller, for existing clients, and their dry, full-bodied Cabernet Sauvignon, and their Cabernet Sauvignon Reserve for newer clients. "We are looking to add Pinot Gris to our portfolio, and some Chilean varietals such as Malbec and Carmenere," he says. "It all requires hard work, passion, and consistency.

ThornCreek Winery & Gardens 🌿

Directions Take I-480 east and exit onto US 422 east, Exit onto Ohio 306 south for 5.5 miles. Turn right on Treat Rd. to the winery

Hours Fridays 4 PM–11 PM; Saturdays: 4 PM–11 PM

Tours By appointment

Tastings By appointment

Gifts Seasonal and holiday gourmet gift baskets

Highlights at Winery Award-winning wines; warm Old World Tuscan tasting room; magical floral, herbal, terraced gardens, environments, and reflection pools

Events Wine and food pairings and musical events for public, Unique themed Spice of Life catered events

Restaurant Gourmet board, Midwestern cheese board, artisan cheese board, pizza, focaccia, ice cream sandwich, warm apple pie

Prices $12–$31.99; 10 percent case discount

Brand Names ThornCreek Winery, Dankorona Winery

Type of Production Traditional

Method of Harvesting Machine and hand

Winemaking Traditional

Aging and Cooperage Stainless steel and French oak barrels

Vineyards Sourced juice

AVAs California and Ohio

Varieties Chardonnay, Cabernet Sauvignon, Merlot, Riesling

Wines ThornCreek Winery; Crystal Spring, Aurora Cream, Deft Way, Merlot, Cabernet Sauvignon, Aurora Cream Red, Riesling; Dankorona Winery: Chardonnay, Seyval Blanc, Vidal Blanc, Riesling, Blushing Vidal, Cabernet Sauvignon, Cabernet Sauvignon Reserve, Merlot

Best Red Cabernet Sauvignon

Best White Chardonnay

Best Other Wine Riesling:

Quote My philosophy is hard work, passion and consistency,"—Benny Bucci

Nearby Places to Visit Chagrin Falls, Cleveland Metroparks

VINTNER'S SELECT
TRAMINETTE
OHIO
ALC 12% BY VOLUME

Viking Vineyards & Winery

268 Old Forge Road
Kent, OH 44240
Tel (330) 678-2080
Fax (330) 678-6364
E-mail Viking@vikingvineyards.com
Web site www.vikingvineyards.com
Owners Jeff and Dana Nelson
Winemaker Jeff Nelson
Founded 1999

Just off of Old Forge Road in Kent, a one-lane road passes by two lakes surrounded by wetlands and woodlands and leads to Viking Vineyards and Winery. The winery name honors the region, Scandinavia, and the North American Norse settlement Vinland, described in Icelandic sagas as rich in grapes, timber and wheat.

In 1997, Jeff and Dana Nelson contemplated departing the rigors of travel and corporate life for a more fulfilling existence. "We decided on the wine business," says Dana, a former manager with the Timken Company. They designed their lives around people who shared their love of viticultural and vinification. In 1998, they purchased a twenty-acre property with a house, a pole barn, and lakes. Viking Vineyards and Winery was transformed into a country residence with a rustic winery, an estate vineyard, and water vistas.

The Nelsons consulted a viticulturist from the Ohio Agricultural Research Center to evaluate their Portage County land, soil, and climate and its suitability as a vineyard. "We dug holes and discovered sandy loam, perfect for hardy winter-resistant varietals," says Jeff, who doubles as an environmental consultant for J. Nelson Enterprises. In 1999 the Nelsons planted one-and-a-half acres of Vidal Blanc, Traminette (a first-generation hybrid off of Gewürztraminer), and Lemberger on a northerly, gently sloping vineyard. The trellises are vertical shoot positioned and high cordon, and the typically hot Midwestern climate has no lake effect to moderate it. Additional juice—Chardonnay, Riesling, Cabernet Sauvignon, Chambourcin, Merlot, and Sangiovese—is sourced from Ohio, New York, and California.

A descendant of Illinois dairy farmers, Jeff produced his first wine while he was a student at the University of Illinois. Later, he experimented at home. But the real test of his skills began in

Viking Vineyards, where the wines are fruit-forward & palate-friendly. *Courtesy Ohio Wine Producers Association*

1999 with his first one thousand gallons at Viking Vineyards. "I specialize in small-batch, limited-production wines," he says, pointing out that the pole barn winery had no electricity, water, insulation, or even a floor until they rebuilt it. The wine grapes are harvested by hand, then pressed and crushed in a small bladder-basket press. The wines are fermented in stainless steel tanks with either a variable capacity, a floating lid, or a fixed capacity. Oak staves are used to age some reds; other reds are aged in barrel.

"Viking Vineyards wines are made crisp, dry, and refreshing in the style of Alsatian wines from France," Jeff says. "Typically they are characterized as very drinkable and lighter than other wines on the market, especially the reds."

Dana has used her prior career experience to analyze their wine products and define their target market. "Our wines are fruit-forward and palate-friendly," she says. "And for consumers with wonderful memories of Niagara and Concord, we have other styles of wines we produce."

The Nelsons' strategy to build market share was twofold. They built the reputation of Viking Winery with a good-tasting Viking product. In 1999, they started with a white, thirty-seat, view-oriented tasting room. Jeff's photography of landscapes is on display with other artists' and craftsmen's work. During the early 2000s, the Nelsons built a second hospitality center, lakeside seating, and watched sales soar to 4,000 gallons annually. In 2007, the original tasting room was totally remodeled.

"We've tried to create a relaxed, cozy atmosphere, a place where people can enjoy themselves," Dana says. "People buy wine by the glass or bottle along with imported cheese and meats, or munchies. Sometimes, they bring their own picnic and a pack of cards, or enjoy our hot dog roasts by the lake or live entertainment on the weekends."

Many Viking Vineyards & Winery's wines have won Gold, Silver and Bronze medals in both the Ohio and Indianapolis international wine competitions.

Viking Vineyards and Winery 🌿

Directions Take I-76 to exit 31 (State Route 43 and Kent exit). Proceed south on State Route 43 for 2 miles. Turn right on Old Forge Road for less than 2 miles to the winery on the left

Hours Jan.–Mar., Tues.–Thurs., 5–9 PM, Fri.–Sat., 12–11 PM; April–Dec., Tues.–Thur., 1–9 PM, Fri.–Sat., 12–11 PM, Sun., 1–8 PM, all year

Tours Informal, pending availability

Tastings All wines available for sampling, price depends on price of wine

Gifts Gift shop features wine-related items, many hand-painted and handcrafted

Picnics Encouraged during good weather on beautiful deck by lake

Highlights at Winery Cozy, friendly, relaxed atmosphere; small-batch, award-winning wines

Events Summer bonfires/hot dog roasts and steak cookouts; varietal tastings

Restaurant Light menu

Prices $12.99–$31.99

Brand Names Viking Vineyards

Type of Production Small-batch, limited production

Method of Harvesting By hand

Pressing and Winemaking Small bladder press used to do whole-berry press for ice wine, or crushed-berry press for other wines

Aging and cooperage Wines are fermented in stainless steel; some with oak staves. Some reds aged in barrel

Vineyards Founded 1999

County Portage

Appellation Ohio

Acreage 1.5

Climate Typical Midwestern with no lake-effect moderation

Soil Sandy loam where the grapes are planted

Varieties Vidal Blanc, Traminette, Lemberger

Wines Vidal Blanc, Riesling, Chardonnay, Cabernet Sauvignon, Traminette Chambourcin, Lemberger, Merlot, various blends

Best Red Cabernet Sauvignon

Best White Nordic Myst

Other Best Wine Salmon Run

Quote "Typically, the wines may be characterized as palate-friendly and lighter than other wines on the market—especially the reds."—Jeff Nelson

Nearby Places to Visit Kent State Museum of Fashion and Aurora Premium Outlets

Wolf Creek Vineyards

SUMMIT COUNTY

CABERNET FRANC

2002

ALCOHOL BY VOLUME 12.0%

The Winery at Wolf Creek

2637 South Cleveland-Massillon Road

Norton, OH 44203

Tel (330) 666-9285 or (800) 436-0426

Fax (330) 665-1445

E-mail info@wineryatwolfcreek.com

Web site www.wineryatwolfcreek.com

Owners Andy and Deanna Troutman

Winemaker Carrie Bonvallet

Founded 1980

The steep hills and deep valleys among century-old farmsteads are one of the many great sights to behold in Summit County. The glass and wooden Winery at Wolf Creek, framed by elegant white pines, is yet another sight to see. An expanse of some five hundred acres of cherry and sugar maple, interspersed with rows of vines, swoops down a dramatic hillside to the raging Wolf Creek below. In the distance, the Akron skyline lingers.

The first thought that comes to mind is: What a spectacular place to live! The second: What a great place to build an Ohio winery. Fifty years ago, Melvin Wineberg purchased thirty-five acres of land here as an escape from his career as a chemist. He built a brick house on the ridgeline of the property, distinguished by its New England stone walls, and raised three sons, Andrew, Steve, and Mike. Andrew later founded the vineyard and filled the role of winemaker. His brother, similarly inspired,

established Pleasant Valley Vineyards in Mt. Vernon.

In 1996, Andy Troutman graduated from the Ohio State University School of Agriculture with a BS in horticulture and food microbiology. Recipient of the Lonz Winery Fellowship, he studied at the Ohio Agricultural Research and Development Center in Wooster before Andrew Wineberg hired him as the vineyard manager for The Winery at Wolf Creek. By 1998, Andy and his wife, Deanna, had expanded and started Troutman Winery and Vineyards, a farm winery in Wooster.

The next few years were tumultuous. Andrew Wineberg and his wife divorced, and he died unexpectedly. "I was the only person who knew how the cellar worked," Andy says. "Suddenly, I was the winemaker." By 2002, the Troutmans purchased The Winery at Wolf Creek. Andy made the wine; Deanna marketed it.

There are 15 acres of vines (50 percent vertical shoot positioned and

The view at Wolf Creek. *Courtesy The Winery at Wolf Creek*

50 percent bilateral cordoned) planted in sandy loam, clay loam, and gravel in Summit County. Similar to the climate in the Loire Valley, with the moderating Wolf Creek nearby, the vineyards consist of Cabernet Franc, Pinot Gris, Riesling, and Vignoles.

The grapes are harvested by hand and machine. Afterward, they are transferred into one thousand pound bins and sorted. The grapes are put into the crusher-destemmer and then into an Italian membrane press. The winery uses mostly cold-fermentation fixed-capacity stainless steel tanks. "We age our wines on an average of six to eight months in 80 percent American oak and 20 percent French oak," Andy says, adding new oak barrels every year.

He believes that Cabernet Franc has great potential in Summit County.

Its full capacity as a varietal has yet to be explored. "We do no filtering of our Cabernet Franc," he says. "It is a very stable wine."

"We serve a diverse group of consumers from twenty to eighty years old. Their preference ranges from dry to semi-sweet to sweet," Andy says.

The Winery at Wolf Creek was designed to offer guests and visitors many possibilities. Some come and spend the day outdoors, hiking the vineyards, then enjoying a hillside picnic with a great view. Some gather in the elegant tasting room to pair wine and food. Still others come to celebrate graduations, anniversaries, or weddings in the more formal great room. But regardless of how guests spend their time at Wolf Creek, they all share this magical experience in Ohio wine country.

The Winery at Wolf Creek 🍃

Directions North: I-77 to State Route 21 south. Turn left at Minor Road and follow it to Cleveland-Massillon Road. The winery is 1 mile on the left. South: I-77 to I-76 west. At exit 14, head north on Cleveland-Massillon road 1.5 miles to the winery on the right

Hours Oct.–May: Sun.–Thurs., 12–9 PM, Fri.–Sat., 12–11 PM. June–Sept.: Sun.–Thurs., 12–10 PM, Fri.–Sat., 12–11 PM

Tours Group tours by appointment

Tastings Daily when open

Gifts Wine accessories, clothing, and gift baskets

Picnics Picturesque grounds and romantic vistas for lovely picnics and gatherings

Highlights at Winery Incredible view for miles of reservoir and Akron skyline; quality packaging and quality line of wines

Events Live music weekly, Cooking with Wine, Yappy Hours

Prices $13–$20; 10 percent case discount

Brand Names The Winery at Wolf Creek

Type of Production 70 percent white wine and 30 percent red wine

Method of Harvesting By hand and mechanical

Pressing and Winemaking Membrane press, mostly cold-fermented white wine

Aging and Cooperage 80 percent American oak, 20 percent French oak; one-third new oak per annum

Vineyards Founded 1979

County Summit

Appellation American

Acreage 15

Waterway Wolf Creek

Climate Similar to the Loire Valley soil, sandy loam, clay loam, and gravel

Varieties Cabernet Franc, Pinot Gris, Riesling, Vignoles

Wines Cabernet Franc, Pinot Gris, White Lies, Original Sin, Rhapsody, Vignoles, Redemption, Sweet Revenge, Blue, Space Cowboy, Cabernet Sauvignon, Syrah, Exodus

Best Red Cabernet Franc

Best White Vignoles

Quote "Cabernet Franc has great potential here."—Andy Troutman

Nearby Places to Visit Downtown Akron attractions; Fairlawn shopping complex

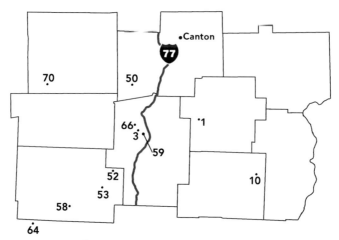

Appalachian Country Tour

AMERICAN
Lakeside Red Wine

A Family of Fine Wines

Produced & Bottled by: Al-Bi Winery Company • 29 North Smith Street • Dellroy, OH 44620

Contents: 750 ml. • Alcohol: 11% by Volume • Contains Sulfites

Al-Bi Winery

29 North Smith Street
Dellroy, OH 44620
Tel (330) 735-1061
Web site www.ohiowines.org
Owners/Winemakers Alan Rummell
and Bill Burrow
Founded 2003

The Al-Bi Winery, founded in 2003, is located in Dellroy in Carroll County, eight miles west of Carrollton, the county seat, on the eastern shore of beautiful Atwood Lake. This quaint hamlet of 350, a dry town until the spring of 2004, represents a modern-day version of life in the agricultural heartland, which began in the early 1800s.

Partner Alan Rummell, an owner of a metal-fabricating shop, had an inclination for business. Partner Bill Burrow, a salesman for a steel company, had a love for home winemaking. While in the steel industry, they crossed paths and their interests merged.

"I made wine for fifteen years as a hobbyist," says Burrow, a Mineral City native. "I bought kits that used either grape concentrate or fresh juice to make wine." In time, Rummell learned of Burrow's winemaking, which aroused his curiosity in mastering this fine art. "One day, we decided we wanted to do something," Burrow says.

So, the gentlemen of Carroll County created a catchy name for their new wine venture. Rummell took the "Al" from his first name and hyphenated it with the "Bi" from Burrow's first name to get Al-Bi. "It had an Italian-sounding name that complemented our new Italian winemaking equipment," Burrows says.

Next, the partners searched for a historic building in tree-lined Dellroy that they converted into a working winery. They were challenged by an archaic county ordinance restricting where wine could be produced and sold on the same premises.

"We purchased a simple wood-frame building on the main thoroughfare that had previously housed other businesses," Burrows says. "We renovated the building ourselves, giving it a rustic look by showcasing some of the natural wood. We designed a rough-sawed poplar tasting bar and a place to display the Al-Bi Winery wines, a focal

Al-Bi Winery, on the shore of Atwood Lake.
Courtesy Al-Bi Winery

point in the main room with tables and chairs for twelve."

Al-Bi Winery contracts its berries from Washington and its cherries from Michigan. Its grape juice originates from several Ohio, Pennsylvania, and New York vineyards, as well as juices from California. "We produce 4,000 plus gallons of wine, roughly 20,000 bottles annually," Burrow says. A small artisan winery, it emphasizes specialty handcrafted berry and fruit wines and two styles of dandelion wines. "Six of our Al-Bi wines are dry, and the rest of our wines are varying degrees of sweet."

The fresh berries and cherries, along with the grape juices, are shipped by refrigerated truck to Dellroy, where they are off-loaded into Italian stainless steel

tanks and American polymer barrels. The berry and cherry wines undergo a classic crushing and destemming before pressing and fermentation. Pending the nature and style of the wines to be made, they are held in barrel for various lengths of time. The wine is properly balanced, then filtered and fined several times before it is hand-bottled, corked, and labeled. Viniferas and more complex wines are aged up to one year in barrel, with additional bottle age.

Al-Bi Winery features thirty wines in its collection. The Foreplay, a four-way blended red wine, Peach, a sweet fruit wine, and Dellroy's Rosé, a sweet blush wine blended of grapes and fruit, are among the most popular in the collection.

"Our customers come from all walks of life—from local construction workers to the woman, eighty-five, who buys cherry wines every two weeks. They are devoted customers who have heard about us by word-of-mouth or through friends," says Burrow, who recently hosted a private tasting for a delegation of future Russian entrepreneurs. "People enjoy coming here!" In addition, the winery wholesales to retail establishments in the region, from North Canton to Killbuck to Steubenville. "We want to make a wine that tastes good and sells. We strive to be friendly and gracious to our customers," he says.

Al-Bi Winery 🍂

Directions Take I-77 to U.S. Route 30 east toward East Liverpool/Canton. Merge onto State Route 43 toward Waynesburg. Turn right on State Route 183/West Libson Street and left onto West Street, which becomes Silver Street, which becomes Morges Street, which becomes Bark Road NW. Turn left on State Route 542 to the winery on Smith Street

Hours Mon.–Fri., 5–8 PM; Sat., 10 AM–9 PM

Tours Self-guided

Tastings Daily when open

Gifts Wine

Picnics Small gazebo in the town of Dellroy

Highlights at Winery Friendly, down-home nature of place & character of owners; rustic, but relaxing, step back in time

Events Ohio Wine Producers Wine Trail

Prices $9–$13; 10 percent case discount

Brand Names Al-Bi Winery

Type of Production Small artisan fruit and berry wines

Aging and Cooperage Predominately stainless steel and polymer

County Carroll

Appellation American

Varieties Chardonnay, Merlot, Chambourcin, Cabernet Franc, Concord, Delaware, Vidal Blanc, Elderberry, Strawberry, Blackberry, Black Cherry, Cherry, Plum, Raspberry, Peach

Wines Cabernet Franc, Chambourcin, Chardonnay, Dark & Dry, Merlot, Vidal Blanc*, Atwood Mist, Atwood Secret, Black Cherry, Concord*, Elderberry, Josie's Plum, Ruby Red, Lakeside Red*, Atwood Sunset*, Atwood Trifecta*, Black Satin*, Bodacious Blackberry*, Cherry*, Dande-Dandelion*, Dellroy's Delaware, Dellroy's Rosé*, Fantasia*, Foreplay, Peach, Ramblin' Raspberry*, Strawberry, Watermelon*
(* Denotes Medal Winners)

Best Red Wine Foreplay

Best White Wine Peach

Best Other Wine Dellroy's Rosé

Quote "We want to make a wine that tastes good and sells. We strive to be friendly and gracious to our customers."—Bill Burrow

Nearby Places to Visit Atwood Queen Cruise Boat; Algonquin Mill Complex; McCook House; Warther's Museum

Breitenbach Wine Cellars

5934 Old Route 39
Dover, OH 44662
Tel (330) 343-3603
Fax (330) 343-8920
E-mail anita@breitenbachwine.com
Web site www.breitenbachwine.com
Owner Dalton and Cynthia Bixler
Winemaker Dalton "Duke" Bixler
Founded 1980

The road west on State Route 39 through Ohio's historic Amish country passes through steep, rolling hills and wide, gracious valleys to Breitenbach Wine Cellars in Dover. The purple and peach winery castle, with its twin towers and gold finials, rises out of the valley and was dubbed "Breitenbach, which means broad or wide stream in German, for the waterway which crosses the 120 acre property.

Founders Cynthia and Dalton "Duke" Bixler, German descendants from Sugarcreek and Bolivar respectively, pioneered the cultivation of the culinary arts and winemaking. The Bixlers began as a retail establishment in 1980 featuring Swiss cheese, quality meats and fresh produce. Today, they share this legacy with their daughters, Anita Davis, marketing and retail manager, and Jennifer Kohler, winemaker and wholesale manager.

Breitenbach evolved out of the Bixlers' creativity and talents. Duke was the designer—he loved to do integrated marketing, sales and public relations. Cynthia was the planner—she thought out each step of the business. "My father did some line drawings that illustrated what he envisioned the place might look like. My mother gave his ideas style, adding the stain glass and antiques," she recalls. The retail environment was conceived to flow from one venue to the next. Each part of the operation—from the market, gift shop, tasting room, picnic facilities and café—belonged to the whole concept. "Sixty percent of our wines are sold at retail at the winery, and the remaining forty percent are sold at wholesale to the trade," explains Anita Davis.

The winemaking began simply enough in the cellar below Der Markplatz, the German translation for "The Marketplace" In 1985, Duke Bixler, then winemaker at Breitenbach Wine Cellars, converted the threshing barn, which had housed the girls'

The culinary arts are an age-old tradition at Breitenbach. *Courtesy Ohio Wine Producers Association/Breitenbach Wine Cellars*

riding and show horses, into a modern wine production center. He outfitted it with state-of-the-art equipment, and implemented the latest research and technology. This included stainless steel fermentors, American, French and Hungarian oak aging barrels, an automated bottling line, and a wine lab.

The wine grapes, which are purchased from premiere growers, are harvested by hand or machine at their prime pH, sugar and acid levels. Once the grapes are transported to Dover, they are put through the crusher-destemmer, then moved to two computerized bladder presses, averaging 30-to-40s ton of wine grapes per day.

The rich color is extracted on the skins during the primary fermentation of the red wine grapes—Cabernet Sauvignon, Merlot, Syrah and Sangiovese. The taste and the flavor

are achieved during the secondary malolactic fermentation. All the white wine grapes—the Viognier, Rieslings, Gewürztraminer, Vidal Blanc, and Seyval Blanc and American varieties are cold-fermented in temperature-controlled, jacketed fermenters. Once the fermentation is completed, the wines are racked off the lees, then held in stainless steel tanks or oak aging barrels in the cellar. "Our wines average nine months to two years in barrel before they are released," says Davis. "We have grown from 1,500 gallons to 150,000 gallons annually. We distribute our wines throughout Ohio. Many of our customers still enjoy making a trip to shop, have lunch, and travel through Amish country."

As one of Ohio's largest producers, Breitenbach Wine Cellars has achieved accolades for its signature line of wines. Among them are its Roadhouse Red; its Frost Fire, and its other best wine, Festival, a blend of red vinifera grapes, that won a prestigious award from the Culinary Institute of America.

"My father takes pride in having pioneered some 15 natural fruit and berry wines. The elderberries and the strawberries are grown by Amish farmers; the raspberries come from southern Ohio; the apples originate from Geneva; and the plums and the peaches come from Michigan. We are proud of the fact that all 40 of our wines have been awarded a gold or silver medal including our specialty Ice Wine, Port, and Sherry," she says.

Breitenbach Wine Cellars 🍇

Directions Take I-77 to exit 83. Go west on State Route 39 to right on Schilling Hill Rd. to winery

Hours Mon.–Sat., 9 AM–6 PM; closed Sun.

Tours Educational, Friday & Saturday at 1 PM & 3 PM, and during special events

Tastings Daily 9 AM–6 PM, special cellar and event tastings

Gifts Extensive selection

Picnics Large patio with views

Highlights at Winery The best of the best in wine, food, and gifts, friendly courteous help and service

Events Annual Dandelion May-Fest; National Dandelion Cook-off

Prices $9.75 to $55

Brand Names Breitenbach

Type of Production Traditional

Pressing and Winemaking Bladder press with traditional winemaking practices

Aging and Cooperage Hungarian and French oak barrels

County Tuscarawas

Appellation American

Varieties 40 total

Wines Johannisberg Rieslings (dry and sweet), Gewürztraminer, Charming Nancy, Frost Fire, Silver Seyval, Café Viognier, Solera Cream Sherry, Breitenbach Ice Wine, Cabernet Sauvignon, Roadhouse Red, Festival, Merlot, Sangiovese, Red Zinfandel, Shiraz, Four Barrel Tawny Port, Old Dusty Miller, First Crush, Sangio Rosso, and a fine selection of fruit, berry and dandelion wines

Best Red Roadhouse Red

Best White Frost Fire

Other Best Wine Festival

Nearby Places to Visit Ohio Amish Country, Roscoe and Zoar villages

Coffee Cake Winery

48018 Giacobbi Road
Hopedale, OH 43976
Tel (740) 937-2572
Fax (740) 937-2053
E-mail ccwinery@windstream.net
Web site www.coffeecakewinery.com
Owners Frank and Janet Kuchan
Winemaker Frank Kuchan
Founded 2001

Coffee Cake Winery, ensconced in the forests of the Appalachians in Hopedale, sits in a peaceful clearing sixteen miles from the Ohio River Valley in southeastern Ohio. Proprietors Frank and Janet Kuchan, educators from nearby Steubenville and Dillonvale, descended from Croatian ancestors who migrated to this isolated territory in the 1800s. Frank's grandfather was a recognized chef at the Fort-Steubenville Hotel, which had a reputation for offering the best accommodations on the toll road between Pittsburgh and Columbus. Proud of this culinary heritage, Frank, a biologist, and Janet, a science teacher, found themselves in the wine industry well over a century later. They honored their forbearers by translating their German surname, Kuchan, into English; the resulting word refers to a type of coffee cake, and named their winery accordingly.

In 1969, the Kuchans purchased a farm on eighty-five acres in Harrison County, where they raised their children, Telicia, Verner, and Julianne. "The place was an absolute disaster," says Frank, who is also a naturalist. "The land was ruined, as no reclamation laws existed in Ohio during the fifties. We were determined to provide our children a country environment."

The Kuchans embarked on a multitude of improvements that characterized the country atmosphere of their home and winery establishment. Their farm provided them a lifetime of unexpected adventures. At first, they industriously maintained a herd of cattle, flocks of chickens, rabbits, and huge gardens. Some evenings, Janet observed Frank with a glass of wine in hand as he surveyed his empty fields. "I saw him look at the wine, then look back across the fields. Then he looked at the wine, and I knew he envisioned a field planted with wine grapes," she says.

In 1991, the Kuchans cultivated the clay soil on their farm and planted a test vineyard. The varietals were

Telicia Kuchan during the harvest, Coffee Cake Winery. *Photo by Annabelle Kuchan, Courtesy Coffee Cake Winery*

De Chaunac, Millot, Foch, Biagio, Baco Noir, Chancellor, Seyval Blanc, Vignoles, Vidal Blanc, Traminette, Aurora, and Cabernet Franc. "We made more wine than we could ever sell," Frank says. Additional grapes were planted in 1994, some two hundred vines in 1996, and one hundred vines each year thereafter. Today there are more than two thousand vines. Coffee Cake Vineyards made its first profit by selling its wine grapes to a vintner friend and to other regional wineries. Their friend encouraged them to start their own winery, and in 2001, the Kuchans opened Coffee Cake Winery and featured their first estate-grown wines.

Today, the gravel driveway leads to a landscaped parking area and a wood-shingled tasting room and gift shop. A sheltered terrace for outdoor wine and food events captures views of the gently sloping vineyards and farm buildings.

Steps lead up to a porch and the family residence, a huge log cabin with wine-making and aging cellars. "We are located out where the fast lane ends," says Janet. Her friendly dogs wag their tails as they escort guests around the property.

Each September, the Kuchans invite three groups of thirty friends to their annual vintage celebration. "People harvest grapes over three days for four hours, then we fire up the grill, relax, and invite our guests to stay for as long as they wish. In appreciation, we give them a gift of wine from our private cellar," Frank says.

Volunteers haul the lug boxes from the vineyards to the crusher-destemmer under the house, where a ton of grapes per day is pressed in an Italian hydraulic basket press. The red and white wines are fermented in 50-gallon plastic drums; the wines remain there until completion of the first settling. All the new wines are racked and pumped over, then clarified in stainless steel tanks. "If the Romans had stainless steel," Frank says, "the oak barrel would never have been invented." The wine is held indefinitely in 15-gallon units, mounted on wheels, and bottled as needed.

Coffee Cake Winery produces 2,000 gallons of wine a year, French American hybrids and fruit. The wines vary from dry to semi-dry and semi-sweet to sweet. "We promote quality Ohio grapes paired with good Ohio food. People often make judgments based on what they are told. At Coffee Cake Winery, we are different. We feature the best wine grapes grown from our wine estate," Frank says. "What we get from other farms is fruit for our apple and strawberry wines."

Coffee Cake Winery 🍃🍂

Directions From U.S. 22 east, take Hopedale exit 151 east in a northerly direction, followed by a quick left onto dirt Giacobbi Road to the winery

Hours June–Oct., Mon.–Thurs., 11 AM–6 PM, Fri.–Sat., 11 AM–9 PM, closed Sun.; April–May & Nov.–Dec., Mon.–Sat. 11 AM–6 PM; Jan.–March, by appointment

Tours Informal

Tasting Daily when open

Picnics Yes

Highlights at Winery Good wine and lots of fun; relaxed atmosphere; lovely setting; friendly people interested in wine

Events Steak Cookouts, ten Saturdays in summer; Wine and Cheese Tastings: cheeses from different countries paired with Coffee Cakes wines; once a month April–Nov. Reservations required for both events

Prices $12–$15; buy 12 pay for 11

Brand Names Coffee Cake Winery

Type of Production French American hybrids and fruit

Method of Harvesting By hand

Pressing Traditional methods

Aging and Cooperage Stainless steel

Vineyards Founded 1991

County Harrison

Appellation American

Acreage 3

Climate Cold winters and hot, humid summers

Soil Clay

Varieties De Chaunac, Foch, Biagio, Vignoles, Vidal Blanc, Traminette, Aurora

Wines Black Knight, Nightfall, Midnight Ruby, Frosted Blush, Crystal Glow, Autumn Gold, Satin, Red Satin, Golden Amber, Strawberry and Apple

Best Red Black Knight

Best White Crystal Glow

Other Best Wine Autumn Gold

Quote "If the Romans would have had stainless steel, the oak barrel never would have been invented."—Frank Kuchan

Nearby Places to Visit Clark Gable & Coal museums in Cadiz; Wheeling Downs

Perennial Vineyards

1187 Poorman St.
Navarre, OH, 44662
Tel (330) 832-3677
Fax (330) 832-3677
E-mail info@perennialvineyards.com
Web site www.perennialvineyards.com
Owner Damon and Kim Leeman
Winemaker Damon Leeman
Founded 2002

The founding of Perennial Vineyards, located in a white 1848 bank barn in the rolling hills of Navarre, marked the advent of viticulture in an Ohio region, long steeped in dairy farms, cheese houses and croplands. "We (his parents and brother Ryan Leeman) were always cheesemakers," says Damon Leeman, a 1992 graduate in food sciences from Ohio State University, who is a co-owner with his wife, Kim, an established veterinarian. "My family always grew grapes and made wine with plans to have a roadside produce stand."

In 1999, the Leemans merged their resources to start a winery in a farming district. They purchased an attractive, 40 acre, 960 foot elevation, Stark County historic farm. It was well appointed with classic architecture dating from the Civil War. An elegant, two story, red brick colonial house dominated the striking tree-lined, property along with a red dairy barn and a lofting

shed. "Earlier, we had worked together and built our own house and Kim's veterinarian office. When we bought Perennial we thought it was a great place, and we knew we wanted our concept for the winery to be compelling," he says.

Perennial Vineyards began as a four acre plot of wine grapes protected by trees on Poorman Rd. at the Leeman's parent's farm. The vineyards were tiled, with a limestone under pan and a clay overlay of topsoil, with a standard, bi-lateral trellising system. Today Perennial Vineyards is 80 percent estate grown comprised of 16 acres that include Vidal Blanc, Cayuga, Chancellor, Riesling, Concord, Niagara, Delaware, Vignoles, Cabernet Franc and Chambourcin. Leeman buys his Chardonnay, Cabernet and Syrah grapes from his brother Ryan Leeman, the winemaker at the Van Ruten Winery in Lodi, CA.

The Leemans strategized how to introduce Perennial Vineyards wines to the public. They wanted their property to come alive. They renovated their barn and lofting shed and did all the work themselves using recycled building materials. Damon contributed his craftsman skills; Kim provided her decorative talents.They built a winery entrance with an oval glass and oak door, accentuated with urns and antiques. They gutted the lofting shed, reused the walnut beams, and poured a concrete and urethane floor. European landscapes by artist Hans Leeman, Damon's Swiss grandfather, were hung on the wall above the walnut tasting bar. The tasting room, furnished with rich mahogany tables, chairs, lamps and oriental rugs, has a viewing window of the wine center. They enlarged the tasting room and added a stone fireplace. They feature their Vidal Blanc and Our Flower, a dry rosé, in hand-painted wine bottles.

A walkway leads to a larger room, which features a quarried river-stone wall (part of the foundation of the bank barn) and reused walls. It is designed for crowds who sit at Leeman's hand-hewn, wooden tables and chairs to listen to an acoustic guitar or a local band. The relaxed atmosphere appeals to an after-dinner crowd, who like to socialize while pairing wine and food. A grape arbor and sunset patio draw groups of people, who enjoy evening bonfires or barbeques and roasts.

The patio at Perennial Vineyards. *Courtesy OWPA/ Perennial Vineyards*

The owners are "going green." A straw grotto, similar to a cave, made from stacked hay sealed with stucco, is their newest project. Forks, knives, plates and cups for the tasting room are made from sugar cane and potato. Waste is composted. Solar panels aid in heating. Grape stems and skins are used for fertilizer in the vineyard.

During the fall harvest, the grapes are handpicked, then brought to the winery where they are put in the crusher-destemmer. Traditional wine practices are followed, using a modern bladder press for the whites and a wooden basket press for the reds. The white and red wines are fermented in stainless steel, then and aged and held in stainless steel or American oak and European oak.

Perennial Vineyards produces Chardonnay, Pinot Gris, Cabernet Sauvignon, Cabernet Sauvignon/Syrah blend, Pinot Noir, Vidal Blanc, True North, a Chardonnay and Vidal blend, a Vino Rosé, a blend of eight varietals; Eclipse, a dry Merlot, Zinfandel and Chambourcin; a bone-dry Eclipse Reserve; and Sangria. The Leemans are both deeply committed to educating the public to new tastes, styles, and discoveries. "Vines are like people," says Leeman. "Some are good and some are bad."

Perennial Vineyards

Directions From Cleveland: I-77 south via exit 172A toward Akron. Merge onto State Route 21 south. Take U.S. Route 30 west toward Wooster. Take Ohio 241 exit to Ohio/Massillon-Brewster. Turn left on 241. Turn left on Ohio 93. Turn left on Poorman St. to the winery

Hours Tues.–Thurs., 2–9 PM; Fri.–Sat., 2–10 PM; Sun., 1–8 PM

Tours Viewing window

Gifts Melted bottles, jewelry

Picnics Encouraged

Highlights at Winery Unique getaway, unusual décor, friendly attitude, Upbeat and fun-loving after dinner crowd, Excellent wine, food and entertainment

Events Wine at the Moon: Music and Art Show in the Vineyard, Dog Days of Summer—Promote Wine Dog White, and Wine Dog Red, Fund raiser for animal groups; pets invited.

Restaurant Gourmet pizzas, cheese plates, and Lapallito

Prices $10–$35; 10 percent case discount

Brand Names Perennial Vineyards; Wine Dog

Type of Production Vinifera and French American Hybrids

Method of Harvesting By hand

Pressing and Winemaking Wood basket for reds; modern horizontal Bladder for whites

Aging and Cooperage Stainless Steel and American and Central European oak

Vineyards Founded 1997

County Stark

Appellation American

Acreage 16

Trellising High cordon, vertical shoot positioned

Waterways Wolf Creek

Climate Cold winters and hot, humid summers

Soil Heavy Canfield with clay underpan. Field tile each row

Varieties Vidal Blanc, Cayuga, Chancellor, Riesling, Concord, Niagara, Delaware, Vignoles, Cabernet Franc and Chambourcin

Best Red Cabernet Sauvignon

Best White Vidal Blanc

Other Best Wine Eclipse

Quote "Vines are like people. Some are good; some are bad." –Damon Leeman

Nearby Places to Visit Akron Art Museum, Wilmot: Stark County Wilderness Center, Ohio Erie Canal National Historic Society & Canal Scenic By-way

Rainbow Hills Vineyards

26349 TR 251
Newcomerstown, OH 43832
Tel (740) 545-9305
E-mail rainbowhillsvineyards@gmail.com
Owner/Winemaker Leland C. Wyse
Founded 1988

As you wind your way off of U.S. Route 36 west onto State Route 751, the Coshocton viticultural district comes alive. By the time you reach Township Road 251, there is a feeling of possibly being lost, but the farms of Newcomerstown seem to say, *Keep going. The winery is just around the corner.*

The road into Rainbow Hills Vineyards is a path to a pot of gold, one of the prettiest places in Ohio. The one-lane road twists and turns past an open meadow with two brooks running through it, around contoured vineyards, and to the winery in the flat of the valley. Up ahead lies an artistic enclave—an enchanting rustic sandstone and wooden tree house, moving flower gardens, and a soaring fountain.

Years ago, after owners Leland and Joy Wyse had lived in Oregon and, later, Australia, where he was a biologist, they were jolted by an unexpected experience. "We were leaving Australia for

good and were near the Outback, some sixty miles from the airport. Off in the distance, we saw a distinct rainbow; the next moment, we drove right through it," Leland says.

It wasn't until much later, when the Wyses returned to the United States, that they began to look for property in Ohio. "We discovered a deserted eighty-two-acre farm and named it Rainbow Hills Vineyards." Suddenly the meaning of their Australian rainbow experience began to bear fruit. The Wyses cleared the land. "It was like a jungle," Leland says. Next, they laid the foundation for their three-level, 3,000-square-foot mountain retreat. "We built every building, we laid every stone, and we planted every grape."

Steep stairs lead past a sandstone foundation, cut as blocks from a quarry on the property, to the tree house. An oak door on a viewing porch graces the exterior of the building, which is cantilevered off the mountain. Walkways and lookouts with sitting benches for tasting wine parallel the hillside and end at the patio, where barbeques and picnics are held. Splendid views take in Joy Wyse's four-hundred-plant perennial garden, which jumps with seasonal color. The woods are teaming with maple, sugar maple, beech, red oak, and white oak trees, which hang over swift streams with dancing waterfalls. There is wildlife everywhere.

The interior, designed for cozy groups, consists of slate floors, paned windows, and poplar and ash walls. A tasting bar serves homemade bread, cheeses, fruit, and, of course, the wines of Rainbow Hills Vineyards. The room ascends some eighteen feet, dominated by a fireplace made of river stone and surrounded by white walls mounted with the Wyses' favorite paintings. An 1831 log cabin on the premises has been newly renovated into a 2,000-square foot, four-unit bed and breakfast.

The south-facing vineyards were planted in 1985, 1986, and 1987. They consist of four acres of three-wired, standard trellising planted in well-drained, shallow-acid limestone soils. Similar to the Ohio River Valley, the climate is suitable for growing Seyval Blanc, De Chaunac, Catawba, Niagara, Cabernet Franc, Riesling, and Chardonel. During the harvest, the wine grapes are hand-picked, then tumbled by a crusher and destemmer at the modern steel winery. ("The ancient barn fell into the creek, so we had to replace it," Leland says.) Next, the grapes are pressed in an oak stave, wooden basket press, then fermented in either stainless steel tanks or American oak barrels. The Chardonel, for example, is aged in American white oak. The red wines, on the other hand, are aged in stainless steel tanks and American oak barrels for up to four years. Afterward, the finished wines are clarified, then bottled, corked, foiled, and properly stored. Rainbow Hills Vineyards has high demand for its Cabernet Franc, its best red, Riesling, its best white, and Rainbow Rosé, a delightful Catawba. Other choices go by poetic names like White Gold, Prism, Spectrum, Drumming Grouse, and Aires. "I believe that for the Ohio wineries to be well known, we must all be careful and keep the quality of winemaking high," Leland declares. "Quality wines, not mediocre ones, reflect on all of us."

Rainbow Hills Vineyards

Directions From 1-77, exit onto U.S. Route 36 west toward Newscomerstown/Coshocton for 6 miles. Turn right on State Route 751 for 2 miles, then left, following signs to the winery

Hours Oct.–May, Mon.–Sat., 11 AM–6 PM, Closed Sun. June–Sept., Mon.–Thurs., 11 AM–6 PM, Fri.–Sat., 11 AM–9 PM, Closed Sun

Tours Self-guided, through vineyards and woods

Tastings Always available

Picnics Welcome

Highlights at Winery Lovely Bed & Breakfast in hills of Coshocton County; extensive outdoor decks

Events Summer cookouts and barbeques—steak/chicken June–September $40; Winter wine tasting dinners $40; Held Fridays and Saturdays, both require reservations

Restaurant Cookouts & wine tasting dinners

Prices $9.75–$13.75

Brand Names Rainbow Hills Vineyards

Method of Harvesting Hand-harvested

Pressing and Winemaking Basket press and traditional winemaking

Aging and Cooperage American oak

Vineyards Founded 1985, 1986, and 1987

County Coshocton

Appellation Ohio

Acreage 4

Waterways Two streams run through property

Climate Central to Ohio River Valley

Soil Shallow acid, well-drained, limestone soils

Varieties Seyval Blanc, Catawba, Riesling, Cabernet Franc, De Chaunac, Niagara, Chardonnay

Wines Grenfell Red, White Gold, Rainbow Rosé, Prism, Spectrum, Drumming Grouse, Aries, Chardonel, Riesling, Cabernet Franc

Best Red Cabernet Franc

Best White Riesling

Other Best Wine Catawba

Quote "We must all be careful to keep the quality high."—Leland C. Wyse

Nearby Places to Visit Roscoe Village

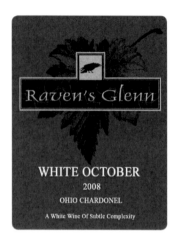

WHITE OCTOBER
2008
OHIO CHARDONEL
A White Wine Of Subtle Complexity

Raven's Glenn Winery

56183 County Road 143
West Lafayette, OH 43845
Tel (740) 545-1000
Fax (740) 545-6930
E-mail erg@ravensglenn.com
Web site www.ravensglenn.com
Owners Robert and Renee Guilliams
Winemaker Beau Guilliams
Founded 1997

The Raven's Glenn Winery sits on the banks of the languid Tuscarawas River at the crossroads of U.S. Route 36 and Coshocton County Road 143 in West Lafayette. The modern winery was named for the raven, a twenty-five-inch-long black Corvid, the largest of the perching birds, common to the west, north, and, recently, the east.

The raven is noted for its vocalizations, intelligence, acrobatics, and love of soaring. For owners Robert and Renee Guilliams, as well as their son Beau, daughter Erika, and grandson Morgan, the legendary bird is the symbol of a family that has launched its winery and is ready to soar.

For years, the Guilliamses owned and operated several long-term care facilities in the area. Each year, the family took a trip to California's Heavenly Valley Ski Resort in South Lake Tahoe. Afterward, they would escape to the Napa Valley, where they enjoyed touring the wineries. The Guilliamses were fascinated by the integrated lifestyle-work ethic and wine products. "I used my digital camera to record details that intrigued me," Robert says. "Certain elements caught my eye—architecture, design, interiors, equipment, cellars, barrels, tasting rooms, retail displays, doors, floors, windows, and gardens. We were inspired!"

In 1996, the Guilliamses purchased one hundred acres so that Robert could plant grapes and Renee could pasture her horses. In 2000, they sold their interests in the health care business and set out to execute their wine venture. Robert contacted a family friend about buying an additional seven acres of real estate—once corn and soy beans—by the river. "The location for the winery was ideal," he says.

A meandering drive leads to the red-roofed Raven's Glenn Winery, a gray structure with white trim and a

The restaurant at Raven's Glenn. *Courtesy Raven's Glenn*

mission-style porch stacked with wine barrels. Robert, the wine ambassador, greets visitors with a short talk followed by an educational tour of their spectacular first-class facilities. The tour includes a look at the wine-production center with its crusher-destemmer and Scharfenberger and Wilmes presses; the fermentation room with its variable-capacity, stainless steel, temperature-controlled, jacketed fermentors; the high-tech lab; the wine cellars; the bottling room; and the case storage warehouse.

A path along the Tuscarawas River invites patrons to the Raven's Glenn Restaurant, a combination full service Italian eatery and tasting bar. "We designed the building and grounds ourselves," Robert says. "We wanted a spacious building with two-by-six wood-plank floors from an old mill and lots of floor-to-ceiling glass." The restaurant, designed for indoor and outdoor dining, has a river-rock fireplace with arched windows and French doors that open to a patio with views of the river and the neighboring golf course. A 200-seat banquet room is popular for weddings and anniversaries and connects to the restaurant, and an 80-seat outdoor pavilion. There is a newly planted two-acre vineyard especially for couples who request being married in the vineyard.

"We have designed our winery and restaurant around tourism. Our site is barrier free with easy in and out for motor coaches. We can accommodate meals, with or without an accompanying winery tour and tasting or simply a stop to enjoy a tasting and gift shop visit overlooking the scenic Tuscarawas River," says Renee Guilliams, hospitality manager.

A short drive through gorgeous hills and valleys bursting with flora and fauna heads up to the one-hundred-acre Sonnet Hills Stables and Vineyards and the Guilliamses' hilltop colonial residence. A friend excavated a winding road through the steep valley, which hides a natural tributary shrouded by trees. "The north side of the hill was created for the horses, the stable, and the pasture of Renee Guilliams, my spouse. The south side of the hill, roughly twenty acres, was contoured for our vineyard, which crests at 987 feet," Robert says.

Currently Raven's Glenn Winery has 16 acres planted to vines. Initially, Robert had the challenge of chisel-ripping the ground and preparing the heavy clay soil before planting the varietals. They include: Vidal Blanc, Chardonel, and Noriet whish is used to produce an award-winning, fortified, Port style wine. Two additional acres were added alongside the restaurant and include two of the aforementioned varietals.

The Guilliamses hired Tony Carlucci, a noted enologist, to help teach the family the advanced side of winemaking. Their son, Beau Guilliams, winemaker, has taken that challenge one step further, adding dry wines, sweet wines, fruit and sweet wines, and dessert wines. With sales in excess of 25,000 cases annually, Beau has created two stunning Ohio Quality Wine Award Gold Medal winners: White October and Vidal Blanc Ice Wine. "Wine should be fun," says Robert, "just keep it simple."

Raven's Glenn Winery 🌿

Directions North: I-77 south to exit 65. Go 7 miles west on US 36 to the intersection of Coshocton County Rd. 143 and the red-roofed buildings. Dresden/Zanesville: take State Route 60 to Route 16 to Coshocton, then proceed 7 miles east on US 36 to the intersection of County Rd. 143 and the red-roofed buildings

Hours Restaurant, gift shop, and tasting bar: Tues.–Sat., 11 AM–8 PM; Sunday Champagne Brunch, 11:30 AM–2:30 PM; Gift shop and tasting bar Sunday, 11 AM–4 PM; Monday, Gift shop and tasting bar only, 11 AM–6 PM

Restaurant Open for lunch Mon.–Sat., 11 AM–4 PM, Fri.–Sat., 10 AM–9 PM, closed Sun

Tours By appointment, tours and tastings for groups of 12 or more, Easy access and accommodations for motor coaches

Tastings Daily when open

Gifts Unique wine related gift shop

Highlights at Winery Ohio's Crown Jewel of Wineries

Events See Web site

Restaurant Italian cuisine; seating inside or on the river deck; banquet seating for 200; hosting weddings, receptions, business meetings, and group events

Prices $9.99–$24.99; 10 percent case discount

Brand Name Raven's Glenn Winery

Type of Production Vitis vinifera, French hybrids, vitis labrusca, fruit wines

Method of Harvesting Hand-harvesting and single row machine-harvested

Pressing and Winemaking Wilmes and Scharfenberger Bladder Press, traditional winemaking

Aging and Cooperage Stainless steel, temperature-controlled, jacketed fermentors; French and American oak barrels

Vineyards Founded 1997

County Coshocton

Appellation Ohio

Acreage 18

Waterway Tuscarawas River

Climate Hot, humid Ohio weather

Soil Heavy clay

Varieties Vidal Blanc, Chardonel, and Noriet

Wines Chardonnay, Pinot Grigio, White October, Merlot, Cabernet Sauvignon, Zinfandel, Syrah, Riesling, Vidal Blanc, White Merlot, White Zinfandel, White Raven, Raven Rouge, Cherry, Raspberry, Blackberry, Passionate Peach, Sangria, Chantilly Lace, Vidal Blanc Ice Wine

Best Red Wine Scarlet Raven

Best White Wine White October

Other Best Wine Vidal Blanc Ice Wine

Quote "If I want things I've never had before, I must do things I have never done before."—Beau Guilliams

Nearby Places to Visit Roscoe Village Wine & Art Garden Festival, co-sponsored by Raven's Glenn Winery

Shawnee Springs Winery

20093 County Road 6
Coshocton, OH 43812
Tel (740) 623-0744
Fax (740) 622-5477
E-mail info@shawneespringswinery.com
Web site www.shawneespringswinery.com
Owners Randy and Cindy Hall
Winemaker Randy Hall and Scott Callahan II
Founded 1997

Shawnee Springs Winery, nestled into the deeply wooded foothills of the Appalachians in Coshocton, is situated within the confluence of the Tuscarawas and Walhonding rivers, where they merge to become the Muskingum River in southeastern Ohio.

Cindy and Randy Hall, natives of Coshocton, chose to name their winery out of respect for the Shawnee Nation, which hunted in the hills on their land above the Tuscarawas River Valley. Shawnee comes from the Algonquin word *shawun,* meaning southerner, in reference to their original home in the Ohio Valley. The Shawnee considered Coshocton, which means "union of the waters," and the Delaware nation that headquartered there as their grandfathers and the source of all Algonquin tribes.

Aside from the occasional glass of holiday wine that the Halls shared with Randy's Italian grandparents, the couple did not know much about wine until they visited Rainbow Hills Vineyards in

Newcomerstown and found themselves thinking, "Why not start a winery on their 95 acres of mountain property."

Randy and his twin sons, Jess and Benjamin, cleared 2.5 acres of prime land by hand. Shawnee Springs Vineyards, in Ohio's Appalachian hill country, were planted in dense clay soils to cold-weather-resistant varieties: Catawba, Niagara and Concord. "Summer days are long, hot, and humid, with the prevailing winds moving west to east. We needed hearty varieties that could adapt to the late Midwestern frosts," he says.

During the vintage, family members and friends harvest the grapes into lug boxes. Tons of grapes per day are processed in a stainless steel destemmer, and pressed in an oak stave, wooden basket press. The white grapes are pressed and fermented the same day, then pumped downstairs in the main house, and cold-stabilized at 55 degrees Fahrenheit in eighty-gallon, stainless steel, jacketed fermentors with variable

The Shawnee Springs entrance. *Courtesy Shawnee Springs*

floating heads. The reds grapes are fermented on the skin to extract character, then pumped outside and held in stainless steel tanks until clarified and aged. All the wines are filtered and fined, before additional bottle age.

"We deal in small lots of handcrafted wines," says Randy. "We try to be consistent. Our fruit varies depending on the quality of a particular vintage. I strive for balanced prunings, and a more vigorous vine."

At Shawnee Springs, the Halls extend hospitality in the tradition of Chief Tecumseh of the Shawnee Nation, who said, "Seek to make your life long, and its purpose in the service of your people." Guests enjoy the red barn, which resembles an Appalachian hideaway, or the outdoor shelter, suitable for picnics or barbeques, or play horseshoes or corn hole. Catered weddings are also popular. The interior has a tasting bar and gifts at one end, and tables and chairs, and a large fireplace at the other. Paintings of Indians,

landscapes, and wildlife decorate the walls. "It is both peaceful and rustic here," Randy says.

Cindy and Randy both work full-time outside of the winery, while Scott Callahan, Cindy's son, is the general manager and oversees the day-to-day operation. Cindy has a background in graphic design and marketing, and created a new logo and sales collateral for the winery. "Our wine sales have expanded by more than half in stores in Coshocton, Newcomerstown, Loudonville, and Zanesville," she says, with guests and visitors coming from 100 miles in any direction to visit the winery.

"People arrive in all sorts of vehicles—including twelve members of the Model T Old Car Club, who chugged up the dirt road in unison at twenty miles per hour," says Randy. "People say they like the friendly and congenial atmosphere and the taste of pure, homemade wines. There are no *vitis vinifera* or French hybrid wines."

Shawnee Springs Winery produces 1,200 gallons of wine per

year—Midnight Mist, Sundown, Sunny Day, Red Dawn, Apple, Elderberry, Cherry, and plans for Red Raspberry, fairly priced between $7.50 and $12. Red Dawn is a refreshingly, fruity, medium-bodied wine with a delightful tart finish. The Elderberry, a deep rich, garnet red dessert wine, with a lush full finish, tops the list. It goes without saying that the guests and visitors, who choose to traverse these ancient Shawnee lands, remember Randy's good, honest wines.

Shawnee Springs Winery 🍃

Directions From I-77, take exit 65 onto U.S. Route 36 west to Newcomerstown/Coshocton. Stay on State Route 16/State Route 83. Turn right on County Road 6 to the winery

Hours Thursday–Saturday 11 AM to 6 PM April through November, December Thursday–Saturday 11 AM to 5 PM

Tours Self-guided vineyard tours

Tasting Daily when open

Gifts Wine-related

Picnics Covered and open decks with grills, light snacks, and wine

Highlights at Winery Peaceful, rustic setting; American wines

Events Appalachian Wine Trail; Fall Foliage Tour

Prices $7.50–$12; 10 percent case discount

Brand Names Shawnee Springs Winery

Type of Production: Vitis labrusca

Method of Harvesting: By hand

Pressing and Winemaking Oak stave-wooden-basket press with water bladder

Aging and Cooperage Stainless steel tanks

Vineyards Founded 1992

County Coshocton

Appellation Ohio

Acreage 2.5

Waterway Shawnee Springs

Climate Temperate

Soil Clay

Varieties Concord, Niagara, Catawba, Fruit

Wines Midnight Mist, Sundown, Sunny Day, Red Dawn, Cherry, Apple, Elderberry

Best Red Midnight Mist

Best White Sunny Day

Other Best Wine Red Dawn

Quote "To fulfill our life-long dream to grow our own grapes and produce a good, local, reasonably priced wine."—Randy Hall

Nearby Places to Visit Roscoe Historic Village

Silver Moon Winery

4915 Old Route 39 NW
Dover, OH 44622
Tel (330) 602-6040
Fax (330) 364-9065
E-mail info@silvermoonwinery.com
Web site silvermoonwinery.com
Owner Judy Eschbacher
Winemaker Ken Eschbacher
Founded 2004

Landscaped with tall pines and low evergreens, the red-gabled, white-trimmed Silver Moon Winery, gaily lit with glowing sconces, is located on Old Route 39 NW in the hills of Dover. The town was laid out in 1806 in what became East Central Ohio. Dover began to grow when a stretch of the Erie Canal was established as a tolling station by the Tuscarawas River in the 1820s. Before the town was incorporated in 1842, Dover was known for its flour mills and, later, its steel mills.

In 1908, when Dover residents voted the city "dry," 22 saloons and 2 breweries were closed down. Repeated violation of the Volstead Act earned Dover an infamous reputation, and city officials resigned in droves. After the Repeal of Prohibition in 1933, Dover restored its good name and permitted the sale of dry liquor.

Judith Eschbacher, a schoolteacher, her husband Ken, who makes the wine, and their son, run Silver Moon Winery together. With a BS in business and a major in marketing from Ohio State University, Ken has owned and operated a chain of clothing stores, a printing/sign company, a chain of video stores, and a label/photo supply business for auto dealers for internet advertising. He also has a consulting business that helps people who are interested in starting a boutique winery of their own.

After a visit to the U-Vin Winery in Canada in 2000s, Ken got interested in the wine business. "Our approach to wine is to have the best wine at the best price. We are a small batch producer, and feel we need a larger variety of wines for our clients to taste and purchase at the winery." Traditionally, the couple buys the juice and ferments it at the winery. When it is ready, they bottle and label the wine for sale.

The Eschbachers initial goal was to provide a warm and friendly gathering place with a wine orientation for residents and visitors. The demographic of people who patronize the winery has made it a coveted destination-winery.

The Silver Moon Winery. *Courtesy Silver Moon Winery*

"Ninety-five percent of our customers, who come from outside of the area, are visiting Tuscarawas County," he says.

The tasting bar was designed as a meeting place for new and existing customers, eager to become educated about wine types and style, characteristics, storage, opening, glassware, pouring, tasting, and pairing wine with food. Customers are invited to taste any of the 35 wines available to determine which wines they like. One of the biggest challenges for people new to wine, according to Ken, is getting them into the winery. Custom wine-making is available, but is a small portion of their business.

All wine categories—whites from Chardonnay to Riesling, reds from Cabernet to Merlot, sweet wines from Romance Red to Kiwi Melon, and dessert wines from Southern Gold to Fire & Ice—are produced in small batches.

The Eschbachers consider themselves improvisers. They take pride in maintaining a small efficient wine facility that contains a number of 15, 40, 100 and 300 gallon tanks that they can turn over in four to six weeks. They introduce French and American oak nuances by adding oak chips and oak planks. Silver Moon Winery's best-selling wines are sweet and require no oak. Typically, their wines are bottled and sold young and affordable. "We produce our wine according to the rate of sale at our winery," he concludes.

Silver Moon Winery 🍇

Directions Take I-77 to the Dover-Sugarbush exit. Proceed west on State Route 39 west for 3.2 miles, then turn right on Old Route 39 NW, .4 mile to winery

Hours Mon.–Sat., 9 AM–6 PM

Tastings Daily when opened

Gifts Soy candles, wine apparel, olive oils, and wine

Picnics Limited

Highlights at Winery Selection of over 20 sweet wine and 35 kinds of wine made on premises

Events Swiss Festival; Fall Canal tour

Restaurant Light fare, olive oil & various breads

Prices $9.99–$22.50; 10 percent case discount

Brand Names Silver Moon Winery

Wines Thirty-five different wines

Best Red Midnight Red

Best White Luna Bianca

Best Other Wine Fire & Ice Red

Quote "We make our wines in small batches so they are all excellent." —Ken Eschbacher

Nearby Places to Visit Reeves Home Museum, Zoar, Atwood Lake Museum

Stone Crest Vineyard

10310 O'Dell Rd.
Frazeyburg, OH, 43822
Tel (740) 828-9463
E-mail stonecrestvine@earthlink.net
Web site www.stonecrestvine.com
Owner Mike and Cheryl Barker
Winemaker Mike Barker
Founded 2006

Stone Crest Vineyard, a 20-acre wine estate with a new wood frame house, stainless steel winery, and sloping vineyards, sits at the crest of rolling hills in Muskingum County in Frazeyburg. After a long search for land, Mike and Cheryl Barker, proprietors, discovered a beautiful property for sale two miles from the house they had just built. "Everything about the place was perfect," says Mike. "All we say, and the people who visit us exclaim is 'what a view!'"

The wine venture takes its name from the sandstone rocks the Barkers unearthed in their vineyard, an elevation of 1000 feet. The breath-taking view from the top of the peak looks out 20 miles across three counties— with the two church steeples in the small community of Perrytown being the most picturesque. The winery is 20 miles from Zanesville; 50 miles east of Columbus; 16 miles south of Buckeye-Newark; and 25 miles west of Coshocton.

A recent Doctor of Audiology, Cheryl, maintains her own Audiology private practice—giving clients hearing evaluations and dispensing hearing aids. "Her goal is to better serve the public, and be sure they get good care," Mike says. Cheryl handles the business details and sells the wine at the winery.

Mike has a degree in mechanical engineer and works full-time at the winery. "All my life I wanted to be a farmer," he says, following in the footsteps of his grandfather, who still harvests hay and maintains a herd of cattle. For their anniversary, spouse, Cheryl suggested they have dinner and visit her friend Dawn, who worked at the lovely four-acre Rainbow Hills Vineyard estate. "To us, it looked like farming on this scale was very doable." Besides visiting wineries across the US, the Barkers attended the Ohio State University Grape Wine Courses. "We learned to grow good grapes, to produce fine wine, and to run a cost-effective business."

The Stone Crest Winery. *Courtesy Stone Crest Vineyard*

From the onset, Cheryl's father, Reece Brown, a home winemaker for about 30 years, furthered the couple's interest. Once Mike made wine, he applied his mechanical engineering and chemistry abilities. "I was good at wine-making. My first batch of Concord wine won a Bronze Medal in the Connecticut International Wine Competition," he says.

In 2006, the Barkers purchased the land, cleared two acres of sand, clay and rock, and cultivated a two-acre vineyard. They planted Chardonnel, Chambourcin, Riesling, Cabernet Franc, De Chaunac, Seyval Blanc, Traminette, Vidal Blanc, and Marechal Foch in the moderate climate of Muskingum County. On one side the vineyards face north; and on the other side the vine-yards face west. The growing conditions on the south-facing hillside result in early bud break and late frost while the growing conditions on the north and west vineyards result in late bud break and avoid the frost. "Though the soil is not fertile, it is good for grapes because it forces the vines to dig way down and stresses them," he says.

A minimalist, Mike preserves the integrity of winemaking by using the fewest chemicals possible, and low-end sulfites. Fermentation takes place in a Pasco Poly Killer Chiller, a large vessel that heats or cools the wine fast. "I can take 240 gallons of wine from room temperature to 32 degrees Fahrenheit in 18 hours," he says. "This improves the quality of our wines simply by chang-ing the temperature at will; the process is precise and can be repeated. Mike practices micro-oxygenation with the reds, a process whereby he uses only the amount of oxygen that is beneficial to the wine. He also controls the amount of oak that is introduced to the wine.

"This tool provides flexibility for the winemaker," he says.

Today, Stone Crest Vineyard produces Gem Stone, a semi-sweet blush; Red Stone, a Concord; White Stone, a Catawba; Bouquet, a semi-sweet Vidal Blanc; Riesling, a dry white; Pinot Noir, a dry red; Chardonnay, a dry white; Waterfall White, a sweet white Niagara; Blue Stone, a blueberry and concord blend; and Cabernet Franc, an oak-aged red wine, plus De Vine, a semi-sweet red wine. "We just want to be known as a small family-owned and operated country winery, where people can come to relax by the waterfall, or look out across the open field to the forest. This is the place to be if you want to have a peaceful day and a glass of wine," he says.

Stone Crest Vineyard 🍇🍂

Directions North: travel south on Ohio 13, to a left and south on State Route 586 for about 25 miles. Turn left onto O'Dell Rd. for one mile, and turn right into the winery. South: travel north on State Route 146 for about 11 miles. Turn right on State Route 586 north for 5.5 miles, then right on O'Dell Rd for about one mile, and turn right into the winery

Hours May–October, Fri., 3–7 PM; Sat., 1–8 PM; Nov.–April, 1–6 PM

Tastings When opened

Picnics Permitted outdoors

Highlights at Winery Great wine; peaceful setting with waterfall and spectacular scenic view

Events Summer Steak and Chicken Cookouts

Wine Prices $ 7.95–$12.95; 10 percent case discount

Brand Names Stone Crest Vineyard

Type of Production Traditional

Vineyards Founded 2006

County Muskingum

Appellation Ohio

Acreage 2

Trellising Vertical shoot positioning

Climate Moderate

Soil Varies from clay, rocky to sandy

Varieties Chardonnel, Chambourcin, Riesling, Cabernet Franc, De Chaunac, Seyval Blanc, Traminette, Vidal Blanc, Marechal Foch

Wines Gem Stone, Red Stone, White Stone, Bouquet, Riesling, Pinot Noir, Chardonnay, Waterfall White, Blue Stone, Cabernet Franc, and De Vine

Best Red Cabernet Franc

Best White Riesling

Best Other Wine Blue Stone

Quote "Patience, attention to detail, and simplicity."—Mike and Cheryl Barker

BACK TO THE 40'S
RED WINE

12% ALC./VOL.   750ML

Swiss Heritage Winery

6011 Old Route 39 NW
Dover, Ohio 44622
Tel (330) 343-4108
Fax (330) 343-1092
E-mail info@broadruncheese.com
Web site www.swissheritagewines.com
Owner Nancy Schindler
Winemaker Chad Schindler
Founded 2002

The Swiss Heritage Winery is cradled in the centuries-old Broad Run Valley. In 2002, entrepreneurs Nancy Schindler and her late husband, Hans, established the winery on the site of the famous Broad Run Cheese House on Old Route 39 in Dover, which was recently honored as Ohio's grand-champion cheesemaker. "Our goal was to marry fine wine and grand-champion cheese," Nancy says.

Broad Run Valley has a strong historic connection to several generations of the Schindler family. In 1933, Amish farmers had built a structure from river stone and formed a successful cheese cooperative. As a young girl in the thirties, Margie Fankhauser, Nancy's mother, used to walk from Sugarcreek past the Broad Run Cheese House to Dover. "Hans was the cheesemaker there during the seventies and bought milk (used in making cheese) from the same Amish farmers," Nancy says. "They were facing hard times due to a declining market."

Subsequently, the Schindlers, who loved the restoration process, purchased the Broad Run Cheese House in 1978. They hired a skilled architect, who replaced the eight-by-twelve-foot retail market with a fancy Swiss Chalet. Over the next twenty years, the Schindlers added retail space and new merchandise five times.

The Swiss Chalet, situated at a bend in the road, was enhanced with two towers topped with weather vanes and highlighted by windows with awnings and dormers with edelweiss shutters. Flags and banners dance in the wind. Bright flowers and green shrubs highlight the landscaped grounds.

"We sell Victorian merchandise and nostalgia," says Nancy, who has created a niche market and following. She gestures to the juxtaposition of lamps, curtains, heritage lace, artwork, china, and accessories with Swiss Heritage wines, cheeses, and meats. "Customers are pleasantly surprised!"

The Schindlers realized they had the location and equipment to start a 4,000-gallon Tuscarawas County winery. Their unchartered approach to winemaking involved relying on their own ideas and their talent for pursuing the unusual.

"We continued with the Victorian theme," Nancy says. "We gave a Canadian design firm ideas for the logo, old photographs of our mother, aunt and uncle, and dog, Dewey. We also showcased Hans as a winemaker and cheesemaker, then Chad Schindler, our son. We took a fresh approach."

Swiss Heritage Winery sources high-quality grapes, fruit, and berry juices from Ohio and surrounding states. The wine grapes are fermented in stainless steel fermentors and held in a mixture of stainless aging tanks. The wines are racked and pumped through a coarse filter. They are then fined and filtered several times before the wine is clarified and ready for bottling.

"Our customers characterize our Swiss Heritage wines as mellow with good feedback after tasting them," Nancy says. "Our market niche definitely prefers sweet wines, and we also produce a few dry ones as well"

Swiss Heritage Winery 🍇

Directions Take I-77 to exit 83. Go west on State Route 39 for 4 miles. Turn right on Old State Route 39 to the winery

Hours 9 AM–6 PM daily

Tastings Monday–Saturday 9 AM–6 PM

Gifts Victorian nostalgia—heritage lace, lamps, china, wine, and accessories

Picnics Encouraged

Highlights at Winery Swiss cheeses and Swiss Heritage wines; eclectic shopping; Ohio wine and cheese gift boxes; gorgeous Amish countryside

Events Fall Ohio Swiss Festival, Spring & Fall Canal Country Wine Trail

Deli Swiss cheeses, domestic meats, and Swiss Heritage wines

Prices $8.95–$13.95; 10 percent case discount; cheeses and meats for $3.99–$13

Brand Name Swiss Heritage Winery

Type of Production Vitis labrusca, vitis vinifera, fruit, and berry wine

Winemaking Original and practical

Aging and Cooperage Stainless steel tanks and other cooperage

Appellation American

Best Red Cranberry

Best White Victorian Lace

Other Best Wine Peach

Nearby Places to Visit Amish Country; Swiss Village of Sugarcreek

Troutman Vineyards

4243 Columbus Road
Wooster, OH 44691
Tel (330) 263-4345
Fax (330) 263-5337
E-mail info@troutmanvineyards.com
Web site www.troutmanvineyards.com
Owners Deanna and Andy Troutman
Winemaker Andy Troutman
Founded 1998

The Troutman Vineyards, nestled on a crest on Columbus Road in leafy Wooster, exemplifies the small-farm winery movement in Ohio.

In the late nineteenth century, many land grant universities, such as Ohio University, had moved away from agricultural and mechanical arts. So, the U.S. Congress passed the Hatch Act of 1887. It provided funds for states to establish an agricultural experiment station under separate federal funding. Wayne County, Ohio, won the bid for an agricultural experiment station, and Wooster's reputation as a plant repository and tech laboratory became known worldwide.

In the 1990s, future devoted founders of Troutman Vineyards, Deanna and Andy Troutman, met at Ohio State University and discovered their mutual fascination with agriculture and farm products. At the time, Deanna was on the fast-track to becoming a marketing executive and Andy was a Lonz Winery Fellow in produce and floriculture. He graduated in 1996 with a BS in agriculture with a specialty in horticulture and microbiology.

Wooster, with its charming homes and century-old farms, arboretums and gardens, and theater and arts, was well known to the Troutmans. In 1997, they purchased a rustic farm outskirts of town.

In essence, Troutman Vineyards rekindled the spirit of the farm and its sense of place. "We reignited the land's natural *terroir*," Andy says. First, the Troutmans renovated the lovely old farmhouse with a new walkway, flower garden, and trellis. Next, they turned the old chicken coop into a winery and outfitted it with stainless steel equipment and oak barrels.

In 1998, the Troutmans launched Wooster's first and only high-quality artisan winery. The red wooden barn and surrounding pasture are home

Wonderful wines, beautiful view. *Courtesy Troutman Vineyards*

After three years of good weather, the Troutmans hand-harvested their first crop of grapes into lug boxes in 2000. The wine grapes were placed in a crusher-destemmer, then pressed in a membrane-basket press. The wine was pumped into stainless steel tanks, racked, pumped over, and lightly filtered. All the wines are held in stainless steel for six to eight months with the exception of Cabernet Franc, which is aged for six to eight months in French oak cooperage.

to their donkey, goats and dog. "We encourage people—families with children—to experience life on a small farm winery with animals." he says.

The superiority of the Wayne County agricultural legacy, which looms large in the eyes of Ohio growers, motivated the Troutmans to reach for the stars. But their stars came with names like Cabernet Franc, Vidal Blanc, Chardonnay, and Chambourcin. In the late nineties, they prepared and tiled six acres of trellised vines, planted in gravelly loam and silty loam, in a true continental climate. What was the result? "Beyond our expectations!" Troutman says. "The fruit in Wooster has a character all its own."

"Our first Troutman Vineyards wines were introduced in 2001," Andy says. The winery produces a variety of still wines. They include a dry but fruity Cabernet Franc with smooth tannins and a long finish; an inky but light and earthy Red Menagerie made from Chambourcin; a medium-flavored Chardonnay; a nearly dry Seyval Blanc called White Menagerie; an aromatic, peachy-apricot German-style Farmer's White; and a sweet Farmer's Red, a swilling wine. Troutman also produces a mineral but earthy Chambourcin Ice Wine. "We spend a lot of personal time crafting these fine artisan wines for our customers."

Troutman Vineyards 🍇

Directions Located southwest of Wooster on State Route 3, 4.5 miles south of where U.S. Route 30/State Route 3 split on the west side of Wooster

Hours Adjusted seasonally; please call or visit Web site

Tours Self-guided tours; group tours by appointment

Tastings Daily when open

Gifts Wine accessories, clothing, and gift baskets

Highlights at Winery 100 percent locally grown wines; farm animals

Events Annual Harvest Festival 2nd week of October, Cherry Festival

Prices $11–$38; 10 percent case discount

Brand Name Troutman Vineyards

Type of Production Classic

Method of Harvesting By hand

Pressing and Winemaking Membrane press and basket press

Aging and Cooperage Half American oak and half French oak; six to eight months in barrel

Vineyards Founded 1998

County Wayne

Appellation American

Acreage 6

Climate Continental

Soil Gravel loam and silt loam

Varieties Vidal, Chardonnay, Cabernet Franc, Chambourcin

Wines Cabernet Franc, Red Menagerie, Chardonnay, White Menagerie, Farmer's White, Farmer's Blush, Farmer's Red, Cherry, Raspberry, Blackberry, Chambourcin Ice Wine, Cuvée "D" Sparkling Wine

Best Red Red Menagerie

Best White White Menagerie

Other Best Wine Cuvée "D" Sparkling Wine

Quote "Cabernet Franc has great potential here."—Andy Troutman

Nearby Places to Visit Wooster shops and restaurants, Amish Country, Mohican Area

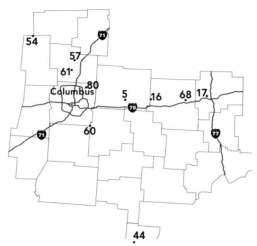

Mountains to the Plains Tour

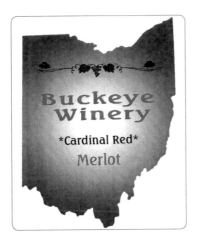

Buckeye Winery

25 North Third Street
Newark, OH, 43055
Tel (740) 788-9463
E-mail winery@buckeyewinery.com
Web site www.buckeyewinery.com
Owner Larry & Kathie Morrison
Winemaker Larry Morrison and son
Andrew Morrison
Founded 2007

The white brick Buckeye Winery with the burgundy awnings, founded in 2007 by Larry and Kathie Morrison, is located across from Courthouse Square in Newark, the county seat of Licking County, near the junction of the forks of the Licking River. The winery lies 35 miles east of Columbus. After construction of the Ohio and Erie Canal in nearby Licking Summit in 1925, Newark prospered in agriculture, publishing, grist mills, iron foundries, and other businesses. The population grew to 15,000 in the 1900s and 50,000 in the 2000s.

Born and raised in Newark, Larry worked for Owens Corning Fiberglass for 37 years. A native of Mansfield, Kathie was employed as a cardiovascular interventional technologist at Good Samaritan Hospital for 15 years. Together, they also ran a successful vending business. "We were always interested in trying new wines and juices from all over," he says. "We made wine at home, and visited many Ohio wineries," she says.

"We wanted to do something different; a fresh concept that involved people."

After the Morrisons visited another custom winemaking establishment, they modeled their business plan and winery after it. It took them a while before they discovered a unique, highly trafficked retail establishment (once a clothing store) on North Third Street in the heart of the Newark revitalization district. "We wanted to be good neighbors, and also support the community," he says. So, the Morrisons got going!

Arriving by car or on foot, one can't help but notice the compelling window displays featuring home winemaking equipment, supplies, kits, books, and other gadgets. One walks into a huge gathering room painted in wine, with tables and chairs for 80, a long tasting bar, and a three-dimensional mural of a beautiful Ohio vineyard by artist Brian Pagas. The Buckeye Winery wines are showcased in wine racks with some bottles standing, and the rest stored on their sides. "Customers love it. We can provide them juice from around the world. If they want to try an Australian Shiraz or an Italian Pinot Grigio, we have that under the Buckeye Winery label," she says.

The winery was designed to accommodate a lot of people at the same time doing different things. These include tasting over 50 Buckeye Winery wines by the glass or bottle with Ohio meats and cheeses; hosting special events and private parties; selling wine at retail, wholesaling wine to restaurants, clubs, or hotels, and making custom wines with personalized labels.

At the back of the Buckeye Winery is the fermentation room, where fun and work meet. It is equipped with standard winemaking equipment and lots of six-gallon glass carboys and 36-gallon wine tanks. The custom winemaking takes from four to eight weeks. It begins with tasting several Buckeye Winery wines—Razzle Dazzle made from Black Raspberry or Intrigue made from Gewürztraminer. Once a choice is made, a starter yeast is added to the juice or concentrate to begin the fermentation of small batches of wine.

"When customers buy by the batch, the price runs $4.83–$7.25 per bottle," she says. "When they buy by the bottle, the price ranges from $8.95–$18.95." Larry oversees the wine during the interim, then invites the customers to return to cork, bottle, and label their wine. Come make some wine with the Morrisons soon. They await your arrival!

Buckeye Winery 🍇🍂

Directions From I-70, take State Route 13 north to Newark. Go right on Church St., then right on Third St., 1 block to the winery

Hours Tues.–Thurs., 12–7 PM; Fri.–Sat., 12–9 PM; Closed Sun.–Mon.

Tours Yes

Tastings Daily when open, over 50 wines

Gifts Wine-related, home winemaking and beermaking products

Highlights at Winery Make your own batch of wine, then cork, bottle, & label it

Events Art Walk first Saturday in Aug.; Holiday Open House first Friday in Dec

Restaurant Light fare, pizzas, Ohio cheeses and meats

Prices $8.95–$18.95; 10 percent case discount

Brand Name Buckeye Winery

Type of Production Custom winemaking over four to eight weeks

Wines Over 30 Buckeye Winery wines from around the world

Best Red Sweet Red

Best White Farmboy (Liebfraumilch)

Best Other Wine Acai Red Raspberry

Quote "We're always interested in trying new wines and juices from all over. We like them all!"—Larry Morrison

Nearby Places to Visit Dawes Arboretum, Octagonal Earthwork Mounds

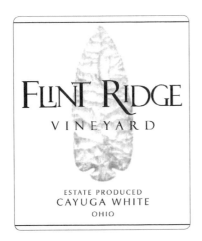

Flint Ridge Vineyard & Winery

8970 Pert Hill Road
Hopewell, OH 43746
Tel (740) 787-2116
E-mail news@flintridgevineyard.com
Web site www.flintridgevineyard.com
Owners The Jahnes Family
Winemaker Ben Jahnes
Founded 2003

Flint Ridge Vineyard and Winery, artistically designed and handcrafted to hug the contours of the Appalachian Foothills in Hopewell, is situated near a huge rock dubbed the Black Hand, which extends out into the Licking River Gorge. This peace rock defined an unspoken boundary of cooperation among ancient and often warring civilizations—Iroquois, Shawnee, French, British, and Americans—who journeyed from near and far to reach these valued lands. Their common interest, which lay five miles to the south, was the "purest flint in the western hemisphere," traded all over North America.

In 1978, Carl and Diane Jahnes, founders of Flint Ridge Winery (with their farm partners), discovered large pieces of different-colored flint in the soils of their newly purchased eighty-acre wooded hillside property. This flint that could break a plow blade was a yet-to-be-realized gift of nature. Wild grapevines naturally covered these lands, which had also been used to grow crops and raise cattle. In this rustic setting, the Jahneses approached their lives as artisans and created products by hand.

The Jahneses were inspired by Wendell Berry, a conservationist and the author of *Gift of Good Land,* who championed the idea of sustainable agriculture. Berry based his thinking on the idea that one should be a steward of the land, keenly aware of all who will follow on the land. In keeping, the Jahneses strive to apply methods of agriculture that are ethically, environmentally, and economically sound.

"Life should be whole," says Carl, a renaissance man and architect. "We nurture people, community, environment, and meaningful work to maintain a healthy ethic."

So, the Jahneses and their friends began to experiment. They raised cows, grew Christmas trees, and planted vegetable gardens and an assortment of blueberries, blackberries, strawberries, and currants. "Nothing we grew was totally disease-resistant," says Diane, a physical therapist for children with disabilities. Carl, Diane, and their children, Ben, Jeff, and Megan, built an Adirondack-style house and a cozy winery by hand with landscaped terraces, floral gardens and a wood-fired pizza oven.

During a visit to Monet's home in Giverny, France, Mike Seiler, a farm partner and artist, noticed the French grew grapes in a topography and latitude similar to Hopewell. Seiler suggested the Jahneses grow wine grapes. David Ferree and David Scurlock, agricultural researchers at the Ohio Agricultural Research and Development Center in Wooster, were asked to evaluate the property as a potential site to grow grapes.

Confirmed to be appropriate, Flint Ridge was cultivated on the northwest edge of a south-facing slope. "The hill starts at an altitude of 1,010 feet to an altitude of 900 feet, and the air drains to the Dillon Reservoir," Carl says. "Our soils consist of gravel, clay loams, pottery grade clay, four to six feet deep, over a shale foundation. The weather comes from the northwest and the Gulf of Mexico."

As artisan producers, the Jahneses hand-craft a wine product expressive of their family spirit and the spirit of this beautiful place. It is a quiet joy for them to look through the mist of morning

across the trellised vines of twelve different grape varieties. Red-tailed hawks soar above the vineyard protecting the fruit that goes into Flint Ridge's 90 percent estate-grown wines. "I am trying to discover which grapes grow easily on our land, and to achieve the best quality wine from our grapes, says Diane, who collaborates with Ben, their winemaker son.

At Flint Ridge Vineyard we are working to develop an ecological approach to wine production, that is a production system of scale and nature that fits into the local ecosystem rather than dominates it," says Ben, also winegrower. "A tree in a forest grows to a fixed size and doesn't continually expand to swallow the woods. In contrast, kudzu . . . is destructive to its ecosystem, and is considered an invasive species. We work on a scale that fits unobtrusively within the landscape, and towards a regenerative form of agriculture that is self-sustaining, and like a healthy ecosystem, grows through diversity. Not all of this may be evident when you sip our wine from afar, which is why we serve a local market, where the holistic essence of our wine can be fully appreciated.

Flint Ridge wines are fresh, dry, usually blended, very earthy wines typical of these flinty lands. "Our plan is to stay a 2,500-gallon artisan producer, improving the overall quality and making drier-style wines while also offering a few in the sweet to semi-sweet range," Diane says.

Flint Ridge Vineyard & Winery 🍃

Directions From I-70 westbound get off at U.S. Route 40. Turn right on U.S. 40, then go right and west on Dillon Falls Road (note convenience store with red roof). Turn right and go 100 yards uphill on Jersey Ridge Road, which winds around and intersects Pinecrest Drive at a T. Go left on Pinecrest Drive for 5 miles. Go right onto Pleasant Valley Road, past a church, over Poverty Run. Take a left on Pert Hill Road to the winery

Hours Sat., 12–6 PM; other days by appointment

Tours Self-guided

Tastings When open

Gifts Wine- and food-related

Picnics Welcome

Highlights at Winery Small Ohio winery producing drier wines than others; hand-built Adirondack house, winery, and landscaping inspired by Wendell Berry's model for sustainable live-work community ethic

Events Fall harvest and luncheon for helpful friends and volunteers: Small group tastings; Pizza days

Restaurant Light fare—fresh bread, cheeses, sometimes soup and pizza

Prices $9–$14; 10 percent case discount

Brand Names Flint Ridge Vineyard

Type of Production Handcrafted wines

Method of Harvesting: By hand

Pressing and Winemaking: Bladder and basket presses

Aging and Cooperage Stainless steel tanks

Vineyards Founded 1995

County Muskingum

Appellation Ohio

Acreage 4

Waterways Poverty Run and Dillon Lake

Climate Breezes blow over the hill and keep vines dry and ventilated on humid days

Soil Clay loam glacial spoil 4–6 feet deep over shale base, peppered with flint

Varieties Steuben, Swenson Red, Cayuga White, Niagara, Marechal Foch, Bianca, Chambourcin, Traminette, Vidal Blanc, Cabernet Sauvignon, Cabernet Franc

Wines Marechal Foch, Traminette, New World White, Cayuga White, Adena White, Red Tail, Hopewell Red

Best Red Hopewell Red

Best White Traminette

Other Best Wine Marechal Foch

Quote "Our goal is to craft distinctive wines which express our spirit and the spirit of the place."—Diane Jahnes

Nearby Places to Visit Hartstone Pottery, Dillon State Park

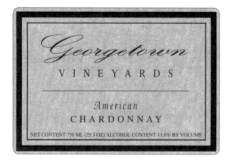

Georgetown Vineyards

62920 Georgetown Road
Cambridge, OH 43725
Tel (740) 435-3222
Fax (740) 439-5995
E-mail info@georgetownvineyards.com
Web site www.georgetownvineyards.com
Owner/Winemaker John Nicolozakes
Founded 1999

Georgetown Vineyards is located in the foothills of the Appalachian Mountains in southeastern Ohio's Guernsey County. A steep drive leads past hillside vineyards to a white farmhouse, an arched pavilion, a hospitality center, and a period winery. This hilltop paradise, which overlooks historic Cambridge, stands on land that President Thomas Jefferson granted to Zacheus Biggs and Acheus Beatty in 1801. Georgetown Vineyards was established there as a joint venture of its founders, Kay and John Nicolozakes, in 1999.

John Nicolozakes's maternal and paternal grandparents hailed from the isle of Crete in Greece. Between 1905 and 1912, one branch of his family immigrated to Ohio, and the other one settled in California. The Greek custom of sharing wine and food among friends in an unhurried environment was a deeply held family tradition. During a creative sojourn in the nineties, John had the good fortune to revive these practices in his own family when he ventured into winemaking.

"I produced my first wine from Cabernet Sauvignon frozen must; I also tried Ohio and Pennsylvania purveyors. I was most encouraged, however, by wine I made from fresh juice from California. I made more batches and bought oak barrels," John says. He was hooked by his discovery.

Between 1989 and 1990, Nicolozakes constructed an eighteenth-century colonial house with an American oak aging room and a wine cellar for his private collection. "This was the heart of our wine production," he says. He made the leap from amateur to professional in 1996 when he applied for a basic wine permit. In 1998, Georgetown Vineyards released its first premium wines—Chardonnay, Niagara, and Concord.

As demand grew, John joined forces with Sam, his son, who manages the retail sales and tasting room. French doors open into a beautiful room with track lighting, white walls, and a green-and-white tiled floor. Sam holds court behind the wine-tasting bar as the resident expert on the winery's newest releases. A black potbellied stove spews warmth in the dead of winter. The gift shop is a treasure trove for the curious, offering fine wines, glasses, corkscrews, baskets, mugs, cards, china, and accessories. "We sell Ohio foodstuffs, like jams, jellies, pastas, balsamic vinegar, and an imported Nicolozakes Olive Oil from Greece," he says.

Kay Nicolozakes, the event planner, lends her organizational skills and creative talents, along with her love of cooking, from fundraising charity events to detailed wine affairs. Occasionally she and her daughter, Emma, the winery bookkeeper, design one-of-a-kind themed parties, and simple culinary dishes to be paired with their wines.

By 2000, John had constructed an outdoor pavilion for parties of up to 35 guests and a handsome winery for his annual 5,000 gallon production. The 50-acre, three-wire trellis vineyards are planted in sandy clay soils. The temperate southern Ohio climate bodes well for the Fredonia, Concord, and Niagara planted in the North Vineyard and the West Vineyard. The bulk of the fresh juice—Chardonnay, Cabernet Sauvignon, White Zinfandel, Cranberry, and Rhubarb—is shipped to the winery in refrigerated trucks from New York and California winegrowers.

"I buy fresh juice, then ferment it into wine in stainless steel tanks in the winery or the barrel cellar," John says. "I rotate the wines, then cold-stabilize them in temperature-controlled, jacketed, stainless steel tanks, then transfer them back into stainless steel vessels. Here they are aged for three to six months until they are clarified, then properly bottled. The red wines are fermented on the skins, then pumped over and racked several times, then held in stainless steel before they are bottled."

Georgetown Vineyards produces one-third dry wine and two-thirds sweet wine. Its typical customer starts with sweet wines, then graduates to dry ones. "Many people go winery to winery doing comparative wine tastings," John says. To satisfy this market, Georgetown Vineyards produces Concord, its best red wine, Niagara, its best sweet white wine, and a dry Chardonnay and a sweet Cranberry, both other favorites.

"It's my philosophy to try to eliminate wine snobbery as much as possible," he says. "I don't believe that certain wines should go with certain foods, but rather people should enjoy what they like."

Georgetown Vineyards 🍇

Directions From I-70, take the Cambridge/Byesville exit (State Route 209). Go north and take the first left (before Bob Evans Restaurant) on Georgetown Road. Continue to the first stop sign. Turn right and go up the hill. As you descend, Georgetown Vineyards is located on the right

Hours Tues.–Sat., 11 AM–5 PM

Tours By appointment

Tastings Twenty-five cents per sample

Gifts Local food items; gift baskets; glasses and mugs with winery name

Picnics Two tables with scenic view and outdoor grills

Highlights at Winery Great wines and spectacular views

Events Harvest and Holiday Season

Restaurant Greek cuisine; Vineyards Catering provides catered meals for small groups

Prices $8–$12; 10 percent case discount

Brand Name Georgetown Vineyards

Type of Production Vitis vinifera, vitis labrusca

Method of Harvesting By hand

Pressing and Winemaking Bladder basket press with standard fermentation and winemaking practices

Aging and Cooperage American oak barrels

Vineyards Founded 1999

County Guernsey

Appellation American or Ohio

Acreage 50

Trellising Cordon, double wired

Waterways Wills Creek

Climate Temperate

Soil Sandy clay

Varieties Fredonia, Concord, and Niagara

Wines Chardonnay, Cabernet Sauvignon, Sauvignon Blanc, White Zinfandel, Cranberry, and Rhubarb

Best Red Concord

Best White Sauvignon Blanc

Best Other Wine Cranberry

Quote "It is my philosophy to eliminate wine snobbery."—John Nicolozakes

Nearby Places to Visit The Wilds, Seneca Lake, and Salt Fork Lake

Merry Family Winery

2376 State Route 850
Bidwell, Ohio 45614
Tel (740) 245-9463
E-mail lmerry@peoplepc.com
Web site www.merryfamilywinery.com
Owners Timothy and Lisa Merry
Winemaker Tim Merry
Founded 2006

The Merry Family Winery in Bidwell was named in tribute to the Merry family, which dates from 1219 in Yorkshire, an historic rural emerald green county in northern England, and the largest in Great Britain. The surname, Merry, was a nickname that described the personal characteristics of many generations, who were playful, carefree, and happy. That same joy is seen again in the current Merry Family wine labels, a replica of the historic Merry family crest. Three lions representative of kingship dominate the top of the shield, which is divided by a sash that runs through the middle; below it are two drinking vessels and the motto, "I stand fast and hope."

A native of Mason County, VA., Lisa was always interested in becoming a registered nurse. "I have great respect for nurses," she says. At the University of Rio Grande in Gallipolis, Lisa completed a Bachelor of Science in nursing. Later, she advanced to nurse

manager at Pleasant Valley Hospital in Point Pleasant, West Virginia. Tim, on the other hand, grew up in the small college town of Rio Grande, and had the good fortune of meeting Lisa when they were teenagers in high school. He later pursued a successful career as a union construction worker.

Along the way, family and friends influenced the Merry's interest in grape growing and winemaking. On Tim's paternal side his father, uncle, grandfather, and great grandfather all made wine at home. Together, they had a lot of good fun experimenting with brandy, fruit wines, and cold duck produced from any fruit they could grow. On Tim's maternal side his family originated from Slovakia, and they brought their winemaking traditions to the US and also inspired the couple.

But there was an older gentleman Rodney Facemire, the proprietor of Kirkwood Winery in Summerville,

A center of real joy. *Courtesy Merry Family Winery*

VA. that had the greatest impact on the young couple. For years the Merrys would make the four hour trip to visit Facemire, talk wine, and taste his latest wine releases. He would always respond in kind to their natural enthusiasm and encouraged them to start a commercial wine venture. "One day on our return drive home, my husband turned to me and said, "Let's try it!" So, they did!

The Merrys remembered that on this occasion, they wasted no time. Lisa got out her favorite notebook, which she carries everywhere, and started jotting down ideas for the vineyard, the winery, and the wines. They used their common sense and some good luck.

First, the Merrys took a hard look at the forest near their family home and realized that it was perfect for a hillside vineyard. They had a choice piece of land with sun exposure, red and yellow clay soil, and good drainage in the Appellation Ohio River Valley.

"We cleared the property of trees, ordered the vines, and planted a four acre, high-tensile wire, vitis labrusca vineyard—Catawba, Niagara, and Concord," Tim says. "We purchase Pinot Grigio and Pinot Noir, or buy the grapes or juice for the other wines such as Cabernet Sauvignon and Chardonnay," says Lisa.

After work and fun, the Merrys, entrepreneurs by now, took the Merry family name to new heights when they established the Merry Family Winery in 2006. People come from near and far to enjoy a grilled steak dinner paired with Merry Family wines at sunset. They love sitting outdoors at the former Jewell Evans grist mill, with the sound of a saxophone playing light jazz. "Give to the world the best you have, and the best will come back to you," they say.

Merry Family Winery 🍇

Directions Just off interstate 35 in Gallia county, at the 850 Rodney Pike At the end of the exit ramp turn toward Bidwell. Travel just a few feet and you will find the Winery on the right

Hours Tues.–Sat. 10:30 AM–8 PM, Closed Sun.–Mon.

Tastings Daily when opened

Gifts Wind & Willow products, tee shirts, Amish baskets, wine-related accessories

Highlights at Winery Live saxophone

Events Summer steak grill outs; Valentine Celebrations

Restaurant Steak and ribs

Wine Prices $10.99 except for Blueberry and Late Harvest Riesling; 10 percent case discount

Brand Name Merry Family Winery

Type of Production Handcrafted

Method of Harvesting By hand

Pressing and Winemaking Oak basket press, small batch production

Aging and Cooperage Stainless steel and oak barrels

Vineyards Founded 2003

County Gallia

Appellation Ohio River Valley

Acreage Four

Waterways Ohio River

Climate River effect

Soil Red and yellow clay

Varieties Cayuga, Niagara, Concord

Wines Janet's Medley (Red Raspberry and White Zinfandel), Miranda (Cranberry Shiraz), Shelby (Black Sherry Pinot Noir), Gewürztraminer, Merry Frost, Moonlight, Fireside. Cranberry Sherry, Strawberry White, Black Cherry Pinot Noir, Red Raspberry, White Zinfandel, and Blueberry Blush and several others

Best Red Gallia County Concord

Best White Gallia County Niagara

Other Best Wine Kiwi Watermelon Pinot Grigio

Quote "Give to the world the best that you have, and the best will come back to you."—The Merrys

Nearby Places to Visit Our House Museum, Bob Evans Farm, Gallia County Bike Trail

Ravenhurst Champagne Cellars

34477 Shertzer Road
Mt. Victory, OH 43340
Tel (937) 354-5151
Fax (937) 354-5152
E-mail raven_ink@hotmail.com
Owners Chuck Harris and Nina Busch
Winemaker Chuck Harris
Founded 1997

Ravenhurst Champagne Cellars, the only Buckeye State establishment with emphasis on the production of classic methode champenoise champagne with still wine as a by-product, lies on the outskirts of Mount Victory, a charming, rural 1800s village in central Ohio. "We are the only one who uses free run juice for the champagne and press for the still wine. Everyone else uses the whole grape for either process. And this accounts for our wines, with bubbles or not," say entrepreneurs Nina Busch and Chuck Harris, natives of Van Wert, Ohio, who established their wine venture in 1997 after starting an artisanal accessories business.

"I met a woman who wanted to drink more champagne than I could afford, so I needed to learn to make good champagne," jokes Chuck, an Ohio State University graduate in history. "Fortunately, Nina was a graduate in chemistry, also from Ohio State University." Both are organic gardeners and accomplished cooks, so having their own wine on the table when they entertained was merely an extension of that lifestyle.

In 1980, the couple relocated to their cedar-sided farmhouse to grow grapes at this unique spot, just east of the 1,549-foot-high Campbell Hill in Bellefontaine, the highest point in Ohio. "The storms come out of the West, and as they hit Campbell Hill, they progress north and south, then reconfigure near Marion," Chuck says. "Our vineyard is like a pebble in a stream. We miss the fall storms, but get rain the rest of the year. Between August 1 and October 1, the place is as dry as Death Valley."

The 4,000-case Ravenhurst Champagne Cellars, which owns three Union County vineyards, benefits from the warmer climate, good air, and proper drainage. The two-acre estate vineyard is predominately Cabernet Sauvignon with some Pinot Noir, Chardonnay, and Chambourcin; the four-acre Clayborn Vineyard, is mainly Pinot Noir, Chardonnay, and Cabernet Sauvignon; and the five-acre Chalamar Vineyard, has Chardonnay, Cabernet Sauvignon, Cabernet Franc, and Pinot Noir, Vidal Blanc, and Seyval. "We are vineyard driven," Chuck says. "We find what our *terroir* gives, and we maximize that aspect of the place."

A pink magnolia brightens the door-way to the cedar-sided winery, trimmed in white paint. It opens into a bright white California-style tasting room, featuring Columbus artist Brooke Hunter-Lombardi's Sunrise Over Ravenhurst and accentuated by vaulted ceilings and natural skylights. The room has hand-hewn cross-beams and a board and batten (stained with Pinot Noir) tasting bar, held together by handcrafted pegs and pins. "During a storm, our century-old red oak tree was downed. Once the tree was milled, it took four years before it was dry enough so we could work with it," recalls Chuck, who, with some help, did all the winery construction.

French doors open to a covered deck into a dining room, site of a new restaurant with vineyard views. Though Chuck and Nina know enough chefs, it's most likely you'll find one of them cooking in their new kitchen. "We're fond of the folks who come this way," he says, "They're like family—the twenty percent, who buy eighty percent of our wine."

Harris and Busch team up to make champagne and still wine in their stainless steel production center and their American and French oak aging cellars. Chuck points to the gold, bronze, and silver medals they have won in more than fifty-four wine competitions from coast to coast, including prestigious events in Los Angeles, San Diego, Riverside, and by the American Wine Society.

The Ravenhurst Champagnes are all hybrid, with the exception of the Grand Cuvée. La Terre Riche Grand Cuvée consists of a blend of three vintages of Chardonnay and two Pinot Noir vintages. Cellared for five years, the champagne is approximately seven years old. Grand Rouge Champagne is produced by bleeding the juice off the skins of Chambourcin grapes to achieve the color of garnet. With aromas of mandarin orange, this Grand Rouge exudes delightful flavors of cherry and strawberry.

Frequently an Ohio Gold Medal winner, the Busch-Harris barrel-fermented Chardonnay Reserve is aged on the lees to produce a silky, papaya-mango-flavored premium wine. The garnet red Cabernet Sauvignon Reserve, with a berry nose and taste and soft tannins, is ready to consume. And the richly blended Cabernet Sauvignon called "Velvet Hammer," an unfiltered wine of some magnitude, is produced from exceptional lots, with additional French oak barrel aging.

Open two weekends a month on Fridays and Saturdays, Ravenhurst

Champagne Cellars bills itself as a tempting destination for wine lovers with the most discriminating of palates.

"Winemaking, like life, is a constant source of miracles," Chuck says. Truly, Ravenhurst is one of them.

Ravenhurst Champagne Cellars 🌿

Directions From Cleveland, take I-71 south to State Route 30 west, Mansfield exit, to State Route 309 west to Kenton. Take State Route 31 south through Mt. Victory, 3 miles south to Yoakum Road. Turn east (left) to first stop sign. Back up 50 feet to the winery. From Columbus, take State Route 33 northwest toward Marysville to State Route 31-State Route 4 exit. Take State Route 31 north toward Kenton, approximately 15 miles, through Byhalia. Turn on the second road to the east, then right on Yoakum Road to the last stop sign. Back up 50 feet to the winery

Hours Open two weekends per month, Fri., 12–7 PM, Sat., 12–6 PM, call for dates

Tours No organized tour

Tastings When open

Gifts Wine-related items

Highlights at Winery Lovely central Ohio farm country; one-of-a-kind destination champagne cellars

Wines $9–$34; 10 percent case discount

Brand Names Busch-Harris and Ravenhurst Champagne Cellars

Type of Production Methode champenoise champagne and still wine

Method of Harvesting By hand

Pressing and Winemaking Italian bladder and hydraulic press

Aging and Cooperage American and French oak cooperage

Vineyards Founded 1980

County Union

Appellation Ohio

Acreage 11

Waterway Headwaters of Scioto River

Climate Located on the leeward side of Campbell Hill in Bellefontaine, the highest point in Ohio, different from most of central Ohio

Soil Clay

Varieties Chardonnay, Pinot Noir, Cabernet Sauvignon, Cabernet Franc, Chambourcin, Vidal Blanc, Seyval

Best Red Velvet Hammer

Best White Chardonnay Reserve

Other Best Wine Le Corbeau

Quote "Winemaking, like life, is a constant source of miracles."—Chuck Harris

Nearby Places to Visit Mount Victory for antiques; Piatt Castles

Shamrock Vineyard

111 Rengert Road
Waldo, OH 43356
Tel (740) 726-2883
E-mail Shamrockmail@aol.com
Web site www.shamrockvineyard.com
Owners Thomas Van S. and Emily Creasap
Winemaker Thomas Van S. Creasap
Founded 1984

The long, perpendicular north-central Ohio county roads bisect the flat soybean and grain fields of Morrow County until they reach Shamrock Vineyard in Waldo. A one-lane dirt road curves through gracious vineyards to an 1800s atelier, barns, and a summer swing shrouded by elegant pines and leafy maples. Tom and Mary Quilter, now both deceased, were the first growers in the district to pioneer hardy European-American varietals. The mantle was passed to their grandson, Thomas Van S. Creasap and his spouse, Emily Creasap, now owners.

The Quilters attributed their appreciation of wine to Tom's chiropractor father, a gregarious wine aficionado who often invited Sandusky vintners to the Quilter home to compare Ohio Grape Belt wines in the 1930s. These vivid memories stayed with Quilter through medical school and his time serving in the U.S. Navy through 1954.

Thereafter, Quilter accepted a urology assignment in Marion and a teaching appointment at Ohio State University. Quilter often said, "We grew beautiful roses in our garden, but in time we had an urge to plant French and American hybrids—possibly even *vinifera*, though it was difficult due to the extreme cold."

The Quilters joined Dr. Richard Miller, a medical colleague, to scout sites for vineyards. "There is no right climate around here for anything," Miller often said. "Growing grapes is worthless!" He withdrew from the wine project. The Quilters were undaunted, and persevered. "We had so much desire that we purchased 150 grapevines, but naturally we had no place to plant," Tom often said.

So, how did the Quilters resolve their challenge? They bought an old German farmhouse and eighty acres of land near Waldo from their friends Winnie and Albert Baker. Their first

Grapes on the vine. *Courtesy Shamrock Vineyards*

Tom & Mary Quilter. *Courtesy Shamrock Vineyards*

task was to plant an eight-acre test vineyard in clay soils to see if they could grow grapes in a climate not perfectly suited for the cause. They learned that some kinds of grapes did well.

They consulted the wine experts for advice. An early influence was the Ohio Agricultural Research and Development Center in Wooster. Journalist Philip Wagner from Boordy Vineyard, who pioneered East Coast wines from French hybrid varieties, recommended Seyval Blanc. Tom often said, "He just didn't know how cold it was here." A fourth generation grape grower ,Chris Stamp of Lakewood Vineyards in western New York, suggested Seyval Blanc, Cabernet Sauvignon and Cabernet Franc after a mild winter.

What the Quilters discovered was how to grow other vines and not cater to any one specific vine. "We dabbled, testing some forty-five varieties," Tom often said. "We gave up any previous notion what a specific fruit might taste like in Waldo. Some dry red wine might taste very differently. In the same way, we

learned that different yeast, for example, Epernay, produced different whites."

After decades of experimenting, Shamrock Vineyard settled on Seyval, Delaware, Vidal, Niagara, Horizon, Marechal Foch, Chambourcin, Cabernet Franc, and Chancellor. At harvest, grapes are picked by hand and brought to the grape-processing barn, where they are put in the crusher-destemmer. Then the grapes are separated and cleaned to utilize the best grapes, free from rot and spoilage. Tom's goal was to produce classic, old-style, handcrafted premium wines in their cellar beneath their house. The white wines are cold-fermented in stainless steel tanks. The red wines are fermented on the skins, also in small stainless steel tanks, and are aged for two years in small 60-gallon American and/or French oak barrels.

Shamrock Vineyard produces Seyval, Seyval D, Delaware, Shamrock Rosé, Vidal, Royal Gold, Buckeye Red, Windfall White, Marechal Foch, Waldeau Red (a derivation of Waldo), and Chancellor Noir. The Quilters up-beat, can-do attitude continues at any age to this day. "We willingly try new things," Tom always said. "When consumers demanded sweet wine, we changed in a heartbeat!" What a legacy!

Shamrock Vineyard 🍃

Directions See Web site

Hours Mon.–Sat., 1–6 PM

Tours Customers are given personal tours by the winemaker with a history of the vineyard and the winemaking process. Customers may leisurely stroll through the vineyard and enjoy nature at its best

Picnics Guests provided picnic tables, or encouraged to bring their blankets for a picnic in the vineyard. Groups of eight or more please call in advance

Events Summer Twilight Dinners at Vineyard: wine tasting, catered steak dinner, sounds of mountain dulcimer, and beautiful sunset over vineyard

Prices $9.35 to $20; 10 percent case discount

Brand Name Shamrock Vineyard, Chateau Shamrock

Type of Production Classic, old-style

Method of Harvesting Hand harvested by family, friends and customers. Fun and educational for all ages

Pressing and Winemaking Wooden basket press

Aging and Cooperage Italian stainless steel and French and American oak

Vineyards Founded in 1971

County Morrow

Appellation The Heartland

Acreage 4.5 acres

Waterway "The Crik," part of Olentangy Watershed

Climate Central Ohio—brutally cold winters; late spring frosts; unforgiving, hot, humid summers

Soil Three types of clay

Varieties Seyval, Vidal, Marechal Foch, GR-7, Niagara, Concord, Delaware, Edelweiss, Aurore, Norton, Traminette

Wines Seyval D, Delaware, Shamrock Rosé, Vidal, Royal Gold, Buckeye Red, Windfall White, Marechal Foch, Waldeau Red, Chancellor Noir

Best Red: Waldeau Red

Best White Delaware

Best Other Wine Buckeye Red

Nearby Places to Visit Harding Home & Memorial, Delaware State Park, Mt. Gilead State Park

Slate Run Vineyard

1900 Winchester-Southern Road
Canal Winchester, OH 43110
Tel (614) 834-8577
Fax (614) 834-5751
E-mail info@slaterunwine.com
Web site www.slaterunwine.com
Owner/Winemaker Keith Pritchard
Founded 1997

Slate Run Vineyard, defined by the rural-suburban farms in Canal Winchester, is named after the waterway Slate Run, which is part of the greater Scioto River and Walnut Creek Watershed just outside of Columbus. During the growing season, the nearby reclaimed Slate Run Wetlands, waterlogged areas covered by water or land, are abundant in wildlife—owls, frogs, ducks, and herons—that depends on the native grasses, flowers, and trees for sustenance.

Keith and Leslie Pritchard, natives of the Buckeye State, had the good for tune to sharpen their goals in mid-life. They searched for an outdoor environment that better embraced their family ethic and their children's lives. The Pritchards settled in Fairfield County, a region new to viticulture, and in 1997 opened Slate Run Vineyard. Keith Pritchard was born and raised on a livestock farm near Bucyrus, where he experienced the rigors of caring for animals as a child. His talents rested with the art of nurturing plants. "I enjoyed the fruit trees and tomato garden," he says.

During the seventies, Keith got hooked on the growing American passion and fervor for wine. While at Ohio State University, where he graduated with a BS in business administration with emphasis on production operations management, Keith also worked for a carryout in Columbus. "I attended trade tastings and developed a taste for wine," he says.

Keith's post-college career included distribution and packaging management, wine store management, and inside and outside sales. A wine hobbyist, he joined the American Wine Society and the Amateur Winemaker's Guild. Meanwhile, Leslie Pritchard pursued an upwardly mobile fast track as a human resources executive. The couple lived happily in a Reynoldsburg townhouse, where Keith crafted wine and Leslie critiqued it.

During the eighties, Keith's interest in wine grew in stages. In 1983 and 1984, he apprenticed for Tom and Mary Quilter at Shamrock Vineyard in Waldo. There he harvested grapes and pruned vines. "I actually collaborated with and learned to grow vinifera grapes from Dr. Robert Pugliese at Darby Creek Vineyards near Plain City from 1985 to 1992," he says.

That same year, the Pritchards purchased one acre of land and moved with their young children to a home in the countryside. They removed the trees and ploughed the earth to plant Vidal Blanc, Cayuga, Chancellor, Chambourcin, Cabernet Sauvignon, and Cabernet Franc. In 1988, the Pritchards acquired six additional acres, which they finished in vines. "Our plan was to sell grapes to amateurs and acquaintances, whom we befriended through societies and guilds. We had no intention whatsoever of becoming a winery. Amateurs interested in science, we experimented with a lot of varieties," Keith says. But it was Leslie who urged Keith to obtain his wine permit. "She mentioned it once. I guess that was all it took," he says.

The now four-acre Slate Run vineyards consist of a three-wire, multiple-trunk trellis system featuring fifty-eight varieties of vitis vinifera, vitis labrusca, French, German, Hungarian, and American Hybrid, planted in silt loams. "We make small batches of 14 blended grape wines, one fruit wine, and an apple wine," Keith says. Their primary emphasis is on classic, elegant, complex wines that age well, and they plan to upgrade the volume of semi-dry and sweet wines. Their secondary emphasis is to upgrade the quality but selectively reduce the volume of dry wines.

Friends voluntarily harvest the wine grapes, which are transferred into a crusher-destemmer, then put into a Wilmes bladder press. The white wines are cold-fermented in the fifty-degree-range for better balance and proper aging. The red wines, which are aged in part oak barrels and part stainless steel (with oak chips), are skillfully blended before bottling.

Slate Run Vineyard produces a vinous apple wine, a mild to sweet labrusca series, a hybrid German-style series, and its premium European vitis vinifera and high-quality hybrid series, which includes Premblage, Premcru, Prembourg, Premblanc, Premcess, and Finale, a 13 percent residual sugar late harvest Vignoles. "We like our red wines, and some white wines, well aged to taste like wine, not fruit," Keith says.

Slate Run Vineyard 🍃

Directions From downtown Columbus, take I-70 east to U.S. Route 33 toward Lancaster to State Route 674. Drive 6.5 miles south to winery

Hours Mon.–Sat., 1–7 PM

Tastings During business hours and by appointment

Gifts Wine- and grape-related items

Picnics Picnic tables available

Highlights at Winery Quality proprietary wines from 60 varieties of estate-grown grapes; unique, traditional stylized wines made from blended grapes

Events Holiday Open House first Saturday in December

Prices $8.99–$19.99

Brand Names Slate Run Vineyard

Type of Production batches of 15 grape wines and one fruit wine, an apple wine

Method of Harvesting: Hand-harvested by friends and volunteers

Pressing and Winemaking Wilmes bladder press and SK membrane press

Aging and Cooperage Variable capacity, stainless tanks, and small barrels

Vineyards Founded 1985

County Fairfield

Appellation Ohio

Acreage 4

Waterway None on premises; nearest creek is Slate Run

Climate Cold winters; warm to hot, humid summers

Soil Celina and Miami series of silt loams

Varieties 58 varieties of labrusca, French, German, Hungarian, and American hybrids; vitis vinifera varieties

Wines Apple Wine, Winsome, Rosily, Rurban Red, Slate Gem, Slate Blanc, Slate Rouge, Slate Garnet, Premcess, Premblanc, Premblanc Reserve, Premblage, Premblage Reserve, Premcru, Prembourg, Finale

Best Red: Premblage Reserve

Best White: Premblanc

Other Best Wine Finale

Quote "Don't make wimpy white wines—like oak as spice, not a dominant flavor. Make wines in a classic, elegant style for complexity, not for fruit bombs. Make wines that age very well and do not fall apart in a couple of years."—Keith Pritchard

Nearby Places to Visit Slate Run Metro Park & Living Historical Farm; Barber Museum and Mid-Ohio Doll Museum; Hidden Lakes Winery

Soine Vineyards

3510 Clark Shaw Rd.
Powell, OH., 43065
Tel (740) 362-5741
E-mail soinevineyards@aol.com
Web site www.soinevineyards.com
Owners Eric, Cherie, Tim and Sandy Sainey
Winemaker Eric Sainey
Founded 2003

Fifteen miles north of Columbus in the rolling farmlands of Central Ohio is the six-acre wine estate, Soine Vineyards. Two generations of the Sainey family—Tim and Sandy and Eric and Cherie collaborated together in 2003. An odyssey to the wineries along the western shoreline of Lake Michigan one Labor Day Weekend inspired their decision to explore going into the wine business.

"During a vineyard tour, we went on a hayride. We tasted the grapes and associated differences in the grapes and the wines. The winemaker talked about the process of crushing, pressing, fermenting, making, and aging wine. I had a chemistry background, and it all made sense to me," Eric says.

Willing to take risks on the learning curve, each person contributed their creativity and expertise. A resident of Westerville with a bachelors and masters from Ohio University, Tim is a geologist who loved to experiment with grape growing. "My father, the vineyard manager, became enthused as he started looking at the parameters and flavor profiles," he says. Also from Westerville, Tim's wife Sandy, is a retired teacher, with a bachelors from Ohio University and a masters from the University of Dayton. She provided the educational component.

Also a native of Westerville, Eric graduated with a bachelors and masters in geological sciences from Ohio State University; he also became a geologist and for years was a passionate homewinemaker before becoming a winemaker. A native of Youngstown, Cherie, a graduate of Ohio State University, has a bachelors in animal science and food science. "My wife has the most qualifications," says Eric.

There was no way the Saineys were going to relocate to California or the East Coast, so they visited Shamrock Vineyard and Slate Run Vineyards.

Eric and Tim Sainey, Soine Vineyards. *Courtesy Soine Vineyards*

"We needed to figure out which grapes we could grow and which wines we could market and sell," he says. "We came back and looked for land close to Columbus, and near where we lived then in Westerville and Hillard."

In 2004 the Saineys planted a two-acre, two percent, north sloping vineyard situated on the uplands between the Olentangy and Scioto River valley basins, which provides some air-drainage. The climate is continental with cold winters and hot summers. Nine cold-hardy cultivars consisting of vitis vinifera, vitis labrusca, and French-American hybrids are cultivated in Blount clay soils that hold the water. The Saineys use lime and fertilizer to help with nutrient deficiencies and drainage

tiles to divert the water away from the vines. The longer the Saineys are in Powell, the more they believe that the waterways have only a modest influence on the vineyard.

"From my perspective as a wine-maker, it is key to know which varieties to plant," he says, naming the varieties—Cabernet Franc, Chambourcin, Traminette, Marechal Foch, Cayuga, Seyval Blanc, Steuben, Vidal Blanc, Riesling and Landot Noir.

By 2007 Eric and Cherie Sainey had finished their family home on the property, and in 2008 the farm winery was constructed. They built new structures—such as their beige barn that blends in with the agricultural landscape, but captivates the visitor with its warm contemporary interior earthtones. The house and the winery both have a country feel with sitting porches. There is a crushing and pressing area, a fermentation room, an aging cellar, and a tasting room. Eric makes small batches from estate grapes and grapes from local vineyards—60 percent white and 40 percent red. Chambourcin is their best red, and Cayuga White their best white. "We are an urban center that grows grapes and makes wines. Our customers are pleasantly surprised," he says.

Soine Vineyards 🍃

Directions Take I-270 to SR 315 north for 5 miles, then left on Home Rd. for 2 miles, then right on Liberty St. for 3 miles, then left on Clark Shaw Rd. for 1.5 miles to winery on right

Hours Fri., 5–9 PM (varies seasonally); Sat., 1–7 PM, 1–5 PM (winter). Check the Web site for latest hours

Tours Upon request. Wine education courses offered quarterly and posted on Web site

Tastings When opened, or by appointment

Gifts Signature wine glasses, home decorations

Picnics Area next to winery in the vineyard

Highlights at the Winery Excellent quality wines in a warm and friendly atmosphere with an emphasis on fun. Customers experience a rural getaway in an urban center

Events Annual Fall Harvest Event— tours of the vineyard; Annual Spring Release Event—food, wine and music

Prices $10–$14; five percent case discount

Brand Name Soine Vineyards

Type of Production Small batches from estate grapes and grapes from local vineyards. 60 percent white and 40 percent red

Method of Harvesting By hand

Pressing and Winemaking Wood basket bladder press and traditional

Aging and Cooperage Stainless steel with oak alternatives, American oak barrels

Vineyards Founded 2003

County Delaware

Appellation Ohio

Acreage 3

Trellising Scott Henry, Geneva Double Curtain, Lyre, Vertical Shoot Positioning, and High Wire Cordon

Waterways Scioto River Valley & Olentangy River Valley

Climate Classic continental, cold winters and hot summers

Soil Blount clay loam, 2 percent slope

Varieties Cabernet Franc, Chambourcin, Traminette, Marechal Foch, Cayuga, Seyval Blanc, Steuben, Vidal Blanc, Riesling, Landot Noir

Wines Cayuga White, Riesling, Fusion, Autumn, Harvest, Chambourcin, Soleil, Seyval Blanc, Marechal Foch, Traminette, Cranberry, Vidal Blanc, Duové

Best Red Chambourcin

Best White Cayuga White

Best Other Wine Traminette

Quote "To increase awareness while building a prestigious reputation for quality Ohio wines."—The Saineys

Nearby Places to Visit Columbus Zoo, Zoombezi Bay, Olentangy Indian Caverns, Perkins Observatory, Delaware State Park

OHIO
Chambourcin
Red Table Wine
ALCOHOL 12% BY VOLUME

Terra Cotta Vineyards

2285 Rix Mills Road
New Concord, OH 43762
Tel (740) 872-3791
Fax (740) 872-3790
E-mail terra@clover.net
Web site www.terracottavineyards.com
Owners Donna and Paul Roberts
Winemaker Paul Roberts
Founded 1995

The hills and valleys along Rix Mills Road in New Concord take the traveler past quaint cattle farms where black Herefords reign as kings of the mountain and freshly mown hayfields become a canvas for art. Visitors who experience Terra Cotta Vineyards' striking panoramic views say they are overcome with awe. "It is where lasting memories begin," proprietors Paul and Donna Roberts say.

During the mid-eighties, the Robertses began to realize their dream to start a winery. "We visited many Ohio wineries," says Donna, a business manager for a Zanesville hospital, "and for three years we looked everywhere for acreage." In 1995, after an exhaustive search, the Robertses purchased fifty-three acres of land overlooking a lovely valley. "The site was ideal for wine grapes, with good air drainage and wind flow," says Paul, a talented welder.

Over time, the Robertses and their daughters, Alysia and Misty, saw the ideas for their wine venture take shape. They creatively drew on New Concord's rich history, its people, its land, its crafts, and their personal experience with these elements. The Robertses rejuvenated their property by replacing hayfields with vineyards—and derived the name, Terra Cotta Vineyards, from the red clay soils that penetrated their property to a depth of forty feet. The name also is meant to honor the region's reputation as a center for ceramics and Alysia's interest in making pottery.

Terra Cotta Vineyards was built with the help of family and friends and is characterized by rustic architecture and a windswept landscape. The grounds include the Robertses' spacious residence, a two-story wooden winery with a peaked roof and lovely porches, a covered shelter for picnics and cookouts, and various farm buildings.

The interior of the winery, a great gathering hall and tasting room done in a Tuscan décor, has a cathedral ceiling,

The view at Terra Cotta Vineyards. *Courtesy Ohio Wine Producers Association*

wide poplar-plank floors, and paned windows.

The gift shop features local pottery and also some personalized Terra Cotta Pottery, daughter Alysia Roberts' painted glassware, and other artisanal crafts. Daughter Misty Roberts conducts wine tastings and assists with wine and food events. Alysia works in the vineyard, wine cellar, and helps with food events.

The two and one-half-acre Terra Cotta Vineyards is planted along Rix Mills Road on a flat hilltop and down a steep hillside in red clay. The hardy, winter-resistant vines are planted to Chambourcin, Vidal Blanc, Seyval Blanc, Steuben, De Chaunac, Baco Noir, Catawba, Riesling, Cabernet Franc, and Traminette. "The climate is typical Ohio weather, hot, humid, but we always have a breeze on the hill, especially during thunderstorms," Paul says. After five

years, the Robertses' biggest challenge is how to quell the influx of deer in Muskingum County, which has one of the highest populations in the state.

At harvest, the wine grapes are handpicked and put in a crusher-destemmer, then pressed in a screw press and fermented in stainless steel tanks. The wines are pumped over and racked, then filtered and fined. They are aged in stainless steel tanks for one year with additional time in bottle.

Paul attended the Ohio State University wine short course for many years and obtained practical experience by observing the winemaking process at Willow Hill Vineyards in Johnstown. "Our goal is to produce quality wines that people will enjoy with family and friends," says Paul. "The emphasis was sanitation and chemistry—pH, acids, and residual sugars."

The wines at Terra Cotta Vineyards are mostly French hybrids and American natives. The Robertses have received several awards for their wines that range from dry to sweet. "Even though winemaking is hard work, we are living the dream we had for 15 years of owning a winery and making quality Ohio wines," Donna says.

Terra Cotta Vineyards 🍃

Directions Five miles south of RT 40 on Rix Mills Rd in New Concord, OH. For specific directions check the Web site

Hours Jan.–Mar., Fri., 2–6 PM; Sat., 11 AM–6 PM; April–Oct., Tues.–Thurs., 2–7 PM; Fri., 2–8 PM; Sat., 11 AM–8 PM; Nov.–Dec., Tues.–Thurs., 2–6 PM; Fri., 2–6 PM; Sat., 11 AM–6 PM

Tours By appointment

Tastings Daily when open or by appointment

Gifts Wine related, logo clothing, custom designed pottery

Picnics Outside shelter, porches, and side patio

Highlights at Winery Gorgeous view of Muskingum Valley; 53 acres of rolling countryside; informative wine discussions with owners and staff

Events Cookouts May–October; Valentine's Day; Chef in Vineyard Dinners with Flaming Dessert finale

Restaurant Nosh plates, wine and cheeses, other fare

Prices $8–$11.99; 10 percent case discount

Brand Names Terra Cotta Vineyards

Type of Production Traditional

Method of Harvesting By hand

Pressing and Winemaking Bladder press

Aging and Cooperage Stainless steel tanks and oak barrels

Vineyards Founded 1995

County Muskingum

Appellation Ohio

Acreage 2.5

Trellising Vertical shoot positioning

Waterway Muskingum River

Climate Hot, humid, constant breeze

Soil Clay

Varieties Chambourcin, Seyval Blanc, Vidal Blanc, Concord, Steuben, De Chaunac, Baco Noir, Catawba, Riesling, Cabernet Franc, Traminette

Wines Chambourcin, Seyval, Chambourcin Rosé, Country Ridge, Vidal Blanc, Terra Rosa

Best Red Chambourcin

Best White Vidal Blanc

Best Other Wine Chambourcin Rosé

Quote "Our goal is to produce quality wine for people to enjoy with family and friends."—Paul Roberts

Nearby Places to Visit John and Annie Glenn Museum; Ohio Pottery

Wyandotte Winery

4640 Wyandotte Drive
Columbus, OH 43230
Tel (614) 476-3624
E-mail valerie@wyandottewinery.com
Web site www.wyandottewinery.com
Owner Robin & Valerie Coolidge
Winemaker Robin Coolidge
Founded 1977

Wyandotte Winery is nestled in a neighborhood setting in northeast Columbus, Ohio, just minutes from Easton Town Center. The native stone, brick, and cedar gabled winery was built by Amish builders for Floyd and Peggy Jones in 1976, and Jones Wyandotte Wine Cellar started producing wine in 1977.

Current owners, Robin and Valerie Coolidge, began a love affair with wine after a visit to the Napa Valley. Valerie's Italian ancestors had long made their own wine and their visit inspired the Coolidges to learn more about winemaking. They began producing many batches of homemade wine. They experimented with different varieties of juice and fruit wines, and Robin honed his skills with each batch. After several years, the couple began to look for opportunities to start their own winery. A friend mentioned that there was a winery for sale, and through a series of fortuitous events, the Coolidges purchased Wyandotte Winery in 2006.

Robin and Valerie never imagined they would one day run a family-owned and-operated winery. It was a huge change for them. Valerie was a former owner of Gourmet Gifts, a retail store, who completed a degree in theology in 2005. Robin was a semi-professional cellist with a love of wine and the arts with a career in Information Technologies. After intense renovation, the Coolidges opened the new Wyandotte Winery in 2007.

Wyandotte Winery has the simple elegance typical of the Amish style. A pathway surrounded by a beautiful garden leads to an inviting green door that opens to a tiled wine shop and tasting room. The intimate wine shop features cedar wine racks, a well-lit tasting bar with stools, high-top tables and chairs, and a warm and inviting wine-themed décor. One can browse for or purchase wine gifts, partake in a wine tasting, or relax with a glass of wine paired with unusual cheeses. The comfortable

Wyandotte Vineyards. *Courtesy Ohio Wine Producers Association*

tasting room, available for special events, features soft lighting, a big screen television for game time, movie nights and corporate presentations. Guests also delight sitting at the picnic tables on the stone patio, and using the porch swing with views of the new Marquette wine grapes. "Our customers are both local and from all over the world. Some are tourists, some business travelers, and many are local residents," says Valerie Coolidge. "A wine tasting at Wyandotte is a fun and educational experience. We try and help people understand how to taste and appreciate wine in a non-intimidating way."

The winemaking facility at Wyandotte is in the cellar, and Robin can be found there most days crafting their fine wines. Wyandotte Winery sources grapes from Ohio vineyards, and fruit from around the US and the world. The details are what counts, combined with time-honored and time-consuming winemaking practices. Robin places an emphasis on making high-quality, small batches of handcrafted wine. "It is my goal to produce a wide variety of wines from red to white, grape to fruit, dry to sweet, so that everyone who visits can find something that they can enjoy," says Robin.

In the winery Robin adds yeast to the wine juice which converts the sugar into alcohol and in the process nurtures the environment to produce outstanding wines. The winemaking process can take several months to years depending on the fruit and the style of wine. "Winemaking is a continuous learning process, and every vintage we produce teaches us a little bit more," he says.

Wyandotte features several brands of fine wines. The "Columbus Classics" labels feature beautiful original watercolor artwork produced by local artist Bonnie Weir, each depicting familiar landmarks around the city with matching botanicals. The "Winemaker's Select" brand of wines are small production, first release wines that are very individual.

In 2010 the winery launched the "Wyandotte Wine Club." Wine Club members receive shipments of wine every quarter, get special gifts, invitations to special events, and credits for everything they purchase at the winery that can be exchanged later as discounts.

Reflecting on their winery, Robin says, "We are working hard to produce great wines that are accessible to many tastes, and that are fun for people to try and drink. We want people to be comfortable experiencing wine and feel at home at the winery. We like to say that people "enter as customers, and leave as friends."

Wyandotte Winery 🍇

Directions Take I-270 to Morse Road, head east on Morse Road, then turn left on Cherry Bottom Road, and left onto Wyandotte Drive to winery.

Hours Tues.–Sat., 1–7 PM

Tours Free every Saturday at 12:30 PM

Tastings When opened, $5 for six wines or $1 per taste

Gifts A well-stocked wine shop with wine-related gifts, a variety of Gourmet Wine Cakes made by Valerie, and custom wine labels for special occasions

Highlights at Winery Special events including: Murder Mystery Dinners, Wine & Food Pairing Dinners, Summer BBQ Series, Women Who Wine, Hump Day Happy Hour (Wyandotte Wednesdays)

Events Check the web site

Prices $9.99–$14.99; 10 percent case discount, free gift with a six pack of wine

Brand Names Columbus Classics, Ohio Classics, Winemaker's Select

Wines Statehouse Cabernet/Merlot, Carmenere/Malbec, Blue Grotto Chardonnay, Glass Garden Vidal Blanc, Graystone Riesling, White Roses Niagara, Grandstand Catawba, Ice House Gewürztraminer, Sweet William Red, Raspberry Summer, Cranberry Harvest, Hope–Pomegranate, Ohio Apple Wine, and Concord Wine. (See web site for availability.)

Best Red Statehouse Cabernet/Merlot

Best White Graystone Riesling

Quote "Wine should be easy to enjoy. Drink what you like!"

Nearby Places to Visit Blendon Woods Metro Park, Easton Town Center

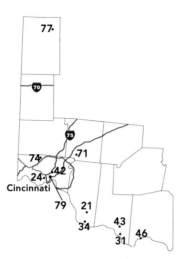

Ohio River Valley Tour

Harmony Hill Vineyards

2534 Swings Corner / Point Isabel Road
Bethel, OH 45106
Tel (513) 734-3548
Fax (775) 402-7424
E-mail wine@hhwines.com
Web site hhwines.com
Owners Bill Skvarla and Pat Hornak
Winemaker Bill Skvarla
Founded 2003

Just off of Swings Corner / Point Isabel Road, in the still of Bethel, lies Harmony Hill Vineyards and Estate Winery, one of Ohio's most treasured artisan wineries and country entertainment destinations. Established in 2003 by healers Bill Skvarla and Pat Hornak, the winery was named for the sacredness of the 70 acre National Certified Wildlife Habitat that surrounds their wine estate and their harmonious approach to maintaining it. The Skvarlas have long shared a reverence for their environment, a passion for flora and fauna, and a love of learning. Their mere presence on this land gives sustenance to their commitment to grape growing and winemaking.

Natives of Pittsburgh, Pennsylvania, Bill graduated from the College of Mount St. Joseph, and Pat matriculated from St. Francis Hospital. Both institutions encouraged open inquiry and free thinking with respect for all humanity. As they grew from a Cincinnati

apartment in the late seventies to a Withamsville Cape Cod, the couple added Amber and CJ, golden retrievers, who, like their owners, loved East Fork State Park. But alas, dogs without leashes were not welcomed, and the Skvarlas shopped for country property.

By 1989, they acquired a Clermont County Ohio River Valley farmhouse, horse, and grounds, where they planted medicinal herbs and raised horses, donkeys, several rescue dogs, and cats. Their peaceful country life balanced Bill's schedule as a Bethesda Hospital, ER-nurse and Pat's profession as a Christ Hospital nurse-anesthetist.

Experimentation in 1996 as a home winemaker, and winning medals as an amateur winemaker were the reasons they went into the wine business. "I won a Bronze Medal for my Riesling in 2002 at the Indiana International Wine Competition, and a second Bronze Medal for my Chambourcin in 2003.

The wine cave. *Courtesy Harmony Hill Vineyards*

We have consistently won medals in numerous major international competitions every year since then," he says. As they planned for their retirement, they diversified into wine grape production, and out of medicinal herbs.

By 2000, with the help of an experienced winegrower, the Skvarlas identified a three and one-half-acre site, rich in glacial soils, in the hot and humid modified climate of southern Ohio. "We found a prime spot for a Cabernet Sauvignon and Cabernet Franc vineyard, and an experimental French-American hybrid plot in search of our signature white wine—grapes like Riesling, Traminette, Vidal Blanc, and Seyval Blanc," Bill says.

"Our plan was to only sell red wine grapes. We were driven then by the high market value of Cabernet Sauvignon, and its positive health benefits, espoused by doctors we knew in the medical community. Our quest for an off-dry white was driven by local flavor."

Harmony Hills was built on its reputation for producing handcrafted, uniquely blended artisan wines with a maximum capacity of 1,500 cases and a present production of 1,000 cases. "We believe in an inviting, low pressure approach to wine. We don't get hung up on rules or protocol. If a customer likes a wine and likes what they are eating, we suggest they put the two together. It is all about having fun," he says.

Inside a unique midwestern wine cave. *Courtesy Harmony Hill Vineyards*

The 1,700-square-foot horse barn was transformed into a white winery with green trim, with a fenced paddock and a cupola on top, accentuated by flowers, shrubs and trees. The exterior features an outdoor café with views of the vineyard landscape. The high-ceilinged tasting room is the site of acoustic light seventies rock or gigs that frequently feature Bill on the guitar. The winery is well-equipped with a high tech lab, crushing-pressing facilities, stainless steel and oak barrel fermentation room, and a bottling line. The winery's spectacular Ohio oak aging barrel cellars is located in their new arched concrete wine cave. This style of cave is unique to the midwest. "With only four found nationally, our wine cave is the only one within a 40 state area," Bill says.

Guests and visitors are encouraged to experience Harmony Hills Vineyards with their friends and families—tasting wine in the cellar, enjoying a picnic in the vineyard, walking the trails, viewing the herb and flower gardens, sharing a juice tasting with their children, or helping their kids ride the donkeys.

"We hand-harvest our grapes and oversee the wine production. We use fermentation bins and send three-fourths of the red grapes through the primary fermentation. The grapes are then racked off and put in a basket press. We squeeze the grapes once and never want to overdo the tannin. We specialize in small batches of premium wine that our marketing manager distributes," he says.

Harmony Hill Vineyards makes wines with intriguing musical names. Rhapsody, a Cabernet Sauvignon and Cabernet Franc blend, is a favorite Bordeaux-style red wine. Concerto, a 100 percent Vidal Blanc at 1.8 percent residual sugar, is a Germanic-style white wine with flavors of apples and pears. Their fruit dessert wines are also gaining in popularity.

Harmony Hill Vineyards 🍇

Directions Take I-275 to State Route 125 east to Bethel. Turn right at the first light onto State Route 232, and then take the first left onto Swings Corner Point Isabel Road to the winery

Hours May–Sept., Fri., 5–9 PM; Sat., 2–9 PM

Tours During regular hours

Tastings When open

Picnics Welcome

Highlights at Winery Relaxing country atmosphere; excellent customer service; underground wine cave; daily live entertainment

Events Summer Kick-off Weekend; Thanksgiving Saturday Barrel Tasting Sampling Event

Prices $10.95–$16; 10 percent case discount

Brand Name Rhapsody, Rubato, Chamber Suite, Concerto, Ovation, Woodwind, Rhythm & Blues, Dawnsong, Berry Suite

Type of Production Artisan, handmade Bordeaux-style

Pressing and Winemaking Basket press/bladder press

Aging and Cooperage Ohio oak barrels in cave

Vineyards Founded 2001

Acreage 3.5

AVA Ohio River Valley

Waterway 1.3 acre lake

Climate Glaciated Rossmoyne

Varieties Cabernet Franc, Chambourcin, Traminette, Vidal Blanc, Seyval Blanc

Wines: Dry red, semi-sweet and dessert wines

Best Red Rubato

Best White Concerto

Other Best Wine Estate Peach, dessert wine

Quote "Harmony Hill, where no one leaves a stranger."—Bill Skvarla

Nearby Places to Visit Nationally Certified Wildlife Habitat with 1.5 mile walking trail on-site

Henke Winery

3077 Harrison Avenue
Cincinnati, OH 45211
Tel (513) 662-9463
Fax (513) 662-9444
E-mail info@henkewine.com
Web site www.henkewine.com
Owners Joe Henke
Winemaker Joe Henke
Founded 1996

The present-day Henke Winery is ideally located in a white 1880s two-story residence on Harrison Avenue, the old east-west corridor between Cincinnati and Indianapolis, in Westwood, a neighborhood of stately homes, wrought-iron gates, and green lawns. Joe Henke, a native Ohioan, established the urban winery and restaurant as a home away from home for friends and neighbors.

Joe's wine odyssey, one of learning by doing, began with his first batch of sweet rosé in 1973, expanded after he won a commendation in his first amateur wine competition in 1989 and moved into the noble varietals in the nineties. "My band of followers supported me," he says. Henke Winery was launched in 1996 in an old-fashioned nineteenth-century confectionery and ice cream parlor in Cincinnati's Winton Place. By 2001 the winery had outgrown this first location and moved to Westwood.

The response was substantial. Upon arriving in this old German, tree-lined neighborhood, surrounded by ethnic eateries, antique stores, and ski shops, one quickly realizes that this urban wine experience is unlike a trip to any country winery.

Thus, Henke Winery's success unfolded. Today, a trellised vineyard of varietals borders the parking lot. The foyer into the main house features wine barrels and wine bottles decorated with colorful ribbons and distinguished medals the winery has received. "Each artifact tells a piece of our wine story," Joe says. The European-style, windowed meeting room is tastefully decorated with a mahogany bar filled with glassware and Henke wine bottles, a faux marble tasting bar, softly draped chairs and glass tables, and artwork by featured artists in the Grapevine Gallery. "People literally stay all evening," Joe says. "And we welcome this practice."

A warm and friendly tasting room designed for wine lovers at Henke Winery. *Courtesy Henke Winery*

Henke's logo, a bird of paradise resting on a dogwood above a glass of claret, is a reproduction of an original ebony glass etching featured at the winery's first location. Over the logo is a quote: "From the heart and the vine," which explains the winemaking philosophy. Below the logo are concepts representative of the Henke Winery's European style of winemaking: passion, quality, and pride.

The 4,000-gallon, boutique Henke winery has grape contracts in Ohio, New York, and California. It exemplifies a uniquely urban winery that creates French-style wines without owning a vineyard, and treats guests to a gourmet restaurant that caters to groups up to 115 in period dining rooms.

Joe explains his small-bin technique: "The dry white wines are barrel-fermented, then aged on the lees to give the wines body and structure. The sweet white wines are fermented cold-style to retain the fruit flavors. The red wines, however, undergo a longer maceration to expose the grape's tannins and flavors, often cellared in American and French oak, with additional time in bottle."

Henke Winery focuses solely on vitis vinifera and French hybrid wines, and has its highest sales at the winery and within Ohio. The label of Cin Zin, its first slightly sweet Zinfandel from Lodi, California, depicts the Cincinnati skyline. The label of its coveted Cabernet Sauvignon Reserve features a taxicab with a reserve sign against the Cincinnati hills. The next time you are on the wine road, head for Henke Winery in Westwood for fine wine and good food. Cheers!

Henke Winery 🍇

Directions From North, South & East: Take I-75 to I-74 west. Proceed to Montana Ave. exit and turn left. Go 2 miles to Harrison Ave and turn right. At next light, turn left onto Epworth Ave., and directly into parking lot on right. From West, take I-74 to North Bend exit and go right. Travel 3 miles until North Bend Rd. dead ends at Harrison Ave. Turn left, and go ½ mile to Epworth Ave., then right and immediately into parking lot on right

Hours Mon.–Thurs. 5–9 PM; Fri. 3–11 PM; Sat. 11 AM–11 PM; closed Sun.

Tour By appointment

Gifts Wine-related

Highlights at Winery Handcrafted, world class wines paired with food made from scratch by a chef with the same passion for cooking as Joe has for winemaking, Best Wine in State of Ohio for Henke Winery 2009 Riesling and Best Red Wine in State of Ohio for Henke Winery 2009 Vin De Rouge

Events Amateur Home Winemaker's Contest; cork-sculpting competition; Grapevine Gallery featuring local artists monthly; Annual Barrel Tasting in November

Restaurant Casual to gourmet dining— pan-seared cheddar, garlic bread, soups, salads, pizzas, steamed mussels, crab cakes, salmon, baked cod, herb-grilled chicken breast, New York strip steaks, and filet mignon

Prices $8.50–$29.95; 10 percent case discount

Brand Names: Henke Winery

Type of Production European-style vitis vinifera and French hybrid

Pressing and Winemaking Traditional

County Hamilton

AVA Ohio River Valley

Varieties Chardonnay, Seyval, Vidal Blanc, Riesling, Cabernet Sauvignon, Cabernet Franc, Cabernet Sauvignon, Zinfandel, Merlot, Norton

Wines Chardonnay, Seyval, Vidal Blanc, Riesling, Cellar Blush, Vin de Rouge, Cabernet Sauvignon, Cabernet Franc, Red Zinfandel, Merlot, Vendange a Trois, Sparkling Chardonnay, Cin Zin, Norton

Best Red Norton

Best White Vidal Blanc

Other Best Wine Seyval

Quote "Our wines have passion, quality, and pride."—Joseph Henke

Nearby Places to visit Cincinnati Art Museum; Paramount's Kings Island

Kinkead Ridge Estate Winery

904 Hamburg Street
Ripley, OH 45167
Tel (937) 392-6077
Fax (775) 416-9184
E-mail NBentley@KinkeadRidge.com
Web site www.kinkeadridge.com
Owners Ron Barrett and Nancy Bentley
Founded 1999

The road to Ripley, a fifty-five-acre National Historic District on the Ohio River Scenic Byway, heads over hills and through valleys along the Appalachian Trail. It was in this southernmost viticultural district in 1823 that Nicholas Longworth, "the father of American wine," successfully planted the first Catawba vines and made the state's first sparkling wine. Just east of Ripley in the Ohio River Valley American Viticultural Area stands Kinkead Ridge Estate Winery, where in 1999 Ron Barrett and Nancy Bentley came to prove that world-class red wines could be grown on these unglaciated limestone soils.

Descended from a Columbus farming family, Ron was an electrical engineer before he was employed by Knudsen Erath Winery in Oregon. In 1987, he purchased the forty-acre Chehalem Valley Vineyards, which he planted to Pinot Noir, Riesling, and Chardonnay and later sold to Pacific Northwest vintners. In Portland, he met his partner, Nancy, who had careers in graphic design and technical support before becoming a Cordon Bleu chef. They settled permanently in the picturesque Ohio River Valley, where they purchased the 126-acre farm and a Gothic Revival farmhouse built in 1880.

"Our goal is to make high-quality wines exclusively from vinifera," Ron says. The five-acre Kinkead Ridge Estate Vineyard is planted on a ridge rising more than four hundred feet above the nearby Ohio River in bluegrass country. It was named for the Kinkead family from Scotland that settled the road in the 1790s. Once the bottom of a prehistoric inland sea, this district consists of ancient limestone soils that are unmodified by glaciation. Nearly thirty inches of well-draining calcareous clay soil tops the broken limestone. In this warm and humid but forever-changing climate, the growing season turns drier and cooler at harvest time. It is ideal for most Rhone and Bordeaux varieties

Nancy Bentley oversees hand-harvested vintage wine grapes. *Courtesy Kinkead Ridge Winery*

during late September, but the winters can be cold and hard on vitis vinifera.

The primary varieties planted are Cabernet Sauvignon, Cabernet Franc, Syrah, Petit Verdot, Viognier, Roussane, Riesling, and Sauvignon Blanc. The vines are cane-pruned and vertically shoot positioned at a density of fifteen shoots per meter. The practices of leaf pulling and crop thinning selectively maximize the overall potential for high-quality wine grapes. Additionally, the vines are spaced seven-and-a-half feet apart to minimize their vigor and maximize their fruit intensity. "Harvest parameters vary, but in general, fruit will be harvested with high sugars and low acids at full maturity and optimum flavors," Nancy says.

Typically, the grapes are left to hang until fully mature without excessive concern for brix, acid, and pH levels. The grapes are then harvested by hand and transported to the Kinkead Ridge Estate Winery, a small, yellow, wood-and-stone artisan house near the 126-acre estate. "Our focus is to make select premium wines in very limited quantities," says Ron. "We have complete control of our estate from hand-grafting our own vines to making our handcrafted, estate-grown wines."

Ron and Nancy are deeply committed to revitalizing this historic grape-growing district. The couple advocates for limited production of fine vitis vinifera wines. The white wines are cold-fermented to preserve any volatile components. The fruit from the vineyard defines the white wines, and no oak is used in white wine production. Red wines are made in small lots, a time-consuming and labor-intensive practice. The combination of cold maceration and hot fermentation produces robust wines with intense fruit and chewy tannins that are aged in both French and American oak.

These dedicated wine enthusiasts say their motto is encompassed in a quote from Goethe: "Whatever you can do or dream you can, begin it." They have experienced a profound response to their vintages from the Ohio River Valley. Their wines include Cabernet Sauvignon, Cabernet Franc, Syrah, Viognier/Roussane, and a Sauvignon Blanc/Semillon blend. In some vintages, varietal blends are named Revelation. "We pick the fruit ripe, and people cannot believe these wines are from Ohio," Nancy says. Try them and see for yourself!

Kinkead Ridge Estate Winery 🍃

Directions. The winery is east of downtown, three blocks behind McDonalds

Hours Holiday weekends, tastings and retail sales by appointment, when quantities permit, the winery is open on summer Sat.; see Web site

Tours Annual Vineyard Tour, Labor Day Weekend

Tastings Holiday weekends, group tastings by appointment; see Web site

Gifts Glasses with logo

Picnics Picnic area along Ohio River in Ripley

Highlights at Winery World-class estate grown vitis vinifera; joint effort with Kentucky to improve Ohio River Valley AVA; two wines made Tom Stevenson's international Top Ten List of Exciting Wine Finds

Events White wine release, Memorial Day; red wine release and annual vineyard tour, Labor Day; Saturday after Thanksgiving, Annual Barrel Tasting

Prices $10.95–$19.95; 10 percent case discount

Brand Names Kinkead Ridge and River Village Cellars

Type of Production Hand-grafted vines to handcrafted premium, estate-grown wines

Method of Harvesting By hand

Pressing and Winemaking Bladder press, with limited production of vinifera wines

Aging and Cooperage French and American oak; reds are barrel aged 18 months

Vineyards Founded 1999

County Browns

AVA Ohio River Valley

Acreage 5

Waterways Proximity to Eagle Creek, which drains to the Ohio River

Climate Modified continental

Soil Calcareous clay over ancient unglaciated limestone

Varieties Syrah, Cabernet Sauvignon, Cabernet Franc, Petit Verdot, Viognier, Roussanne, Riesling, Sauvignon Blanc, experimental plantings of Nebbiolo and Sangiovese

Wines Cabernet Sauvignon, Cabernet Franc, Petit Verdot, Riesling, Viognier/Roussanne, red Revelation blend, white Revelation blend, Syrah

Best red Cabernet Sauvignon

Best white Viognier/Roussane

Other best wine Petit Verdot

Nearby Places to Visit Rankin and Parker houses; Ripley antique shops

Lakeside Vineyard & Winery

3324 State Route 756
Felicity, Ohio, 45120
Tel (513) 876-1810
E-mail info@lakesidevineyard.com
Web site www.lakesidevineyard.com
Owners Tim and Lynn Downey
Winemakers Tim and Lynn Downey
Founded 2007

The classic Lakeside Vineyard and Winery in Felicity stands less than a mile from the highest point in Clermont County at 950 feet and four miles from the lowest point in Clermont County at 450 feet. In 1993 Tim and Lynn Downey, owners, purchased an easterly positioned 105-acre farm property on gently rolling land and named it Bluebird Meadows.

The Downeys are from families with several generations from the area. Tim, a native of Goshen, works for Duke Energy in Cincinnati in information technology. Lynn, a native of Loveland, taught high school biology, and now works in consumer and sensory research for Proctor & Gamble in Cincinnati. "I tend to take a more logical approach while Lynn is more consumer-oriented," he says.

Over the years, the Downeys experimented with their farm and got interested in fruit, wine and other foods. In

1997 Tim read an article published by Ohio State University that stated that the 34 wineries in Ohio had imported 1,000 tons of grapes for the 1996 harvest. This focused their thinking about becoming winegrowers, then eventually winemakers.

"Our goal is to provide a relaxing atmosphere for wine drinkers, new or knowledgeable, that allows for opportunities to learn more about wines and vineyard management. Our wines range from easy-to-drink sweeter wines to something the more educated and critical consumers can enjoy. Meeting new people each week, having them sample our wines, and then watch the smiles and nods of approval is heartwarming," he says.

Located in the heart of the Ohio River Valley AVA, Lakeside Vineyard, is influenced by the moderating climate due to its proximity north and east of the Ohio River. The well-drained

Avonburg and Rossmoyne silt loam soils are planted with 17 varieties of grapes, including American and French American hybrids that produce dry, off-dry, and semi-sweet wines.

In 1999, the Downeys began planting 50 vines each of Niagara, De Chaunac, Cayuga, Cynthiana, Vidal, and Chambourcin on one-third of an acre. By the winter of 1999–2000, they erected a high-wire quadrilateral cordon trellis for three additional acres of grapes. That spring, the Downeys drilled over 2,200 holes suitable for planting Traminette, Reliance, Seyval and Marechal Foch. The vineyard was expanded in 2001 and again in 2002 to reach the current seven acres.

"We have complementing but overlapping palates, which meet in the floral zone. I can pull out oaks and earthy characters while Lynn is able to pick up on lighter notes. I also will drink sweeter wines, so that's a good benchmark; when she says it's too sweet, I know to go half a percent," he says.

The Downeys researched wineries in several states during their two-year winery operations research project. Several owners, some that purchased their grapes and produced award winning wines, encouraged them to build a winery. Construction commenced in 2002 on their energy-efficient, 6,200 square foot facility. The building features a drive-through crush pad, a production area, an aging room for their oak barrels, case storage, a wine lab, a commercial kitchen and a tasting room that can seat 50 guests.

Lakeside Vineyard & Winery 🍃

Directions Take I-275 to State Route 32 East, to State Route 133 South to State Route 756 East

Hours Saturday: 12 PM–9 PM

Tours Vineyard tours vary with season: cover pruning, flowering, cluster thinning, shoot positioning, leaf pulling and harvesting; winery tours cover equipment and winemaking

Tastings When open, $0.50 per one ounce sample

Gifts Wine games, charms, racks, bottle lamps

Picnics Welcome in vineyard

Highlights at the Winery Goal is to educate consumer by putting them at ease by taking extra time, not to intimidate; adjust our approach to meet consumer's comfort level

Events Summer Festival & Family Day

Restaurant Light fare, Italian emphasis

Wine Prices $8–$14; 10 percent case discount

Brand Name Lakeside Vineyard

Type of Production Hands on, 300 liter to 2,000 liter batches

Method of Harvesting By hand

Pressing and Winemaking Stainless steel basket press, two types of crusher-destemmer

Aging and Cooperage Stainless steel, French and Hungarian oak

Vineyards Founded 1999

County Clermont

AVA Ohio River Valley

Acreage 7

Trellising High-wire quadrilateral cordon

Climate Ohio River influence

Soil Well-drained, Avonburg and Rossmoyne silt loam

Varieties: Niagara, De Chaunac, Cayuga, Cynthiana, Vidal, Chambourcin, Traminette, Reliance, Seyval, Marechal Foch

Wines Brilliance Therapy, De Chaunac, Cynthiana, Crazy, Enchanted, Vidal, Traminette, Amoré, Splash, Chill, Reggae, Temptress, Masquerade

Best Red Therapy

Best White Brilliance

Best Other Wine Chill

Philosophy "As a winegrower, I think of myself as a teacher, my students are the grapes and their parents are the vines. My job is to help my students reach their full potential by supporting their strengths and limiting the negative influences in their growing environment."—Tim Downey

Nearby Places to Visit: Living and Working with the Ohio River, Harmony Hill Dairy House & Historical Museum

Meier's Wine Cellars

6955 Plainfield Road
Cincinnati, OH 45236
Tel (513) 891-2900 or (800) 346-2941
Fax (513) 891-6370
E-mail info@meierswinecellars.com
Web site www.meierswinecellars.com
Owner Paramount Distillers, Inc.
Winemaker Bob Distler
Founded 1865

In 1856, the visionary John Michael Meier, founder of Cincinnati's Meier's Wine Cellars, the oldest and largest winery in Ohio, journeyed from Bavaria's vineyards by train, across the Atlantic by schooner, and over the Appalachian Mountains by horse-cart to Reading, a German settlement near Cincinnati, in search of a better life. Meier and Kunigunde Seidenbaden, his new spouse, established a 164-acre homestead with a farm, livestock, and vineyard in Kenwood on the Cincinnati-Zanesville Pike.

Meier longed for aspects of his European homeland, especially the fine wines and plentiful bounty. Rhine winegrowers shipped him healthy German rootstock, but when he planted them, they died from the severe winter temperatures. Meier's son John Conrad Meier, the vineyard manager, contacted aristocratic lawyer Nicholas Longworth, one of the wealthiest winegrowers in

America. Longworth had had legendary success growing Catawba, a native American grape, in Cincinnati, and the Meiers wished to share in his good fortune. So, they replaced their German varietals with six hundred acres of Catawba. This decision defined winegrowing and winemaking at Meier's Wine Cellars for the next 140 years.

As Cincinnati prospered in the late 1800s, so did Meier's Wine Cellars. In 1895, John Conrad's sister tasted some unfermented wine and unintentionally discovered that Catawba grapes make excellent fresh grape juice. Thus, the John C. Meier Grape Juice Company was born.

In 1900, John C. Meier sold the Kenwood property and purchased six acres of Silverton land along the Baltimore & Ohio Railroad line. A winery was built—and it remains Meier's Wine Cellars' present location today. The winery features a wood-and-stone

The interior features hand-hewn beams and stone fireplace. *Courtesy Meier's Wine Cellars*

great room, hand-hewn beams, a stone fireplace, and an elongated tasting bar. The bookcase, by far one of the most interesting historic features, displays Meier's wines, labels, medals, awards, and photos. The outdoor terrace, with hanging flower baskets, leads to what was once a posh 1920s garden with pedestals and statuary, now used for entertaining. There is a gift shop, which sells books, baskets, gadgets, glasses, and wine. The winery also features a five-acre wine-production center and an aging cellar equipped with stainless steel and oak tanks.

During Prohibition, Meier's Wine Cellars survived by making grape juice. By 1941, the winery had expanded its reach and purchased vineyards on the Isle of St. George, the northernmost of the Erie Islands northwest of Sandusky.

The island's century-old winegrowing legacy in glacial limestone soils, with a growing season six weeks longer than the mainland, produced Catawba, Delaware, Concord, Niagara, and other grapes. Meier's also buys grapes from winegrowers throughout Ohio, New York, and Pennsylvania.

In 1976, Robert Gottesman, the owner of Paramount Distillers in Cleveland, acquired Meier's Wine Cellars along with two hundred acres of vineyard on North Bass Island in western Lake Erie.

Paramount also owned Firelands Winery, Lonz Winery, and Mon Ami Restaurant and Historic Winery. A founding member of the Ohio Wine Producers Association, Gottesman contributed to the rebirth of the Ohio wine industry and preservation of the Erie Islands. After his death in 2000, Paramount Distillers sold all its wine and vineyard holdings to John Kronburg, an Ohio and Florida real estate developer, with the exception of the Meier's Wine Cellars.

In 1995, Bob Distler, who had been champagne maker at Weibel Champagne Cellars, then winemaker at Taylor and Great Western, was hired as one of several winemakers at Meier's Wine Cellars. "People have been drinking Meier's wines all their life," he says. "Our goal is to deliver them the best glass of wine. Thirty-year Pink Catawba customers expect a consistent product."

Meier's Wine Cellars 🍃

Directions From I-71, take exit 12, Montgomery Road. Head west on Montgomery Road and turn right on Plainfield Road to the winery

Hours Tues.–Sat. 9 AM–5 PM

Tours Video presentation in lieu of tours

Tastings See hours above

Gifts Wine accessories, books, glassware, wines, jewelry, and clothing

Picnics Garden and patio

Highlights at Winery One of Ohio's oldest and largest wineries

Events Annual June Art Festival; Halloween Party

Prices $4–14; 10 percent case discount

Brand Names Meier's Wine Cellars, J.C. Meier Sparkling Non-Alcoholic Juice, Reiem

Type of Production Still wine, bulk-process champagne, and sparkling juice

Aging and Cooperage Stainless steel tanks and American oak

Appellation American

Varieties 42 types

Wines Sauternes, Haut Sauterne, White Catawba, Walleye White, Concord, Red Seedling, Spiced Wine, Black Berry, Pink Catawba, Lakeside Vines Rosato

Champagnes Reiem Brut, Reiem White, Reiem Pink, Reiem Spumante

Best Red Red Seedling

Best White White Table Wine

Other Best Wine No. 44 Sherry and No. 44 Port

Quote "We make a wine product our loyal customers will always enjoy." —Robert Distler

Nearby Places to Visit Kings Island; Newport Aquarium

Meranda-Nixon Winery

6517 Laycock Rd.
Ripley, OH 45167
Tel (937) 392-4654
Fax (937) 392-4654
E-mail seinavineyards@myway.com
Web site www.meranda-nixonwinery.com
Owners Seth & Tina Meranda
Winemaker Seth Meranda
Founded 2003

South of Georgetown, and north of Ripley, just off of the north-south US 68, not far from the Ohio River in southern Ohio, is the home of the Meranda-Nixon Winery.

Owners Seth and Tina Meranda acquired the 170-acre tobacco farm once belonging to Seth's great-grandfather James Laycock, from Seth's grandfather Elroy Laycock, in 1999.

Seth, one of five boys, grew up in Georgetown in Brown County, with views of the Ohio River Valley. His family grew tobacco and raised pure-bred, black-with-a-white-belt Hampshire hogs, imported from Scotland to America in 1825. He excelled in the U.S. Department of Agriculture 4-H Club, where as a youth he learned citizenship, leadership, and life skills through experiential learning. Twice Seth was recognized and appeared on the *David Letterman Show* for cultivating some of the largest pumpkins, watermelons, and cantaloupes in the United States. "That experience expanded my horizons," he says. In 1994, he graduated with a B. S. in food sciences from Ohio State University.

Tina, whose brother introduced her to Seth in the 1990s, was raised on a standard-bred horse farm in Lebanon in Warren County. Standardbreds are a breed of horse known for their ability to race in harness at a trot or pace. A descendant of one of the most powerful political families in Warren County's history, Tina's grandfather Corwin Nixon, was a 30-year Ohio legislator and 14-year Republican minority-leader. "Tina is very people-oriented and outgoing," he says. In 1995, she received a B. S. in surgery technology from Cincinnati State University. Seven years passed before Seth and Tina met again, then married in 1998.

A driveway wends its way between the four-acre-European vineyard, past the Meranda's Cape Cod family home, to a tan building with a sloped roofline, covered veranda, trimmed in natural wood with big windows, outdoor lighted sconces, benches and ornamental shrubs. Inside is the Tuscan tasting room with its decorative murals and comfortable gathering place, which overlooks a 3.5 acre American vineyard. Adjoining it is a renovated winery barn for crushing, pressing, fermenting, aging, bottling, and case storage. The Merandas attribute their do-it-yourself spirit to their early hands-on learning passed down by their parents and forebearers.

As the tobacco market dissolved in the mid-1990s, the Merandas explored other economic options for their land. They attended courses and conferences on viticulture and vinification at the University of Missouri and Ohio State University. In 2003 Seth and Tina selected a location for their vineyard—a glaciated plateau over limestone at the top of a watershed with superior air drainage to Straight Creek and Red Oak Creek in Brown County. They also benefited

from the Ohio River Valley AVA—its moderated Ohio River climate and vertical shoot positioned and high cordon trellised vines. This included three acres of Traminette and Cabernet Sauvignon planted in 2003; one acre of Cabernet Franc and Chardonnay planted in 2005; one acre of Norton and Catawba cultivated in 2006, and one acre of Traminette in 2007.

The Merandas enjoy the back and forth stimulation and exchange that customers bring to their wine enterprise. Tina heads the marketing operation and works at retail in the tasting room. "She handles the people, the product, and shares daily feedback," he says. Seth manages the vineyard and oversees winemaking. "As I am independent by nature, I like to make my own decisions." Seth prides himself in producing a new world style of wine. He is taking the best wine grapes and showcasing a new range of possibilities for the Ohio River Valley. "We are revitalizing the Ohio River Valley one vine at a time," he says.

Meranda-Nixon Winery 🍁🍂

Directions From Cincinnati, take State Route 471 south to I-275 northeast, to State Route 125 east to Ohio 68 south to a right on Laycock Rd. to the winery. From Dayton, take I-75 south or I-71 south to I-275 southeast to Ohio 32 east to a right on Laycock Rd to second driveway on the right to winery. From Maysville, cross the bridge into Aberdeen, then take State Route 52 to State Route 68 north to a left on Laycock Rd. to second driveway on the right to winery

Hours Thurs., 11 AM–7 PM; Fri.–Sat. 11–9:30 PM

Tours Self-guided, educational and historic

Tastings Thurs., 11 AM–7 PM; Fri., 11 AM–9 PM; Sat., 11 AM–9:30 PM

Gifts Corkscrew, hats, cards, charms, lighted wine bottles and wine glasses

Picnics Welcome

Highlights at Winery Top quality, award-winning wines; quality for every palate

Events Christmas & Fall Harvest

Restaurant Cheese trays, fresh bread and olive oil; Thursday: pizza; Friday: pizza or pork tenderloins; Saturday: grill your own steak or Atlantic salmon with choose of sides and beverages

Prices $8.50–$35; 10 percent case discount

Brand Name Meranda-Nixon Winery

Type of Production Handcrafted

Method of Harvesting By hand

Pressing and Winemaking Bladder press and hand-produced

Aging and Cooperage American and French oak barrels

Vineyards Founded 2003

County Brown

AVA Ohio River Valley

Acreage 7.5

Trellising Vertical shoot positioned and high cordon

Waterways Red oak Creek and Straight Creek

Climate Moderated by Ohio River effect

Soil Glaciated Plateau over limestone

Varieties Chardonnay, Cabernet Sauvignon, Cabernet Franc, De Chaunac, Traminette, Norton and Catawba

Wines Chardonnay, Cabernet Sauvignon, Cabernet Franc, Red Oak Creek, Traminette, Catawba and Norton

Best Red Cabernet Sauvignon

Best White Traminette

Best Other Wine Catawba

Quote "We are revitalizing the Ohio River Valley one vine at a time."—Seth Meranda

Nearby Places to Visit Ulysses S. Grant Memorial; Old Train Depot; Covered Bridges

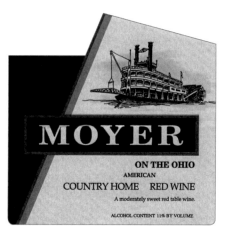

Moyer Vineyards, Winery, & Restaurant

3859 U.S. Route 52, P.O. Box 235
Manchester, OH 45144
Tel (937) 549-2957
Fax (937) 549-4795
E-mail moyervineyards@yahoo.com
Web site ohiowines.org
Owners Robert & Cindy Gilkison; Jim & Wanda Bowman; Les & Kay Grooms; Tom Hamrick; Ben & Carol White; & Brett & Sherry Spencer
Winemaker Jim Bowman
Founded 1972

The green Appalachian foothills rise from the earth as you travel over rushing waterways and through cypress-lined byways along the banks of the Ohio River Valley toward Manchester, home of Moyer Vineyards, Winery & Restaurant.

Decades ago, one of Manchester's highlights was The River-By, a once-fashionable 1926 restaurant and dance hall on the Ohio River reached by motor coach or steamboat. The River-By pulled in droves of people with its nickelodeon music, square dancing, and prohibited bootleg beer. In 1935 Ezzard Charles, called the "Cincinnati Flash," who would become a world heavyweight boxing champion, fought a boxing match on the site. But the dramatic 1937 Ohio River flood buried the place in six feet of mud, leaving silty streets and twisted flood debris. By the late forties, this landmark building had been renamed The Top Hat, a private gambling club; through the late sixties, the place reinvented itself several times.

In 1972, Texas wine enthusiasts Ken and Mary Moyer refurbished the site of The River-By and established Moyer Winery and Vineyards, one of a handful of producing vineyards located along the fertile banks of the Ohio River. In addition to renovating the building, they added a lovely deck and landscaped the grounds. Soon Moyer Vineyards, Winery & Restaurant was showcasing Ohio River Valley wines and foods. Among its most loyal customers were Jim and Wanda Bowman, Terry and Peggy Ayres, Les and Kay Grooms, Ben and Carol White, Brett and Sherry Spencer, Tom Hamrick, and Robert and Cindy Gilkison. "When the Moyers put the place on the market in 1998, we decided to purchase it as a group in 1999," says Jim Bowman, proprietor and winemaker.

These friends redesigned Moyer Vineyards, Winery & Restaurant with style. They started by landscaping the gazebo and flower gardens with color. The exterior received a new roof,

An enchanting view of the Ohio River from Moyer Vineyards. *Courtesy Ohio Wine Producers Association*

burgundy board-and-batten siding, and an enlarged deck with moveable windows. "The views of the Ohio River became the focus," Bowman says. They brightened the interior, installed new floors, and accented the room with purple fabrics and fresh flowers to add flair. The kitchen was newly equipped, and the menu recalibrated to account for Midwestern tastes. Appetizers, salads, sandwiches, pastas, beef, seafood entrees, and deep-fried dishes were perfected to accompany the new Moyer wines. The new owners even booked a piano player and singer to entertain on the weekends.

The historic, thirty-year-old metal-post-and-wire trellised vineyards, interspersed with red roses, are located in sandy Adams County's riverside soils and planted to Vidal Blanc, Chambourcin,

De Chaunac, Chardonnay, and Cabernet Sauvignon. The Ohio River Valley AVA at this locale has a hot and humid growing season cooled by summer river breezes. "Our goal is to make fine wine and make a success of this place," says Bowman, who is assisted in the vineyards and the cellar by Jeffrey Riggs and Jonathan Bowman.

Below the restaurant lies the friends-and-family-oriented winery. The winemakers do pressing, crushing, and fermenting in stainless steel; bottling, corking, and labeling are done by hand. "Down here in the cellar, there is always something going on," Bowman says. "I like wine and food, but I especially like the people. The reason I am doing this is for my enjoyment—from creating fine wine to making the place look good. As a 1,200-case producer, we make small batches of handcrafted wine with a capacity of 2,500 to 3, 000 cases annually."

Moyer Winery produces Merlot, Cabernet Sauvignon, Chambourcin, River Valley Red, Country Home Red, Chardonnay, Vidal Blanc, and River Valley White along with rosé wines and fruit wines—raspberry, strawberry peach, a Brut Champagne, and a semi-sweet champagne. "Our market, five to one, prefers a sweet wine to a dry one," Bowman says. "Our major sales are at the winery and the remainder at stores in Manchester, Ripley, Aberdeen, Portsmouth, and Georgetown."

Moyer Vineyards, Winery & Restaurant

Directions From Columbus, take I-71 south toward U.S. Route 62 south to U.S. Route 52 at Ripley. Turn left and proceed 15 miles to the Moyer Winery on the right in Manchester. From Cincinnati, take I-275 south to U.S. Route 52. Follow U.S. 52 for 70 miles along the Ohio River to the Moyer Winery in Manchester

Hours Mon.–Thurs., 11:30 AM–9 PM; Fri.–Sat., 11:30 AM 10 PM; May–Oct., Sun., 12–5 PM

Tours By appointment

Tasting Daily when open, at table or at tasting bar

Gifts Wine, wine bags, and boxes

Highlights at Winery High quality wine paired with good food at reasonable prices, views of the vineyards and of the spectacular Ohio River

Events Vintage Car Festival; Riverboat Day

Restaurant American cuisine; known for bean and bacon soup, steaks, seafood, chicken, pasta dishes, and desserts

Prices $8.50–$13.75; 10 percent case discount

Brand Name Moyer Winery

Type of Production Handcrafted wines

Method of Harvesting By hand

Pressing and Winemaking Basket press

Aging and Cooperage Stainless steel

Vineyards Founded 1972

County Adams

AVA Ohio River Valley

Acreage 8

Waterway Ohio River

Climate Four seasons

Soil Sandy

Varieties Vidal Blanc, Chambourcin, De Chaunac, Chardonnay, Cabernet Sauvignon

Wines Cabernet Sauvignon, Merlot, Chambourcin, River Valley Red, Country Home Red, Chardonnay, River Valley Blush, Raspberry Wine, Strawberry Wine, Peach Wine

Best Red Country Home Red

Best White Chardonnay

Other Best Wine Raspberry

Quote "Come once; you will come back!"—Cindy Gilkison

Nearby Places to Visit Serpent Mound; Amish Country; President Ulysses S. Grant's Birthplace; Point Pleasant

Valley Vineyards

2276 East U.S. 22
Morrow, OH 45152
Tel (513) 899-2485
Fax (513) 899-9022
E-mail info@valleyvineyards.com
Web site www.valleyvineyards.com
Owners The Schuchter Family
Winemaker Greg Pollman
Founded 1970

There is an unassuming sense of longevity about Valley Vineyards in Morrow. A handsome Tudor winery and weathered residence sit in the flat of a wide agricultural valley located along the well-traveled U.S. Route 22, opposite 115-acres of undulating hillside vineyards thriving in the Ohio River Valley American Viticultural Area.

When Lawrence and Evelyn Schuchter, Bavarian immigrants, arrived in Morrow at the turn of the nineteenth century, they were struck by the promise these verdant farmlands held. They successfully cultivated fruits and vegetables for farm markets. But it was Lawrence's son, Kenneth G. Schuchter, and his spouse, Margaret, who decided to take a risk and plant wine grapes in the 1960s. The Schuchters planted twenty-seven varieties of wine grapes, some vitis vinifera—Cabernet Sauvignon, Cabernet Franc, Chardonnay, and Riesling—French hybrids, and three American varieties.

The Schuchter wine legacy was defined by the character of its good-natured and hard-working founders. Patriarch Kenneth Schuchter, an energetic, hands-on man, loved the outdoors. "My grandfather admits being the happiest riding his tractor and tending his vines," says his grandson, Joe Schuchter. The matriarch Evelyn, who was very much a people-person, thrived on her lifestyle choices. "My grandmother was content cooking in the kitchen or pruning the vineyards," Joe says. The Schuchters shaped the culture of Valley Vineyards winery: They emphasized family, they welcomed their friends and neighbors, and they celebrated life with German food and estate-grown wines. This has influenced the modern-day Schuchters and their loyal employees to take a unified approach to their work.

What began as a small family farm mushroomed into a top Ohio restaurant and 35,000 case wine estate. The Schuchters hired contractor Everett

Valley Vineyards replicates a Bavarian wine castle. *Courtesy Valley Vineyards*

Done to replicate a Bavarian wine castle on the Rhine, Germany's famed wine-growing district. A two-story stucco winery with a peaked roof, dormer windows, and a brick foundation was built and framed by trees and decorative landscaping. A large wooden doorway opens into a spacious tasting room at the center of activity. One wing houses a great dining hall in the tradition of a European wine garden, complete with beamed ceilings, brick fireplace, artifacts, and wine murals. Another wing houses a high-ceilinged dining hall, the Cabernet Room, that is used for private parties.

Kenny Schuchter of the third-generation and the vineyard manager, and his wife Dodie, restaurant manager, are now the proprietors. His son Joe Schuchter says his father worked with Cabernet Sauvignon, Cabernet Franc, Chardonnay, Seyval, Vidal Blanc, De Chaunac, Niagara, and Catawba, all planted in clay loam in a typically continental climate. "My father gives the

viniferas extra care, protecting them from winter freezes by utilizing a grape hoe, which ploughs the dirt over the graft. This step ensures a good crop, with yields varying from three-and-a-half to eight tons per acre, pending the specific variety," he says. A brand new 35-acre vineyard planted to Vidal Blanc, now under development, will be harvested in 2013 for the distinctive Vidal Ice Wine.

A 7,200-square-foot stainless steel wine-production center and an American-and French-oak aging cellar lies under the restaurant. Greg Pollman, the present-day winemaker, has pursued quality through experimentation with his winemaking. "Our newest achievements are bigger and better," he says. As examples, he cites the winery's growing volume of Traminette, its launch of Ohio's first ice wine, and its production of its first Cabernet Sauvignon Reserve. The increasing interest in the wines from Valley Vineyards rests in their dry, fruity Chardonnay; dry, oak-aged

Seyval; rich, medium Vidal Blanc; and delightful De Chaunac. Still, another segment of customers supports the purchase of their medium to sweet wines.

The winery has carved out its role as a frequent recipient of commendations and medals and remains a serious contender in the Ohio wine saga.

Valley Vineyards 🍃

Directions Take I-71 to exit 28 (State Route 4). Turn south on Route 48 to U.S. Route 22 and U.S. Route 3. Turn left and east for 3 miles to the winery

Hours Mon.–Thurs., 11 AM–6 PM; Fri.–Sat., 11 AM–11 PM; Sun., 1–6 PM

Tours Self-guided, educational, and historic

Tasting Daily when open

Gifts Gift baskets, VV glasses, T-shirts, and personalized wine bottles

Highlights at Winery Beautiful Ohio River Valley and hillside vineyards; Tudor architecture of winery; historic oak aging cellars

Events Valley Vineyards Weekend Cookouts, Fridays and Saturdays

Prices $7–$40; 10 percent case discount; steak dinners $45 per person

Packages/Specials Gift baskets, gift boxes, personalized labels

Brand Names Valley Vineyards

Type of Production American hybrids, vitis vinifera, French-American hybrids

Method of Harvesting By hand

Pressing and Winemaking Traditional

Aging and Cooperage French and American oak barrels, stainless steel tanks

Vineyards Founded 1970

County Warren

AVA Ohio River Valley

Acreage 115

Waterway Ohio River

Climate Continental

Soil Clay loam, Glacial till

Varieties 20 varieties

Wines Cabernet Sauvignon, Cabernet Franc, Hillside Red, De Chaunac, Seyval, Chardonnay, Blue Eye, Vidal Blanc, Valley Blush, Niagara, Concord, Pink Catawba, Honey Mead, Ice Wine, Champagne, Blanc de Blanc Champagne

Best Red Cabernet Sauvignon Reserve

Best White Chardonnay

Other Best Wine Vidal

Quote "The art of winemaking has been a tradition in southern Ohio for nearly two centuries."—Schuchter Family

Nearby Places to Visit Paramount's Kings Island; Fort Ancient State Memorial

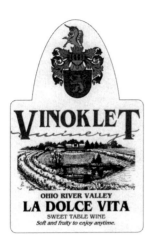

Vinoklet Winery

11069 Colerain Avenue
Cincinnati, OH 45252
Tel (513) 385-9309
Fax (513) 385-9379
E-mail vinokletwinery@fuse.net
Web site www.vinokletwines.com
Owner/Winemaker Kreso Mikulic
Founded 1980

The thirty-acre Vinoklet Winery sits high on a hillside overlooking gently rolling vineyards, cypress-lined ponds, and perennial gardens with spectacular vistas of Cincinnati and the Ohio River Valley. This beloved wine country estate Vinoklet, which means "little house in the vineyard" in Croatian, reflects the artistry of its founder, Kreso Mikulic, who brought a "little bit of heaven" to this remote corner of Hamilton County.

"My father taught me to make wine," says Mikulic, a native of Mimici, a Croatian village of sixteen families and sixteen wineries. He is also the winemaker, and you'll often find him jauntily dressed in a red beret, glasses, a faded shirt, and worn jeans. "If one family didn't make wine in my hometown, everyone would have thought that something was wrong."

At thirty, Kreso departed Europe for the United States, where he pursued his dreams and lived his philosophy—"start and never quit." He reached prominence as an engineer for Reuland Electric, where he built the B-1 bomber fuel pump. As an aerospace engineer at Wilco Corporation, he designed commercial applications and high-speed motors.

"My father had his own winery in Croatia, and he made classical wine. I did what I loved," Mikulic says. "I had land and thought, what could I do?" He hired ten bulldozers to clear seventeen acres for a south-facing hillside vineyard. "Foot by foot, we pulled out every root, then graded and shaped the land, adding topsoil to the rocky acidic clay underpan."

First he planted 150 plants, and none sprouted. Next, he planted two hundred vines, and they died. "I was persistent," he remembers. "Something was wrong with the soil and the climate." Then, he ordered five hundred plants from the Finger Lakes, and every one came up. "I made wine just for friends," he says. Mikulic planted one thousand vines, then two thousand vines, and finally six thousand vines before adding winery

Vineyard view with Vinoklet Winery in the background. *Courtesy Vinoklet Winery*

buildings in 1986 and outfitting them with the latest winemaking equipment.

"Wine helps in this life; it adds to one's health and happiness," Mikulic says. "I wanted to create a winery with ambiance, reflective of the goodness in life."

Along Colerain Road stands a charming tan farmhouse with red shutters, framed by trees and accentuated with boxes of red, purple, blue, and yellow flowers and a patio with a cafe table and chairs. Mikulic's cozy home is a step back in time. A European-appointed Vinoklet Bed and Breakfast, located on adjacent property, is richly decorated in textured fabrics, mahogany furniture, oil paintings, and oriental rugs.

A quarter-mile away, a grape arbor leads into a courtyard, where there is a brick winery and restaurant with elegant lanterns, wrought iron furniture, an ivy-covered flowing fountain, and a gazebo with breathtaking vineyard views. A renovated 25,000-gallon redwood wine barrel suitable for small year-round parties

has a fireplace and air conditioning.

Mikulic invites his guests to dine in their gazebo, solarium or dining room, decorated in green and red with woodcuts and a fourteenth century Italian mural. Customers grill steak, fish, chicken or pork on the high-tech grill, served with a fancy buffet, and paired with Vinoklet fine wines. A strolling violinist adds to the ambiance.

"People like Vinoklet wines. They are light, easy to drink, and not too tart or too soft," he says. With the completion of both the new ponds, the Traminette acreage, the landscaping, and the 100,000-gallon modern steel winery, equipped with a new crusher-destemmer, bladder press, American stainless steel tanks and oak cooperage, Mikulic recommitted to traditional winemaking.

Their grapes are hand harvested, then de-stemmed and crushed in a bladder press. The whites are cold-fermented in stainless steel, then held in stainless and bottle for clarity and flavor. The reds are fermented in stainless steel and /or American oak, with additional barrel and bottle aging. "Our Vinoklet Traminette Master Reserve was a recent Double Gold Medal winner at the Indianapolis International Wine Competition," he says. "People who drink wine are the ultimate judge. The best wine is the one which pleases the consumer the most. Wine is a very personal experience."

Vinoklet Winery 🍂

Directions Take I-275 to exit 33 (Colerain Avenue) north to Old Colerain Avenue. Turn left. Winery is 1.25 miles, on the left

Hours Tues., 12–6 PM; Wed.–Thurs., 12–8 PM; Fri.–Sat., 12–11 PM; Sun., 1–5 PM

Tours By appointment for small groups

Tastings Daily when open

Gifts Glasses, shirts, wine, and accessories

Highlights at Winery Our-you-grill-to-perfection dinners and buffet $35

Events September Art and Wine Festival with 66 artisans and 12,000 guests; outdoor wedding ceremonies, receptions for 160

Restaurant Patrons grill their choice of steak, fish, chicken, or pork with Vinoklet wines

Prices $12–$20; 10 percent case discount

Brand Names Vinkolet Wines

Type of Production Traditional

Method of Harvesting Hand-harvested

Pressing and Winemaking Traditional

Aging and Cooperage Stainless steel and oak

Vineyards Founded 1980

County Hamilton

Appellation Ohio

Acreage 17

Waterways Three lakes, some surrounded by cypress trees

Climate Hot, humid spring and summer; fair to cold winter

Soil Rocky, acidic clay with excellent drainage

Varieties Catawba, Chambourcin, Niagara, Vidal Blanc, Concord, Traminette

Wines Tears of Joy (comparable to Chardonnay), Sunset Blush (comparable to White Zinfandel), Dreamer (comparable to Chablis), In Vino Veritas (comparable to sweet Riesling), La Dolce Vita (comparable to Port), Traminette Master Reserve, Brother Joe (Cabernet Sauvignon)

Best Red La Dolce Vita

Best White Traminette Master Reserve

Other Best Wine Brother Joe

Quote "Wine helps in this life; it adds to one's health and happiness."—Kreso Mikulic

Nearby Places to Visit Cincinnati Zoo; Cincinnati Art Museum

The Winery at Versailles

6572 State Route 47
Versailles, OH 45380
Tel (937) 526-3232
E-mail mikewav@bright.net;
       carolwav@bright.net
Web site www.wineryatversailles.com
Owners Carol and Mike Williams
Winemaker Mike Williams
Founded 2002

The road weaves its way through beautiful open stretches of Ohio farm country before it reaches The Winery at Versailles. The only winery in Darke County, it was established in 2002 by Pennsylvanians Mike and Carol Williams, who relocated to this elegant Midwestern hamlet to be near their children.

While stationed in Germany with the US Army, Mike began his love affair with wine. It was Mike's mechanic who first turned him onto the idea of winemaking. "My mechanic, a failed master wine taster, was unsuccessful in identifying over 85 percent of Germany's three thousand vineyards by flavor," Mike says. However, he successfully advised Mike to buy a pricey German Trockenbeerenauslese, a rich, nectarous wine with concentrated sugar and flavor made from overripe, nearly dry grapes left on the vine and harvested at maturity.

For an impressionable young man from St. Mary's, Pennsylvania, the town that produces the all-natural Straubs Beer, it was the perfect incentive. From there, Mike began to read voraciously about centuries-old German wineries and breweries, and his love of wine unfolded.

In 1974, the Williamses met and married in Wisconsin and returned to Germany while Mike completed a tour in the Signal Corps. They returned to the United States in 1978. Mike pursued several endeavors: He raised quail, worked with the handicapped, and managed factories. For relaxation, he made wine at home for his seven siblings, who were among his best and worst critics. "As the wine got better, my reputation improved," he says. "By the early 1990s, I was making more and more wine."

In 1994, the Williamses established the Winery at Wilcox in the Allegheny National Forest. Under the Presidential Proclamation of 1923, a 513,000-acre forest of hardwoods, since replaced by black cherry and maple, was created in the heart of the oil and gas region. "We produced 1,000 gallons of eight varieties, and by 1996 expanded to 25,000 gallons, or thirty wines," Mike says.

In 2000, the Williamses relocated to Versailles, a gentrified farm community recognized for eggs, shipping, and medical equipment. They purchased a historic ten-acre farm (which had a grand old manor house where Annie Oakley—Darke County's own Phoebe Moses, who shot the ashes off Kaiser Wilhelm's cigarette—spent her summers), an 1850s tobacco barn, and land for winegrowing. The Williamses and son Jamie, vice president of operations in Pennsylvania, run the Wilcox and Versailles operations.

Four miles west of town stands the Winery at Versailles, a renovated pale green barn trimmed in dark paint with an overhanging porch and rail fence. The bright main room is appointed with a wrought-iron chandelier, a right-angled tasting bar, and tables and chairs covered in rich, red-patterned fabrics. Merchandise available for purchase—winemaking equipment, gift baskets,

myriad wine accessories, and fashionable clothing—is displayed everywhere.

With two of ten acres in Versailles under development, Mike has gambled on the Darke County clay soils, the moderate yet humid climate, and the absence of severe cold and partnered with local farmers to plant Steuben, Chancellor, Traminette, Chambourcin, Seyval Blanc, and Vidal Blanc.

Until Versailles's Vineyards bear fruit, Mike sources grapes from growers in northwestern Ohio and Pennsylvania, destemmed and crushed. Within eight hours, the juice is shipped to Versailles, where it is fermented in stainless steel temperature fermentors. "I am a minimalist and do very little fiddling," Mike says.

The Winery at Versailles showcases some twenty-six fruit-forward wines. They are an American Pinot Grigio, a stainless steel-fermented Chardonnay, a fragrant Viognier, a classic Cabernet Sauvignon, and a rich Cabernet Franc. The Williamses also produce semi-dry and semi-sweet wines, a collection of sweet sparkling fruit wines, and Old Fort Port, and Proprietor's White.

The Winery at Versailles 🍃

Directions From I-75 head west on State Route 47 for 24.7 miles, west of Versailles

Hours Mon.–Thurs., 10 AM–6 PM; Fri.–Sat. 10 AM–9 PM; closed Sun.

Tours Daily educational tours when open

Tasting Daily when open

Gifts Winemaking equipment, wine accessories, glassware, and clothing

Highlights at Winery Variety of unique and innovative wines; steak fry weekends; all levels wine education and winemaking classes; personalized labels

Events Monthly, see web site

Restaurant Eclectic, catered dinners

Prices $10–$25; 10 percent case discount

Brand Names The Winery at Versailles

Type of Production Traditional

Method of Harvesting By hand

Aging and Cooperage French and American oak

Vineyards Founded 2005

County Darke

Appellation Ohio and American

Acreage 2

Climate Moderate but humid with air drainage but no severe cold

Soil Deep clay with stone

Varieties Steuben, Chancellor, Traminette, Chambourcin

Wines Pinot Grigio, Chardonnay, Viognier, Cabernet Sauvignon, Merlot, Darke Red, Autumn Leaves, Buckeye Blush, Hunter Red, Celebration Sparkling Wine, Blueberry Sparkling Wines, Peach Mist Sparkling Wine, Wedding White, Rodeo Red, Niagara, Old Fort Porte, Traminette, Schwartzbreeren, Framboise, Mustang Rosé, and Schokoladenkirschwein

Best Red Port of Chambourcin

Best White Traminette

Other Best Wine Sparkling Blueberry Wine

Quote "As for me and my family, we will serve the Lord"—Joshua 24:15

Nearby Places to Visit Inn at Versailles, Garst Museum in Greenville, Bear's Mills

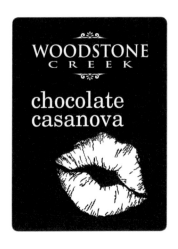

Woodstone Creek Winery

3641 Newton Avenue
Cincinnati, OH 45207
Tel (513) 569-0300
E-mail woodstonecreek@yahoo.com
Web site www.woodstonecreek.com
Owner/Winemaker Donald R. Outterson
Founded 1999

The brick Woodstone Creek Winery, headquartered in a former stamping factory at Newton and Dana Avenues in Cincinnati's Evanston, is the first and only winery/microdistillery combination in Ohio. As a winery, it produces 100 cases per year. The distillery has a maximum production of 500 barrels under Ohio law, but generally doesn't make more than one barrel a month. Woodstone Creek has Ohio's only quadruple threat winemaker. Don Outterson is a Certified Brewmaster, Master Distiller and mead mazer as well as a winemaker.

The idea to combine the winery and distillery ventures was a natural one for owner Donald Outterson. "I made beer and wine in 1979, after legislation permitted for home production," he says. He then spent time as an exchange student, which he says further defined his styles of making beer and wine. Once back in the United States, Outterson

won the New York State Amateur Beer Championship in 1982. This led to an apprenticeship at the William S. Newman Brewing Company in Albany, New York, where he made English ales.

Outterson is a Certified Brewmaster who received his credentials from the Siebel Institute of Chicago in 1986. A member of the Master Brewers Association of America, he also partook in Alltech seminars in distillation. "This began my journey of running breweries," Outterson says. At James Page Brewing in Minneapolis, he formulated a wild-rice-based European lager. At the Great American Beer Festival, Don won Gold, Silver and Bronze medals.

As a consultant, Outterson did contract work for brewpubs in famous places, such as Telluride Lager Beer. These upscale designer brew products resulted in an Australian multinational chain of breweries hiring Outterson as their brewmaster through 1989.

While in Canberra City, Australia, Outterson acquired the U.S. importation rights for the Adelaide Malting Company floor malts, originally made by the historic Cooper's Brewery, Australia's last family-owned producer of beers, ales, and stouts. "I honed my malt-analysis skills as it pertained to varieties, species, and grains, with an inroad to distillation," he says. Outterson began to study the industrial application of distilled alcohol. Over the course of a decade, he progressed from brewmaster to winemaker to distiller. "I now had completed my training as a fermentation technologist."

Just as the brewpub fad was fading, Outterson's desire to make wine was blossoming. He started a company selling production equipment to wineries, distilleries, and brewpubs. He established lasting business contacts with the quality people he met in the wine business. As was customary among many brewers, Outterson produced mead, the most ancient of fermented beverages made from honey, water, and yeast. Mead is regulated by the U.S. government and categorized as a wine. If he wanted to produce it commercially, he had to open a winery. When Outterson discovered that mead was little understood and difficult to market, he tried his hand at adding wine from grape varietals to his budding wine list, and Woodstone Creek Winery took form.

Today, Woodstone Creek Winery welcomes friends and neighbors to share in the culture of art and wine. Outterson's wife Linda, a graphic designer and artist, designs their wine labels and paints oils—landscapes and florals—that are displayed with her handmade jewelry and crafts in the tasting room. Comparative wine tastings with commentary by the owners commence at the curved 1930s maple tasting bar with a paneled front and butcher-block top, accented by a solid mahogany rail. The shop retails varietals, blends, ports, sherries, brandies, honey wines, spirits such as bourbon, whisky, vodka, gin, rum, and bierschnaaps, and accessories. The owners share the building with a home winemaking and brewing supply store.

"We produce small batches," Don Outterson says. He challenges himself by introducing new concepts and innovative techniques in his winemaking while he conducts experiments in his wine cellar. "I shop for the best quality…from the mountains to the valley…on our economy of scale."

"We now offer Ohio varietals and honeywines from local honey as our list of contract growers has expanded to fill our needs. The dessert wines contain our pot-stilled brandy, also made from Ohio varietals," say the Outtersons. "Here we make dreams come true."

Woodstone Creek Winery 🍇

Directions From I-71, take the Dana Avenue exit, then proceed west for two blocks to the winery

Hours Sat., 1–5 PM

Tours None

Tasting When open

Gifts Handmade jewelry, craft items, artwork

Highlights at Winery American-Ohio wines of different tastes, styles, varieties, blends; dessert wines fortified with potstilled brandy; specialty Ohio ports and port-style honey wines

Prices $9–$34.95; 10 percent case discount

Brand Names Woodstone Creek Winery

Type of Production Innovative

Method of Harvesting By hand

Pressing and Winemaking Traditional

Aging and Cooperage Stainless steel and American and French oak barrels

Appellation 70 percent undesignated Ohio growing region, 30 percent Ohio River Valley

Varieties Vidal Blanc, Chardonnay, Riesling, Cabernet Sauvignon, Merlot, Sauterne, Cabernet Franc, Niagara, Aurore, Cayuga, Syrah

Wines Vidal Blanc, Diva, Riesling, Chardonnay, Haut Sauterne, Mead, Traditional Honey Wine, Raspberry Honey White, Aurore, Chocolate Casanova, Honey Mist, Ginger Honey, Royale, Rialto Red, Cabernet Sauvignon, Taliesin, Niagara, Ambiance Port, Laureate Port, Crowne Amber Spiced Honey Dessert Wine, Legacy Honey Port, Eden Apple Dessert Wine, Three Trees Cherry Wine, Pomegranate Honey and Blueberry Honey

Best Red Royale

Best White Diva

Other Best Wine Crowne Amber

Quote "Give a person a bottle of wine and one can waste an afternoon. Teach a person to make wine and one can waste a lifetime."—Donald R. Outterson

Nearby Places to Visit Xavier University; Krohn Conservatory; Cincinnati Zoo, Art Museum, Music Hall

Other Wineries of Interest

Burnet Ridge Winery
6721 Richard Avenue
North College, OH, 45224
Tel (513) 522-4203
Web site www.burnetridge.com
Hours Available by appointment to the trade only, not the general public

This is a small family-owned and -operated winery in North College Hill, Ohio. Owner Chip Emmerick, a transplanted Californian, sources the Golden State's north coast grapes to produce artisanal European-style oak-aged wines.

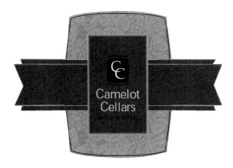

Camelot Cellars
958 North High Street
Columbus, OH, 43201
Tel (614) 441-8860
E-mail wine@camelotcellars.com
Web site www.camelotcellars.com
Hours Tues.–Thurs., 1–9 PM; Fri.–Sat. 12–10 PM; closed Sun. and Mon.

Camelot Cellars is a Columbus-based, service-oriented winery that proudly provides its customers the opportunity to design, produce, package, and label their own wine from an array of foreign and domestic wine juice and concentrate sources. Owner Jeff Anderson and Boutique Manager Rick Mitchell also sell Camelot Cellars quality wines.

Heritage Vineyards & Guest House
27561 TR 45
Warsaw, OH, 43844
Tel (740) 824-4314
E-mail info@heritagevineyardwinery.com
Web site www.heritagevineyardwinery.com
Hours Mon.–Sat. 11 AM–7 PM

The Endsley family started Heritage Vineyard, a small winery, a three-acre hillside vineyard, a family home, and a guest house in the foothills of the Appalachians. Randy got interested in winegrowing, and their son Brent pursued winemaking, all with the goal of making fine Heritage Vineyards wines.

Paper Moon Vineyards
2008 State Route 60
Vermilion, OH, 44089
Tel (440) 967-2500
E-mail adam@papermoonvineyards.com
Web site www.papermoonvineyards.com
Hours May–Oct., Tues.–Wed., 12–6 PM, Thurs.–Sat., 12–10 PM; Nov.–April, Thurs., 4–10 PM, Fri.–Sat., 12–10 PM

The Paper Moon Vineyards, a fourth generation family business, is located on 50 acres west of the Vermilion River in Vermilion, Ohio. With five acres of wine grapes, and more to be planted, owners Richard and Sheryl Cawrse, and their son Adam, the winemaker, are focused on the production of high quality handcrafted wines.

Red Horse Winery
5326 Fairland Road
Barberton, OH, 44203
Tel (330) 807-8600
E-mail joe@redhorsewinery.com
Web site www.redhorsewinery.com
Hours Please call for information

A warm and friendly getaway in Barberton, this winery stands on a knoll with beautiful views west to Cleveland. Founders Joe and Gayle Semansky, home winemakers and horse breeders, dubbed Red Horse Winery for their famous chestnut (red) show horses. Guests and visitors are encouraged to stop by for a glass of one of their California or Ohio wines.

Vermilion Valley Vineyards
11005 Gore Orphanage Road
Wakeman, OH, 44889
Tel (440) 965-5202
E-mail info@vermilionvalleyvineyards.com
Web site www.vermilionvalleyvineyards.com
Hours Wed.–Thur., 12–6 PM. Fri.–Sat., 12–11 PM. Please check the Web site for seasonal hours.

A striking wooden winery reminiscent of an earlier time sits on a 23-acre site with sweeping views of vineyards, farmland, and ponds. Here, owners Larry Gibson, David Benzing, and Jack Baumann produce premium vitis vinifera wines grown from their vineyards—including Pinot Noir, Cabernet Franc, Gewürztraminer, and Muscat Ottonel—vitis labrusca from other local vineyards, and local fruit wines from nearby orchards and markets.

Selected Bibliography

Adams, Leon D. *Wines of America*. 3rd ed. New York: McGraw Hill, 1985.

Boker, Kurt. *A History of the Kelleys Island Grape and Wine Industry*. Kelleys Island Library, Kelleys Island, Ohio.

Cahoon, Dr. Garth A., to Patricia Latimer, March 8, 2005. In the author's possession.

Church, Ruth Ellen . *Wines of the Midwest*. Athens, Ohio: Swallow Press Books, 1982.

Esterer, Arnie, to Patricia Latimer, August 4, 2004. In the author's possession.

Gallander, Dr. James F., to Patricia Latimer, March 9, 2005. In the author's possession.

Geraci, Victor W. *Salud! The Rise of Santa Barbara's Wine Industry*. Reno: University of Nevada Press, 2004.

Hammer, A. J. Conversation with and interview by Patricia Latimer. Cleveland, Ohio, December 2004.

Hatcher, Harlon. *Lake Erie*. New York: Bobbs-Merrill Company, 1945.

Heck, Gary, to Patricia Latimer, February 11, 2005. In the author's possession.

Johannesen, Kyle J. *The Winegrowing Industry of the Lake Erie Island Region*. Bowling Green, Ohio: Bowling Green State University, 1983.

Latimer, Jean Francis M. Conversation with and interview by Patricia Latimer. Cleveland, Ohio, 2004 and 2005.

Latimer, Patricia. *California Wineries of Sonoma and Mendocino*. St. Helena, California: Vintage Image, 1975.

Longworth, Nicholas. *To the members of the Cincinnati horticultural society, on the cultivation of the grape*. Cincinnati, Ohio: L'Hommedieu & Co., 1846.

Morton, Marian J. *Cleveland Heights: The Making of an Urban Suburb*. Chicago: Arcadia Publishing, 2002.

Orkin Rosenthal, Judith. Conversation with and interview by Patricia Latimer. Cleveland, Ohio, July 6, 2004.

Pinney, Thomas. *A History of Wine in America: From Beginnings to Prohibition*. Berkeley, California: The University of California Press, 1989.

Reemlin, Charles. *Vine-Dresser's Manual: An Illustrated Treatise on Vineyards & WineMaking*. New York: C.M. Saxton, Barker & Co, 1860.

Shaker Heights Collection. Shaker Heights Historical Society. The Elizabeth Nord Library, Shaker Heights, Ohio.

Silverman, Sanford. Conversation with and interview by Patricia Latimer. Cleveland, Ohio, July 6, 2004.

Silverman, Sanford. *Geneva Jewish Farmers, Reunions*. Cleveland, Ohio, 1990–1991.

Acknowledgments

It is with appreciation that I thank the many people who have given so generously of their time and thought in assisting with this creative work. And it is with respect that I honor those who shared their sight and insight over the years along the wine trail and made this book possible.

Leon D. Adams
Bouvier Beale Jr.
Darrell Corti
Jose Ignacio Domecq Jr.
Arnie Esterer
James Gruber
Louise Gund
Gladys Horiuchi
Geoff Kenway
John Kithas
Jean Miller Latimer
Phil Masturzo
Tom Mc Carthy
James Miller
Bonsal Seggerman
Sharon Till
Amy Wilson
Mary Wilson
Donniella Winchell

My thanks to my colleagues at the University of Akron Press: Thomas Bacher, director; Amy Freels, editorial and design coordinator; Carol Slatter, coordinator of print manufacturing and digital production; and Julie Gammon, marketing coordinator.

About the Author

Patricia Latimer is founder of Patricia Latimer Associates, a public relations and strategic planning company located in San Francisco with a presence in Cleveland. Latimer also served as the Director of the Sherry Institute of Spain and advocated for Spain and Sherry in the Western United States, representing the Asociacion de Criadores de Sherry, S.A. in Jerez de la Frontera, Spain.

She is the author of *California Wineries of Sonoma and Mendocino* in addition to being a one-time political writer and scriptwriter. Latimer has been published in more than one hundred national and regional magazines and newspapers, including *Connecticut, Colorado Magazine,* and the *San Francisco Chronicle.* She was a columnist on wine for the *Nob Hill Gazette, Bayviews,* and *Coast,* and was a columnist on women in business for the *San Francisco Examiner.* She began her career in New York as an editor for one of the Hearst Corporation magazines.